Diversity, Difference and Dilemmas

SOCIAL WORK SKILLS IN PRACTICE

Series editors:

Ruben Martin, *Honorary Senior Lecturer in Social Work, University of Kent*
Alisoun Milne, *Professor of Social Gerontology and Social Work, University of Kent*

About the series:

The social work profession is constantly evolving and adjusting to changes in the policy, professional and care contexts and to wider issues such as demographic and structural shifts. The *Social Work Skills in Practice* series aims to explore core skills and knowledge needed to practise effectively as a social worker. Initiatives to address perceived challenges and concerns within the profession have included reforms, new standards and reviews of social work education. The foregrounding of evidence-informed practice and recognition of the complex nature of social work will be increasingly important in the future. There is therefore a need for textbooks addressing new and developing requirements and expectations that will help practitioners respond to practice requirements in an informed, effective, agile and critical way. This series is targeted at Masters level students, Newly Qualified Social Workers (ASYE and CPD), professionals and undergraduate students in their second placements. All books in the series adopt a critically reflective lens on the development and deployment of social work skills, are theoretically grounded and address issues of relevance to all service user groups, families and carers, different settings and sectors and the increasingly varied context of social work practice.

Titles in the series:

Professional Writing Skills for Social Workers: Louise Frith and Ruben Martin
Diversity, Difference and Dilemmas: analysing concepts and developing skills, Kish Bhatti-Sinclair and Chris Smethurst (eds.)

Forthcoming titles:

Evidence-Informed Practice for Social Workers: Hugh McLaughlin and Barbra Teater
Social Work Skills with Networks and Communities: Martin Webber

Diversity, Difference and Dilemmas: analysing concepts and developing skills

Edited by Kish Bhatti-Sinclair and
Christopher Smethurst

 Open University Press

Open University Press
McGraw-Hill Education
8th Floor, 338 Euston Road
London
England
NW1 3BH

email: enquiries@openup.co.uk
world wide web: www.openup.co.uk

and Two Penn Plaza, New York, NY 10121-2289, USA

First published 2017

A catalogue record of this book is available from the British Library

ISBN-13: 978-0-335-26182-6
ISBN-10: 0-33-526182-5
eISBN: 978-0-335-26188-3

Library of Congress Cataloging-in-Publication Data
CIP data applied for

Typeset by Transforma Pvt. Ltd., Chennai, India

Printed and bound by CPI Group (UK) Ltd, Croydon, CR0 4YY

This book is dedicated to our fathers:

Nazir Bhatti

and

Jack Smethurst

Contents

About the contributors

Kish Bhatti-Sinclair (Principal Lecturer, University of Chichester)
Kish is Head of Social Work at the University of Chichester. Kish has an established reputation in researching race and racism with a focus on how racist attitudes or behaviour can impede social work practice. Kish co-ordinates the Anti-Racist Social Work Education Group (ARSWEG) which comprises social work academics in the UK.

Chris Smethurst (Principal Lecturer, University of Chichester)
Chris is Deputy Head, Department of Childhood, Social Work and Social Care at the University of Chichester. Chris's research interests include inequality, social justice and economic disadvantage. Chris is also concerned about what can be done to support the wellbeing of students and practitioners in the workplace.

Dan Allen (Lecturer, University of Salford)
Dan has background in social work research and practice with Roma, Gypsy and Traveller children, families and communities. Dan seeks to improve service provision and advance the knowledge, values and skills needed to inform social work practices and traditions with Gypsy, Roma and Traveller people.

Lisa Armstrong (Senior Lecturer, University of Chichester)
Lisa's research interests include service user and carer involvement and co-production, citizenship studies and care ethics. Lisa is a practice teacher and has worked as an approved social worker in forensic and community mental health teams with young adults experiencing psychosis and eating disorders.

Vida Douglas (Social Work Consultant and Educator)
Vida has extensive experience of taking responsibility for leading change and developing teams within social care and higher education settings. As a policy and performance manager Vida has considerable experience of developing and implementing policies, processes and structures in local authority and higher education work contexts.

Jan Fook (Professor, Leeds Trinity University)
Jan Fook is currently Professor of Higher Education Pedagogy and Director of the International Centre for Higher Education Educational Research at Leeds Trinity University. She is most well known for her work in critical reflection and critical social work. She has held professorial positions in Australia, Canada, Norway and the UK.

Lucy Jaques (deafblind teacher and trainer)
Lucy works in the areas of diversity, disability and sensory impairment awareness and manages her own social care support and has experience of social work interventions. Lucy's particular interests are around breaking down the barriers

of understanding and enabling communication between deafblind and hearing sighted people.

Rebecca Long (Independent social worker and practice educator)

Rebecca is also a registered Interpreter for deafblind people and has a range of qualifications in sign language and deafblindness. She is particularly interested in the ways that social work and therapeutic practitioners understand and respond to situations where there is a need for communication and other support.

Bridget Ng'andu (Tutor, Ruskin College, Oxford)

Bridget's research interests include international volunteer groups, volunteering and HIV/AIDS social policy and HIV/AIDS in Botswana. Bridget has worked as a frontline social worker and senior practitioner and is a member of the Anti-Racist Social Work Education Group, the Social Work Action Network and the European Social Work Research Association's Special Interest Group on Migration.

Jon Old (Senior Lecturer, University of Chichester)

Jon has experience of frontline social work with children and families, youth offending and asylum seeking young people, acute mental health, learning disabilities and substance misuse. Jon's research interests focus on the social-psychological aspects of practitioner experience and cognitive dissonance/decision-making, values and ethics.

Gerry Skelton (Social work lecturer, trainer and counsellor)

Gerry's background is in animating and championing a plethora of often marginalised social justice issues. These have ranged from working in and through community development and community work, training and education, religious and political arenas. Gerry has also supported carers and service users in meaningful involvement in education, training and practice.

About the editors

The series is edited by Ruben Martin and Alisoun Milne.

Ruben Martin is Honorary Senior Lecturer in Social Work at the University of Kent, where he was Director of Studies for the BA (Hons) Social Work programme for seven years. He has been a probation officer and national training officer for a voluntary organisation. Since his retirement from his full-time academic post in 2010 he has continued work as part-time lecturer and tutor, consultant, freelance practice educator, writer and editor.

Dr Alisoun Milne is Professor of Social Gerontology and Social Work at the University of Kent's School for Sociology, Social Policy and Social Research. She has managerial responsibilities for, and contributes to delivering, the university's undergraduate and post-graduate social work qualifying programmes. Alisoun is widely published in both academic and practice-related journals. Her key research interests are: social work with older people and their families; older carers; mental health in later life; and long-term care. Before becoming an academic in 1995 Alisoun worked as a social worker and team manager in two London boroughs. She is a member of the Standing Commission on Carers, the Association of Professors of Social Work, and was on the Executive Committee of the British Society of Gerontology from 2009–15. She is registered with the Health and Care Professions Council.

Series editor's foreword

It is pleasing to be able to introduce another book in the *Social Work Skills in Practice* series. As social workers practise their varied skills, they cannot avoid relating to diversity and difference since these characterize and shape human experience and are critical to the formation of individual identity. While exploring this book you will be able to consider dilemmas, analyse concepts and be challenged to develop skills for responding to diversity and difference.

Social work practice takes place within a socio-economic and political context. This leads to conflicting factors impacting on social workers. Recent political developments in the UK have included the election of a Conservative administration in 2015, following five years of coalition government, giving momentum to an increased age of austerity. A referendum on whether the UK should remain a member of the European Union in 2016 led to strident concerns being voiced about levels of immigration. Disturbingly, an increase in incidents of racial abuse and hate crime were reported following the vote to leave the EU.

With this backdrop, Kish Bhatti-Sinclair and Christopher Smethurst have edited and contributed to a timely collection of chapters that in themselves represent diversity among contributors and content. Kish and Chris's commitment and enthusiasm have permeated what has been an ambitious project. As a reader you will find that many issues resonate with your own experience. The topics are challenging and some uncomfortable to consider. There are no easy answers. Exploring the chapters will help you to better understand historical developments, theoretical ideas and practice implications. Considering relevant case studies, pausing for reflection and undertaking suggested activities will enable you to engage with the material.

The book acknowledges the vast remit of diversity and difference generally, but also puts forward particular examples of themes relevant to contemporary practice, including class, religion and spirituality. These are important aspects contributing to our human identity. Some chapters explore very specific experiences, such as those of Roma and deaf-blind people. Discussion of these areas is welcome as there is probably no other social work literature focusing on them. However, they are also examples of marginalization and discrimination that can be applied to many other service users either collectively or individually. Learning points will therefore be transferable. In keeping with principles of acceptance and inclusion inherent in the concept of diversity, the ideas put forward support and encourage the meaningful participation of service users and carers in social work education and practice.

This book is a welcome contribution to current debates around diversity and difference, confronting dilemmas, analysing concepts and developing relevant skills.

Ruben Martin
Honorary Senior Lecturer in Social Work
University of Kent

Introduction

*Kish Bhatti-Sinclair and
Christopher Smethurst*

This book seeks to explore diversity and difference within the context of recent changes and challenges to the social work profession. Its specific focus is to address themes that are contentious and under-explored, but essential to understanding the complexity of contemporary social work practice.

It has been primarily written for students on undergraduate and postgraduate social work training courses. However, the themes addressed are intended to be relevant to experienced practitioners, and all those who struggle with the practice dilemmas posed by diversity and difference.

Why another book on diversity and difference?

We believe that there are two good reasons for another book that focuses on both diversity and difference:

First, that the legitimacy of social work's value base has been subject to an unusually consistent and sustained level of criticism – both from government and from its agents and advisors. Arguably, one of the few constants in social work over the past 30 years has been the anticipation of its impending demise. These predictions have always been premature. Social work has been remarkably resilient as a profession, able to adapt to the ebb and flow of the policies and ideologies of successive governments (Jordan and Drakeford 2012). However, root and branch reforms to the profession may yet radically redefine social work within a narrow range of specified tasks aligned to the ideological whims of the current government. It is clear that social workers will not be driving these reforms; in the absence of a unified voice for the profession, they will be largely imposed, with little consultation or desire to achieve consensus (McNicholl 2016). When it comes to policy formation, social workers may feel that they are no strangers to being marginalized. However, of particular concern is that the involvement of service users, in social work reforms and wider social care policy, is at best cursory and largely notable by its absence (Beresford and Boxall 2012).

Although it would be premature to assume that all impending reforms are hostile to the profession, it should be noted that the perennial criticism of social work's perceived unhealthy obsession with 'political correctness' has been a consistent feature of the British government's narrative about the profession. From adoption processes through to social work training, the government has made bold its intention to challenge that which contradicts its own 'common sense' conceptualization of practice. As the themes of diversity and difference frequently stray into the orbit of what is dismissed as mere political correctness, it seems timely to re-evaluate what 'diversity' and 'difference' will mean in the new, 'reformed' world of social work.

Second, it is our view that there are many aspects of diversity and difference which are relatively neglected within social work literature. Partly, this is because of issues that have emerged fairly recently – for example, the complex and highly emotive tangle of concerns that include child sexual exploitation and extremism which appear to be linked ever closer to ethnicity, culture, racism and Islamophobia (Runnymede Trust 1997). However, we felt that there was a need to address other, arguably more specialist, areas of practice which have transferable messages and possibly a wider significance for the profession as a whole.

Aims and approach

In our experience, we have observed that students and practitioners frequently struggle to fully incorporate, within their practice, the principles and values that are regarded as the sacred tenets of social work training. There is a risk that these may be rejected as unrealistic. Or, practitioners may feel a continual sense of being ethically compromised and insecure. In addition, we believe that social work training has often struggled to address aspects of diversity and difference that pose dilemmas for practitioners. We believe that culture and religion, alongside nationality and citizenship, are overladen with ideas on British values and ways of living which reinforce 'them' rather than 'us', i.e. othering (Masocha 2016). The intention is often unintended or misplaced, but the manner can border on inciting racial hatred, a premise (if acted on) which is outlawed by the 1976 Race Relations Act. Arguably, the 2010 Equality Act provides a further strengthening of legal protection against direct and indirect discrimination. Yet, in the run-up and aftermath of the 'Brexit' referendum, the apparent upsurge in hostility to those perceived as 'outsiders' highlights the potential fragility of this protection. Indeed, this raises the question of a disconnection between the progressive intentions of legislation and the intolerant instincts of a large swathe of the population.

We do not propose a magic solution to these problems. However, we aim to address those themes that are contentious and challenging – which perhaps do not receive the attention they deserve in social work training. Our intent is to assist practitioners when they are unsure of how to respond in situations of complexity, or when they experience the perennial anxiety of doing or saying 'the wrong thing'.

We have not sought to produce a 'How to work with . . .' manual. Our aim is to enable practitioners to enhance their existing skills by developing a deeper understanding of others and themselves. The exercises, throughout the book, are designed to support this process. Finally, we invite readers to explore their own biases and prejudices; we acknowledge that bias, prejudice and discriminatory attitudes are intrinsic features of our existence as fallible human beings. Understanding our own frailties is a prerequisite to gaining the insight required to work with others in a purposeful and meaningful way.

Structure of the book

PART 1: 'Theories and contexts', provides an overview of key themes and theories which underpin the book.

Chapter 1: Chris Smethurst and Kish Bhatti-Sinclair provide a synopsis of the current political, economic and ideological issues facing the profession. The terms 'diversity' and 'difference' will be defined.

Chapter 2: Vida Douglas and Jan Fook explore cultural competence, social difference and 'othering' which relate to reflexive practice, and examine bias in types of behaviour which push people into places which make them different. They suggest that social workers are engaged in complex human relationships and that the process of 'othering' hinders active engagement, rooted in ethical principles such as openness, empathy and acceptance.

Chapter 3: Bridget Ng'andu explores 'whiteness' and being white, and argues that social workers need to develop a deeper understanding of white identity and identification – particularly, when working with Black Minority and Ethnic (BME) families.

Chapter 4: Jon Old proposes that professional power, alongside a mismatch between behaviour and ethical principles, is likely to lead to a high level of cognitive dissonance for social workers. He argues that the human capacity to express thoughts may lead to poor judgements and decision-making, and suggests that theoretical ideas, rooted in social psychology, can enable social workers to understand themselves in a societal context which is diverse and socially different.

PART 2: 'Themes from contemporary practice', further develops the themes in Part 1 by considering aspects of practice that are comparatively neglected in social work literature, yet have a significance that transcends their specific focus. The messages in Part 2 are about the professional dilemmas inherent in day-to-day working with groups marginalized and disempowered by societal antipathy. In essence, the authors are sharing knowledge which can be applied more broadly. We call on the reader to look for parallels with their own experience and areas of practice, even if these would, from a brief reading of their titles, appear to be significantly different from the focus of the chapters.

Chapter 5: Chris Smethurst examines the influence of contemporary class politics upon social justice and inequality. The chapter builds on the themes introduced in Chapters 2 and 4 and asks social workers to consider how class difference impacts on everyday engagement, including assessment and intervention processes.

Chapter 6: Kish Bhatti-Sinclair develops the themes of 'othering' in relation to the developments in Islamophobic thinking rooted in ideas of dangerousness which appear to be increasingly linked to followers of Islam and Muslim traditions. Professional debates on race, religion and the fear of being called racist are related to professional laws on diversity and difference.

Chapter 7: Dan Allen introduces cultural determinism, evolutionary psychology and memetics in relation to social work practice with Roma people. Theoretical understandings of biological determinism, human growth and the epigenetic impact are particularly useful with any group deemed to be different, diverse and disadvantaged. Social workers are urged to consider discrimination as a situational social construct which can act as a contagion, passed from one person to another.

Chapter 8: Gerry Skelton questions the merging of spirituality with religion, and argues that spirituality, as a discrete subject, should be critiqued and embedded in social work education, training and practice.

Chapters 9 and 10 make compelling arguments for greater involvement of service users and carers in social work education, and better understanding of specialist need in practice.

Chapter 9: Lisa Armstrong and Angela Etherington argue that the first-hand, story-based experience offered by service users and carers is an invaluable source of knowledge. They suggest that service users and carer educators enable students to examine ethical dilemmas in detail, and support solution-based practice based on respect, choice and self-determination.

Chapter 10: Lucy Jacques and Rebecca Long introduce an area which is rarely considered in specialist practice – deaf-blind services for people with dual or combined sensory loss. They argue for greater inclusion in the hearing world and the deaf-signing world within all relevant services, and provide a pertinent discussion of social work responsibilities under the 2014 Care Act.

Part 1

Theories and contexts

1 Diversity and difference in challenging times: the social and political context

*Christopher Smethurst and
Kish Bhatti-Sinclair*

Chapter overview

By the end of this chapter you should be able to understand and critique the following:

- The interrelationship of contemporary social, economic, political and ideological themes in social work
- Definitions of diversity and difference
- The importance of theory to improvised social work 'performance'.

Introduction

This chapter provides a concise summary of the some of the societal and political themes which provide the contextual background for the issues discussed in this book. Contemporary understanding of the terms 'difference' and 'diversity' are explored, culminating in a brief analysis of the key challenges for social work practice.

A new era of intolerance?

'Do you worry about Britain's growing Muslim population? You're not alone.' (Kirkup 2015).

This *Daily Telegraph* headline was the perfect illustration as to why we decided to write this book. About six months previously, we had discussed whether we had entered a new era of intolerance – one that threatened to roll back decades of what we had assumed to be progress. Those of us who grew up in the 1970s and 1980s had lived through, what we had thought to be, the high water mark of the careless acceptance of discrimination and prejudice in Britain. Perhaps we had been wrong?

We had observed, with dismay, the increasingly strident attacks on multiculturalism (Cameron 2011; Phillips 2015). This had been accompanied by what appeared to be the casual racism which characterized much of the discussion regarding immigration during the run-up to the 2015 General Election (Kaushik 2015) and the 2016 referendum on the membership of the European Union. In addition, contemporary England seemed to provide fertile ground for increasing antipathy towards those receiving welfare benefits, including disabled people for whom being labelled a scrounger was potentially a precursor to more extreme forms of hate crime (Quarmby 2011).

The *Daily Telegraph* headline enabled us to crystallize our thoughts. We neither considered that the author was being racist, nor that they were intentionally causing offence. Instead, we viewed the headline as indicative of a wider theme: an underlying assumption that difference and diversity are a threat to an assumed homogenous British identity. It seems that discriminatory views can once more be aired openly and aggressively by political leaders and the general public. Interestingly, the newspaper editors either thought that their Muslim readers would agree, or that they did not have Muslim readers. The ICM survey (Phillips 2016) sought opinion from a random sample of 1081 Muslims living in England on issues such as women, homosexuality and social relations with outsiders. Although the analysis of the survey did not focus on the commonalities between the survey respondents and conservative thinkers, the findings suggest that further attention needs to be paid to the common attitudes of some Muslims and some right-wing groups towards equality and human rights.

Kaushik (2015) discusses the continuing expectation that Black and Minority Ethnic (BME) citizens are expected to prove their 'Britishness' – a British identity that is assumed to require giving up one's minority identification (Nandi and Platt 2013). Muslims have been singled out for particular scrutiny, with a strong media and political debate focusing on whether or not the Islamic faith is compatible with secular, British values (Nickels et al. 2012; Cesari 2013). However, it is not only BME communities who appear to be lower down in a hierarchy of belonging. Todd (2014) argues that rights of citizenship are apparently contingent upon participation in the world of paid work. Commitment to 'hard work' seems to have emerged as an unseen addition to the government's definition of British values. Indeed, both the Conservative and Labour governments' apparent fetishization of the 'hard-working family' has placed it at the head of a 'community of worth' (Anderson 2013: 4), thereby devaluing or excluding the unemployed and many disabled people. Additionally, those perceived as not conforming to an economically productive, culturally homogenous ideal have been constructed in government rhetoric and policy as a burden on (or a threat to) an imagined community of 'us' (Hills 2015).

Activity 1.1

Consider the headline:

Do you worry about Britain's growing Muslim population? You're not alone.

1. What is your reaction to this headline? Is the headline problematic? If so – why? If not – why not?

2. For the word 'Muslim' substitute 'Jewish'. Is your reaction the same? Consider why or why not?
3. Now substitute the word 'black' and repeat the exercise.

The purpose of this exercise is to illustrate the apparent ease with which a section of the population can become identified as an out-group in a manner that would be unacceptable for other groups or communities. Stigma and discrimination can become normalized through a process that is both gradual and insidious.

Progress or complacency?

It is easy to focus exclusively on recent trends and forget that discrimination and oppression may not necessarily have got any worse. There have been considerable achievements, particularly in relation to anti-discrimination legislation, which is considerably stronger in Britain than in most European countries (Carvalho et al. 2015). Similarly, McCormack (2012) outlines British successes in tackling homophobia and contrasts the UK experience favourably with that of the USA. However, Walter (2011) sounds a note of caution. When writing in 1999, she believed that 'old fashioned sexism' was on the wane. Yet, she later concluded that policy change, goodwill and aspiration were insufficient to tackle a societal culture that was resistant to change:

> I don't really think sexism ever went away, it's stronger than it was. It's as though something crept in by the backdoor – and we turned around and it's everywhere, and you just think, 'OK, we've got to deal with this again.'
> (Walter 2010)

Walter raises the spectre that hard-won reforms, and an apparent liberalization of social attitudes, may in fact not be as deeply rooted in the fabric of society as is frequently assumed. In fact, Priestland (2013) suggests a degree of complacency on the part of those who define themselves as 'progressives'. A belief in consensus and the power of reasoned argument has perhaps led to an over-optimistic minimizing of the extent of conflicting interests between groups in society. Similarly, the potential for latent conflicts to be resurrected and amplified for political gain has possibly been underestimated. Much of the analysis of the reasons why the British voted to leave the European Union has focused on these themes.

Within social work, it is acknowledged that the New Labour government emphasized the concepts of partnership in child protection and personalization in adult social care, while failing to acknowledge the conflicting agendas of the state, the professional and the service user (Ferguson 2011; Ferguson 2012). The language of 'choice', 'empowerment' and 'independence' has been utilized by Labour, Coalition and Conservative governments, within a policy agenda that redefines service users as consumers (Hugman 1998; McLaughlin 2009;

Gray et al. 2015). Therefore, there is an inherent risk that difference and diversity may be recast as individualized preferences, met through the operation of a market in services. Yet this emphasis on the individual 'customer' finding the best deal, and acting in rational self-interest, is problematic (Carey 2009; McLaughlin 2009). Its focus on individual autonomy fails to adequately acknowledge the impact of structural oppression and the processes of disempowerment (Carey 2009; Dodd 2013). The vision of the empowered *individual* consumer effectively marginalizes the need for collective action in order to address the structural inequalities that undermine lasting social change (Dodd 2013).

As was possibly the case with Walter's (1998) conceptualization of 'The New Feminism', the power of individual agency in achieving wider social change has perhaps been afforded too much significance. Female equality has not been achieved through the medium of consumerism and lifestyle choice (Walter 2011). This suggests that hard-won freedoms may be deceptively fragile – that an inclusive and tolerant society is not an inevitable outcome of economic growth and customer power.

A consequence of the notion of the public as customers is that recent governments have perceived them as 'voters to be pleased rather than citizens to be enlightened' (Thompson 2015: 144). Arguably, this has resulted in a passive and reactive pandering to the vagaries of public opinion and popular prejudice. In response to crises that have challenged the assumed consensus of a tolerant society (most notably: the financial crisis, terrorism, child sexual exploitation and the refugee/migration crisis), the emerging narrative of political parties of government has been an inconsistent mix of expediency and cynicism. Expediency can be clearly demonstrated by the knee-jerk responses to media-induced moral panics. For example, Warner (2013) locates the reaction to the death of Peter Connelly ('Baby P') within a moral panic concerning an imagined, contaminating underclass and its perceived threat to middle-class values. These values are powerfully reinforced through demands on social workers to 'get tougher' with families (Casey 2013), despite the fact that the self-defeating consequences of such punitive social work practice are well documented (Featherstone et al. 2014).

The accusation of cynicism is perhaps justified by examples of government advocating tolerance on the one hand, while fanning flames of prejudice on the other. In the wake of recent terrorist outrages, official commentators have stressed the disconnection of the perpetrators from views held by the majority of Muslims. Paradoxically, terrorism is implicitly located, by those same commentators, within a narrative of cultural dysfunction, with Muslims being collectively held responsible for extremism and their failure to do more to address the problem in their midst (Kassimeris and Jackson 2012; Heath-Kelly 2013; Khan 2015).

Arguably, there is a risk in complacently assuming that the fabled tolerance of British society is resilient enough to withstand the challenges which it has been subjected to. Particularly concerning is the empirical evidence that reveals a close correlation between the impact of economic hardship upon communities and the rising levels of intolerance (Perry 2001; Johnston and Lordan 2015; Tyson and Hall 2015). Hence, it is essential for social workers to have an understanding of the impact of the financial crisis and 'austerity' upon social cohesion and social tensions.

Austerity and intolerance

Within the limitations of this chapter we are unable to provide a detailed analysis of current economic policy. However, 'austerity' can be understood as an approach to economic policy which includes cuts to public spending, imposed by many Western governments, following the financial crisis that began in 2007 (Blyth 2013).

Conceivably, it was not just the financial sector that was caught unawares by the financial crisis. There were those who identified politically as 'progressives' who perhaps failed to understand and address the hardening of social attitudes which accompanied the imposition of the economic policies of austerity.

A clear demonstration of this was the rise to pre-eminence of immigration among a list of voter concerns (Evans and Chzhen 2013; McLaren 2013). This phenomenon was feasibly more complex than a resurgence of visceral grievances against the foreign 'other'. Yet this was frequently understood, particularly by those on the political Left, within the narrow definitions of racism. Indeed, within the political class, opinions somewhat unhelpfully crystallized around two oppositional perspectives: it was either racist to be concerned about immigration; or, public concerns about immigration were merely justified anxieties about economic and social costs. In short, and in a direct echo of the politics of austerity, Britain could not 'afford' immigration.

The likelihood that such a complex and contradictory reality was probably a mixture of both positions remains a contentious issue – one which has been subject to a process of denial and entrenchment. It is a sobering thought that rational discussion appears to have been displaced by the often ill-judged campaigning of the British media (Lirola 2014; Hoops et al. 2015).

This cultural and political trend was starkly illustrated by the British EU referendum campaign. Whatever the complex individual motives of those who voted for 'Brexit', a clear focus on the issue of immigration by the 'out' campaigners framed much of the referendum debate. Arguably, the 'Remain' campaigners could mobilize no convincing response to this overwhelmingly negative focus on immigration.

Certainly, the ideological left has struggled to discover a convincing narrative that addresses this new political reality. Correspondingly, it has singularly failed to mount a convincing defence of the welfare state – this in the face of governmental attacks (Ryan 2015) which have sought to present the interests of an imagined community of working 'strivers' as oppositional to (and threatened by) those deemed to be feckless 'skivers' (Coote and Himmelweit 2013). 'We're all in this together' has been a mantra used by Coalition and Conservative governments to justify economic austerity; but it is not an inclusive one. It is aimed to largely appeal to the self-sacrifice of 'strivers', while implicitly excluding those unable or unwilling to 'do their bit' for the country's finances.

The human consequences of 'austerity' (the discarding of those in poverty, disabled people and those in acute mental distress) have been made anodyne to the majority population by presenting poverty as a lifestyle choice (Patrick 2014; Garthwaite et al. 2015). Similarly, disability and mental distress have been characterized as being surmountable, through a combination of attitudinal change on the part of the individual and motivation to participate in paid work (Verhaeghe 2014; Friedli and Stearn 2015). This presents a false dichotomy of dependence and independence, thereby ignoring the interdependence which is the hallmark of societal cohesion (Smethurst 2012). The vision of 'The Big Society' (Cameron 2011) appeared to embrace the notion of interdependence. However, this is curiously at odds with the competitive individualism implied by the government's narrative of 'strivers v shirkers' in 2016.

Activity 1.2

1. To what extent have you been affected by the economic policies of austerity, both personally and professionally?
2. Consider how austerity has affected the individuals and families you work with.

Research indicates that austerity has not been experienced equally across the population:

- The impact of spending cuts on the poorest tenth of the population has been 13 times greater than for the richest tenth (Haddad 2012).
- Varying according to the level of disability, austerity cuts have a financial impact on disabled people of between 9 to 19 times the national average for non-disabled people (Duffy 2013).
- Through an array of complex factors, the impact of austerity has fallen disproportionately on women (Rummery 2016).

Diversity, difference: what do these words mean in social work practice?

There has been an apparent decline in social work of the use of the robust terminology of anti-racism and anti-sexism in favour of the seemingly gentler terms of 'difference', 'diversity' and 'equality' (G. Singh 2014). The assertive tenets of anti-racism have seemed to be at odds with Western societies' paradoxical desire for sameness *and* difference (Paradies 2016). Within this context, diversity and difference can perhaps be understood as relatively minor individual and cultural variations within the constraints of social conformity. The unwritten rules of compliance are largely defined by the normative expectations of a white, middle-class life course and the willing participation, as consumers and workers, in a competitive market economy (Ciscel and Heath 2001; Skeggs 2004; Lawler 2005; Lazzarato 2009).

This rather opaque and fragile conception has proved difficult to articulate within the contemporary preoccupation of defining notions of 'Britishness' and 'British values'. Definitions of Britishness purport to be inclusive of diversity and difference, yet require connection or assimilation with vague and reductionist definitions of white, Anglo-Saxon culture (Fortier 2013; Nandi and Platt 2013; Keddie 2014). Official definitions of British values give the appearance of inclusivity: 'democracy, the rule of law, individual liberty, and mutual respect and tolerance of those with different faiths and beliefs' (DfE 2014). However, it is difficult to identify what is distinctively 'British' about them. Nevertheless, it is clear that both Britishness and British values are intended as a riposte to what are perceived as the pernicious effects of multiculturalism (Cameron 2007).

Uberoi and Modood (2013) provide a useful understanding of multiculturalism. Firstly, it denotes a culturally diverse population. Secondly, a policy of multiculturalism aims to reduce fear, suspicion, inequality and disadvantage. Thirdly, an ideology of multiculturalism is an aspirational vision of future harmonious coexistence. Meer and Modood (2009) note the widely held belief that the policy and ideology of multiculturalism has been in retreat as a consequence of the backlash from terrorist outrages. However, Uberoi and Modood (2013) argue that this retreat is overstated. Nevertheless, Sealey (2016) illustrates how social policies have retreated from multiculturalism in favour of an agenda of assimilation.

Ideas on racism are also worth re-examining in a context where multiculturalism may have been perceived to have failed in policy and practice. Masocha (2016) suggests that contemporary thinking on colour, nationality and place must be incorporated within theories such as modern racism, a concept which develops the notion of antipathy and suggests that we react to preconceived ideas in the following ways (Hogan and Mallott 2005: 115):

- **resentment** towards the gains made by ethnic minority groups (for example: immigrants get all the resources)
- **denial** that racial discrimination is still a problem (for example: everyone should get the same treatment)
- **antagonism** towards equality (for example: all immigrants should be tested for English).

Modern racism can explain the attitudes of people who perceive themselves as open-minded liberals, but have been shown to privilege some groups above others. For example, child protection professionals have been accused of not carrying out, or perhaps being in denial of, their duties towards victims of child sexual exploitation under the 1989 Children Act and the 1975 Sex Discrimination Act for fear of being accused of racism (Jay 2014).

Antipathy is prevalent towards those seen to receive above average public resources or gains (say through employment laws). If modern racism is developed into the broader notion of modern discrimination, it can also explain the multiple and overlapping dimensions of age, health, disability, ethnicity, caste, class, gender, race, nationality and sexuality.

Within this context, how should we understand the terms 'diversity' and 'difference'?

Definition of 'diversity'

Diversity is multidimensional and includes race, disability, class, economic status, age, sexuality, gender and transgender, faith and belief. Social workers appreciate that, as a consequence of difference, a person's life experience may include oppression, marginalization and alienation as well as privilege, power and acclaim, and are able to challenge appropriately.

(BASW 2015)

Diversity suggests that varied, possibly dissimilar, groups can coexist in close proximity, and share sufficient common, uniting characteristics, traits and qualities. Within British law and social policy, diversity relates to a type of person who is ethnically different because of skin colour, skin shade and regional identity (Bhatti-Sinclair 2015).

Definition of 'difference'

Difference is defined as dissimilar or divergent from the norm, and tends to describe alternative, variant and contrasting behaviour which may be slightly but acceptably edgy, deviant and risky. In societies such as the UK such individuals and groups are seen to share deeper, complex experiences, memories, meanings and backgrounds which intersect and overlap (Law 2010).

In social work practice the words diversity and difference are notionally combined and mainly used to cluster groups who may benefit from professional methods – for example, culturally sensitive or culturally appropriate service interventions (Fook and Gardner 2006). However, these approaches are limited as they focus upon personal and attitudinal change, rather than structural and institutional responsibility for human rights, social inclusion and equality of opportunity (Bhatti-Sinclair 2011). What then are the challenges for social workers, addressing diversity and difference in their professional role?

The challenges for social work

One of the key challenges for social work is the creeping marginalization of diversity and difference in social work policy. The Conservative government is openly critical of the so-called obsession of social work with 'political correctness' (Rogowski 2013). Social work education is singled out as a particularly suspect source of misguided ideas about social justice (Gove 2013). A key belief is that the profession must be depoliticized, and it has been quite skilful in the art of divide and rule, contrasting 'out of touch' politically naïve, social work academics with a select sample of managers and practitioners deemed to represent the 'real world'. As Narey (2014: 11) asserts: 'It is vital that social work education for those working with children and families is not dominated by theories of non-oppressive practice, empowerment and partnership.'

Yet social work professional standards and regulatory regimes have long held a commitment in which the principles of social justice are enshrined, and require professionals to practise ethically and understand the implications of diversity for their practice. Three of the eight Domains of the Professional Capabilities Framework (PCF) focus on 'Diversity', 'Values and Ethics' and 'Rights and Justice'. However, there are concerns that these elements are being marginalized in the current round of social work reforms, particularly in relation to children's social work where values have a diminished profile in the Knowledge and Skills Statement. In addition, there is little apparent commitment to the involvement of service users in the reform of the profession (Stevenson 2016). The absence of explicit references in this book to professional standards reflects the current state of flux and climate of uncertainty.

The second challenge for social workers is working within a residual welfare system which is under a consistent regime of service cuts. The inherent danger here is that addressing diversity and difference may not be seen as a priority, particularly when this is perceived to cost time and money (Pitt 2011). Similarly, bureaucratic and mechanistic assessment practices may fail to take into account the complex reality of service users' lives (Oliver et al. 2012; Mainstone 2014).

Thirdly, there is a risk that professionals may view diversity and difference as singular categories. For example, Muslims are frequently and misleadingly defined as a homogenous 'out-group' within political and public discourse (Peace 2015; Jones 2016). The use of the word 'community' can, in itself, be an unconscious form of 'othering', particularly when referring to individuals with assumed similar characteristics and interests. Therefore, it may be viewed as a means of exclusion *just* as much as inclusion.

Within this context, 'intersectionality' is a useful concept for understanding the relationship between difference, diversity, inequality and exclusion. Intersectionality is when individuals may be excluded or experience discrimination through a multiplicity of dimensions: age, health, disability, ethnicity, caste, class, gender, race, nationality and sexuality (Crenshaw1991; Essed 2001; Walby 2007; Law 2010).

The final challenge for individual social work practitioners is that the application of skills may become disconnected from a deeper understanding of the lived realities of service users' lives. Current social work reforms are privileging specific perceptions of practice which appear to be disembodied from their societal context.

Practitioners will be familiar with the age-old challenges of applying theory to practice. They may struggle with what can appear to be the lofty aspiration to 'challenge oppression', when the realities of practice may seem like they are struggling to stay upright against a constant headwind. We can certainly identify with those conscientious and committed social workers for whom the musings of theorists may merely confirm what they already know: that there are many things wrong with social work. So what is the point of a commitment to gain a deeper understanding of the theories which underpin social work?

In answering this question, we feel that the work of Payne (2007: 85) is very relevant. His conceptualization of the social worker is as a 'wise person': someone who 'knows what to do' in challenging situations. Payne does not privilege theory above practice wisdom; instead, he draws upon the analogy of an improvising musician – one who is not consciously aware of his/her theoretical knowledge but draws upon it to respond, in the moment, in an improvised performance.

The notion of social work as an improvised performance will no doubt have resonance for many practitioners!

For us, Payne's analogy is powerful in providing a means of addressing the perennial question of whether or not theoretical knowledge can be recalled and utilized in the rapid ebb and flow of direct work with individuals. As with the improvising musician, a social worker may not have immediate cognitive recall of their theoretical knowledge. But that is very different from saying it is not there, or that knowledge does not enrich, inform, and is even essential to, virtuoso displays of skill.

We hope that the chapters in this book will contribute something towards your knowledge of 'what to do'.

Activity 1.3

Before proceeding, take some time to reflect on your own thoughts, knowledge and beliefs.

1. Consider these words from Martin Narey: 'It is vital that social work education for those working with children and families is not dominated by theories of non-oppressive practice, empowerment and partnership.' (Narey 2014: 11)

   To what extent do Narey's views support or contradict your own? How might your own views affect how you approach: your reading of the chapters in this book; your day-to-day social work practice?

2. Take an audit of your own skills, knowledge and confidence. What aspects of diversity and difference do you feel confident in working with?

   Are there any aspects where you feel that you particularly lack knowledge, skills or confidence?

2 Cultural competence: towards a reflexive approach to working inclusively

Vida Douglas and Jan Fook

Chapter overview

By the end of this chapter you should be able to understand and critique the following concepts and models:

- Cultural competence
- Reflexivity and how it relates to cultural competence
- Social difference and othering.

Introduction

We live in a world of continuous technological and social change. In reality, the only constant is that our environment and the people within it will be subject to change. Diversity, difference, equality, and the values of social justice and human rights, fundamental principles of social work, are all context specific and subject to flux. In addition, we now recognize that we live in a post-colonial era, when the influence of colonization on forging new ethnic and cultural identities must be considered. Social work is delivered in increasingly complex and changing environments, and has been defined by the International Federation of Social Workers (IFSW) and International Association of Schools of Social Work (IASSW 2014) as follows:

> a practice-based profession and an academic discipline that promotes social change and development, social cohesion, and the empowerment and liberation of people. Principles of social justice, human rights, collective responsibility and respect for diversities are central to social work. Underpinned by theories of social work, social sciences, humanities and indigenous knowledge, social work engages people and structures to address life challenges and enhance well-being.

Social workers are then foremost change agents, seeking to interact and connect with people from a variety of backgrounds, many of whom will be experiencing profound change and challenges in their life. The profession expects you to select from theories of social work and the social sciences, and critically learn to reject, sift, connect and pre-order previously held beliefs and perspectives in order to achieve effective solutions and outcomes to the problems presented by clients. Connecting with the 'voice' of the client or service user to encourage change, and collective responsibility, while at the same time establishing your authentic 'voice' as a social worker, is not without its challenges. As Anaïs Nin said: 'We don't see things as they are; we see things as we are.'

As social workers, we bring to our studies or work context, previous experiences and knowledge – some good and some bad. It is a fact – we are not a tabula rasa – a clean state!

Within social work the need to work with increasing diversity has led to ethical debates about how the profession can encourage the development of a culturally competent and responsive workforce. You may be familiar with the sketch by Alan Fletcher called 'Two-faced friend'. When looking at the picture for the first time you might see an old woman with a hook nose and a wart, or a young woman with her faced turned away. Fletcher commented about his work: 'When the mind has seized one view, it's amazingly difficult to get it to switch one's perception to see it from another point of view' (Newton 2015: 154). Essentially, the image that you see first will be the perspective you will hold and can make it difficult to see the other interpretation. As a social worker, the theoretical and conceptual knowledge drawn upon will help to challenge previously held positions, and encourage alternative opinions and routes to solving a problem. To further assist social workers in practice there are numerous approaches and frameworks to promote personal and professional change, helping to extend previously held perspectives of the world. Cultural competence is one such approach, often used by healthcare and social work professionals to examine previously held assumptions about groups and individuals. When doing so, they seek to reduce the level of biases and prejudices that can occur within the context of social and healthcare practice.

We begin with a brief discussion of what is meant by the term cultural competence. Then, drawing on three approaches to cultural competence, we consider their strengths, limitations and relevance for social work education and practice today. A central question for consideration is whether cultural competence can be practised, improved and changed? Or instead, do we now need an alternative approach to working inclusively in health and social work?

The aim is to enable you to also gain an appreciation of the skills needed to apply a reflexive understanding to oneself and to begin to identify how a reflexive approach might apply in working inclusively.

Definitions of cultural competence

Culture is the extent to which members identify to a particular group in relation to, for example, a common language and behavioural norms. Our understanding of culture is confounded by the fact that culture itself is not static; it is constantly evolving and changing. That said, it is widely acknowledged that, like language and ethnicity, culture shapes all our lives. From the time we are born culture influences our behaviours, thoughts and attitudes.

Cross et al. (1989: 13) define cultural competence as 'a set of congruent behaviours, attitudes, and policies that come together in a system, agency or among

professionals and enables that system, agency or those professions to work effectively in cross-cultural situations'.

Cultural competence is concerned with how we respond to and meet the needs
of people with different cultures to our own, but professional dilemmas can
arise when what we find conflicts with what we would like to see. The mismatch
between the external world and our internal values can lead to incongruence, a
notion explored further by Jon Old in Chapter 4.

Historically, research has focused on cultural competence with African-
Americans and Latinos (Randolph and Banks 1993; Schiele 1996). More recently,
research on cultural competence has evolved to include sexuality and religion,
among other things. The approaches taken have focused primarily on the key
features of cultural competence in relation to **knowledge, skills** and **values**
(Matthews 1996; McPhatter 1997). Knowledge acquisition about various cultural
groups is considered essential for professional competence (Dana et al. 1992;
Mason et al. 1996; Purnell 2002). Skills development, and the development of culturally competent skills, requires the social worker to move from using her/his
own culture as a benchmark for the assessment of behaviour, to incorporating
the perspectives of other cultures (Krajewski-Jaime et al. 1996). Demonstrating
an awareness of how our values and biases might impact on practice is impera-
tive in demonstrating cultural competence. It has been suggested that more
research is still required into the values associated with a culturally competent
social worker (Weaver 1999).

Cultural competence in social work

Social work training is grounded upon the values of social justice and human
rights. Two dominant approaches within this tradition in the UK have been
anti-racist practice (Dominelli 2002, 2008) focusing on power relationships
between black service users and white social workers, and anti-discriminatory
practice (Thompson 2012), articulating other forms of discrimination and oppression other than race. Over the years, several government policies and social work
research have highlighted the importance of addressing the cultural diversity of
the population being served and providing culturally appropriate services. In the
area of child protection, Brophy et al. (2003) suggest that cultural competence is
a necessity for effective child protection outcomes for families from ethnic
minorities. Similarly, the Department of Health strategy document, *the Government's Objectives for Children's Social Services* (DH 1999: para. 16) on children in
need, commented that 'the needs of black and ethnic minority children and families must be identified and met through services which are culturally sensitive
and which recognise and value diversity'. In addition, the Health and Care Professions Council (HCPC) standards of proficiency for social work reinforce the
need for social workers to 'understand the impact of different cultures and communities and how this affects the role of the social worker in supporting service
users and carers' (HCPC 2012: 11).

Below are three models of cultural competence which have been influential
primarily in the USA, but latterly have gained recognition among health and

Table 2.1 Five dimensions of cultural competence

Cultural Awareness	This requires in-depth self-examination of the practitioner's own cultural and professional background, and recognition of own biases, prejudices and assumptions about people from minority communities.
Cultural Skill	This is the ability to collect cultural data relevant to the service user's problems and needs within the assessment process.
Cultural Knowledge	This is searching for and acquiring detailed information about other cultures and ethnic groups.
Cultural Encounter	This is about learning accrued from engagement with service users and carers from culturally diverse backgrounds. It may dispel stereotypes and lead to modification of the practitioner's existing beliefs.
Cultural Desire	This relates to the practitioner's motivation to want to, rather than have to, engage in the above four processes. It includes a real willingness to accept differences, build on similarities, and learn from people as cultural informants.

social care educators in the UK: ASKED; the Prunnell Model for cultural competence; and Organizational Cultural Competence.

The ASKED Model

A process model of cultural competence is articulated by Campinha-Bacote (2002: 182–3) called **ASKED**. Five dimensions of cultural competence are required to achieve cultural competence, detailed in Table 2.1 – adapted from Laird (2008).

It is acknowledged that culture must be recognized within the context of racial prejudice, gender and sexuality experiences. As Laird (2008: 149), comments:

> Over-focusing on culture without appreciating how it intersects with other aspects of identity or without exploring the potential for black-on-black and white-on-white oppression as well as white-on-black racism will result in inadequate assessments and services which fail to meet needs.

The Purnell Model

Within the healthcare professions, and more recently social work education, the Purnell Model for cultural competence has gained prominence internationally since its development in 1998. This approach evolved from the desire to provide student nurses with the tools to assist them with clinical assessments and guide individualized interventions. The model sought to offer insight into the general and cultural-specific knowledge required to work effectively with a client. According to this model, it is only when the health worker is aware of his or her existence, and is able to refrain from allowing their own experiences and values to shape the quality of care delivered, that a worker can become culturally competent. At the centre of the model is the empathy and understanding of the health worker. Four circular rims are denoted to recognize the role that the global society (outlying circular rim), local community (second rim), the family (third rim), and the individual (fourth rim), has on understanding the culture and cultural needs of the client. Within the inner circle are 12 cultural domains/ constructs to help increase understanding of the client's culture and encourage individualized interventions. Table 2.2 describes the domains involved in cultural competence. The table depicts the domains as linear. In reality the process is helical because you may revisit different domains to expand your understanding following new sources of information.

Each domain is interconnected and can be applied differently dependent on the cultures and specific needs of the client (see Figure 2.1 overleaf). The model proposes that there is a process of self-discovery as the health worker journeys towards cultural competence in practice.

Table 2.2 12 Domains for cultural competence

Domain	Key concepts
1. **Overview/heritage**	Relates to current residence, education status, occupation, economics and reasons for immigration.
2. **Communication**	Dominant language, dialect, tone and annotations, non-verbal communication, touch, body language and greetings.
3. **Family roles**	Family roles, roles of older and extended members. Gender roles and social status.
4. **Workforce issues**	Autonomy, gender roles, ethnic communication styles, healthcare practice from country of origin.
5. **Biocultural ecology**	Skin colouration, physical differences, hereditary differences, differences in how the body reacts to drugs.
6. **High-risk behaviours**	Use of tobacco, recreational drugs, lack of physical activity high-risk sexual practices.
7. **Nutrition**	Adequate food, appropriate food choices and rituals. Food substances during illness and for health promotion.
8. **Pregnancy and child-rearing practices**	Method of birth control and view about pregnancy. Restrictive and taboo practices.
9. **Death rituals**	Views on death, behaviours to prepare for death, burial practices and bereavement behaviour.
10. **Spirituality**	Religious practices, use of prayer, sources of strength that give meaning to life.
11. **Healthcare practices**	Responsibility for health, self-medication practices, views on mental illness.
12. **Healthcare practitioner and child-rearing practices**	Use of traditional healthcare practices and gender of healthcare provider.

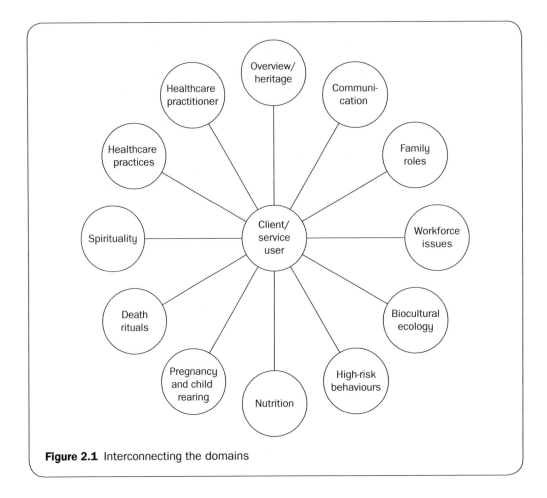

Figure 2.1 Interconnecting the domains

A number of benefits are evident from taking this approach to the delivery of care. Implicit value is given to the diversity and uniqueness of others. The model recognizes that each culture has the potential to influence how an individual client perceives and interprets interventions by professionals. The model promotes a co-production approach to care, in which the voice and wishes of each client are key to good-quality, responsive and appropriate care. While there are obvious merits to this approach, there are several assumptions underpinning the model that require further consideration (Purnell 2002). Firstly, the model is applied to all professionals operating in differing contexts, implying that the same information is required about cultural diversity across all professions and contexts; and, secondly, that all cultures are different but share core similarities. This does not fully account for the fact that culture is evolving and dynamic. It is clear from research that cultural differences can be observed on many levels – i.e. within, among and between (Purnell 2002). Regardless of how comprehensive the tool/resource is, it cannot account for the complexity of culture. Thirdly, it is suggested that equal value is given to each culture, where no one culture is considered preferable or more advantageous than another. The consequences of failing to recognize, preserve and protect the dignity of others may be deemed professional incompetence. However, is it possible to guarantee equal recognition to all cultures given the current structural and economic disparities between certain groups? Finally, understanding and learning about culture is not a one-off event – it is a continual process of discovery promoted through cultural encounters which affirm value and worth (Campinha-Bacote 1999).

Although there has been support for the idea that increased cultural competence can improve the quality of care received, while alleviating the disparities in care experiences between some groups, it has been suggested that cultural competence is limited by the lack of clarity concerning its operationalization (Geron 2002). In response to this criticism, cultural competence in mental health services has been redefined as the 'degree of compatibility between the cultural and linguistic characteristics of a community and the manner in which the combined policies, structures and processes underlying mental health services seek to make these services available, accessible and utilized' (Hernandez et al. 2006: 2).

The Organizational Cultural Competence Model

The final model promotes organizational cultural competence, and suggests that the characteristics of the individual practitioner and the service delivery are integral to the wider context of the organization in which professionals work and exist. According to this model, cultural competence is realized when there is congruence between the following four factors.

1 *Community contexts*

Understanding how some groups come into contact with services might differ (voluntary or involuntary admission). For instance, many Black Minority and Ethnic (BME) groups are more likely to enter the services through involuntary routes.

2 *Cultural characteristics of the local population*

The strategies employed to seek help, identify a problem or the choice of services requested, will vary among cultural groups. A culturally competent organization will be responsive to these issues.

3 *Organizational infrastructure*

The values and vision of the organization that support cultural competence. The quality and quantity of communication that occurs within the organization and between the communities it serves is considered to be crucial to achieving cultural competence. The extent to which the organization promotes user engagement and community participation in the delivery and design of services is a key feature. Equally important are the governance, planning and evaluation approaches within the organization to promote cultural competence.

A diverse workforce backed up by relevant technical support serves to support the vision of a culturally competent organization.

4 *Direct service support*

The availability of the service, the degree of accessibility and the extent to which the usage of these services is monitored against what is known about expressed needs in the community serve to reinforce cultural competence.

In essence, the model provides factors required for culturally competent organizations. Further exploration is required to establish the best approaches to measure the above factors. As Hernandez et al. (2009: 1049) state, future research is needed 'to examine the frequent suggestion that increased cultural competence in mental health services can reduce disparities in the delivery of existing services'.

Cultural competence: criticisms and reflections for future practice

The above models of cultural competence are based on practice experience that, to date, has not been evaluated in a systematic way (Weaver 1999). Furthermore, it has been suggested that cultural competence frameworks currently lack the necessary detail to achieve definite learning and practice objectives (Furness 2005). Lee and Zaharlick (2013) suggest that more understanding is required on how to undertake culturally sensitive social work research, and of the measures of cultural competence within practice.

Cultural awareness encourages a multicultural agenda, but there is a danger that this approach may result in a colour-blind mentality and increase the potential for practitioners to overlook the significance of institutional racism and the impact it has on the lived experiences of many clients (Abrams and Moio 2009). Much of the research on cultural competence has focused on individual attitudes of the practitioner and not fully addressed how institutional racism and oppression can impact on the way clients engage with social workers.

In addition, there is a conceptual problem with models which rely too heavily on knowledge or awareness of differences in order to provide more culturally competent services. The essence of this criticism is that the term 'cultural competence' itself implies an overemphasis on behavioural characteristics (such as in the Purnell Model), rather than perhaps the type of mindfulness which needs to form the basis of any culturally competent practice. Although some of the models include this phase of awareness (see the ASKED Model above), in our experience it is exactly this phase which is the most difficult to teach, but without which the awareness of cultural differences may have little in-depth or sustainable impact on thinking and behaviour.

We believe a major reason for this lack of impact is the clear assumption a 'learning about cultural differences' approach implies. Unfortunately, emphasizing the need to know about the content of social and cultural differences implies that being culturally competent means you need to be aware of all the major details of that culture, in order to practise competently with that particular group of people (the Purnell Model above provides a comprehensive list of the dimensions about which knowledge is needed). The onus in this sense is placed on the person to find out all they can about a particular culture. It is not hard to see the fallacy of this type of approach. (Unfortunately this is the kind of list which is often assumed to underpin professional competence.) For a start, it is impossible to know all details of a culture – most people within that culture would, in any case, have difficulty in articulating it all, since culture, by its nature, can be a hidden or taken-for-granted thing (and can involve much more in-depth thinking than visible social differences may superficially indicate). Secondly, there are always exceptions or modifications to cultural rules, and assuming that all representatives of a cultural group will think and act in roughly similar ways can land a professional person in more trouble than if they just kept an open mind in the first place. Thirdly, the emphasis on knowing about cultural differences has a dangerous possibility of encouraging the phenomenon of 'othering'.

'Othering' (see Fook 2012: 92–5) is the process whereby phenomena (in this case people) who are seen as 'different' are constructed as socially different and, as a result, often 'inferior' or, worse, 'dangerous'. In postmodern thinking, 'othering' can occur as a result of binary oppositional categorizing, a process which seems relatively harmless since we all do it in order to make sense of complex and changing phenomena we experience constantly in our daily lives. In postmodern analysis, binary oppositional thinking is evident in our language, when we often speak as if there are only two major opposing categories of phenomena, such as 'men' and 'women', which in theory make up the whole population. A problem arises in that often the second category is defined in terms of the first and, as a result, the second category is seen as inferior (when compared with the first), rather than simply different. An example might be how men are categorized as 'rational' and women as 'irrational'. Note the choice of words here. Women could be categorized as 'emotional', which does not necessarily imply the same devaluing as the term 'irrational'. Calling them 'emotional' would be using a term which denotes the difference, without the implied devaluing.

Said (1978) wrote about the concept of 'orientalism', perhaps one of the most famous examples of othering. He coined the term to refer to the way white colonizers tended to characterize the people they colonized in unfamiliar (and therefore the implication was undesirable) terms. This implied that their own characteristics were desirable. Such ways of categorizing of course functioned to maintain power distinctions. This type of othering became known as 'orientalism', referring to the ways in which the features of orientalism were constructed in the thinking of white colonialists.

Activity 2.1

Think of the first time you as a social worker might meet a particular service user.

Imagine a particular person.

- What kinds of things will you notice about them? (For example, it might be their ethnic or racial appearance, their gender, their dress, their tidiness.)
- What kind of judgements do you make about them on the basis of these aspects?

Now think about what assessments you have made of them.

- How have you assessed them in relation to yourself (i.e. how much might they be similar to you or not)?
- What is it about them that you have used to make these assessments of similarity or difference?

Activity 2.2

- Now try to picture the same person, but you are meeting them at a friend's place at a party instead.
- Do you notice the same sorts of things, and do they mean the same sorts of things to you? If so, why or, if not, why not?
- How has the situation made a difference to the way you see this person?

Both the above examples are situations which might involve 'othering'. Othering occurs on an everyday level when we look for indicators in other people to provide guidance on how we should relate to them. Often when we meet people for the first time we are looking for points of similarity (or difference) which will subtly indicate whether we should relate to them as equals, or on what exact footing we should relate. 'Othering' becomes problematic when we use these indicators (and make assumptions about them) to reinforce social distinctions, especially those which inferiorize the other person or group in relation to ourselves. We often do this unwittingly of course.

Such 'binary oppositional' categorizing can become harmful in this way, when the categorizing that we do actually functions to protect ourselves from engaging with social differences and, worse, discriminates against and excludes people we feel are different from ourselves. Often it may result because of a perceived need to protect ourselves by surrounding ourselves with, and identifying with, people who we believe to be like ourselves, or who we would like to be identified with.

Towards a reflexive approach

For these reasons we argue that it is far better to develop a more mindful mindset about culture, one that allows a person to be open and more relaxed with cultural differences in order to explore, understand and craft better practices in conjunction with people from different cultural backgrounds. This entails, first and foremost, a curious, humble and familiar engagement with one's own cultural heritage, especially the more hidden and taken-for-granted aspects of this. We would term this a more *reflexive* approach to cultural competence. What do we mean by 'reflexivity' in this sense?

In simple terms, when we speak about being reflexive, we are referring to the ability to be aware of how one's self, in all aspects, influences how one sees and relates to the world (see Fook and Gardner 2007: 27–30). Of course, when we say 'all aspects', that is not so simple, since the self may be made up of a complex array of varied aspects (e.g. physical, emotional, cognitive, gendered, social, cultural, economic, historical and political) which are formed in different contexts and may change according to circumstances. Being reflexive, though, does entail an ability to be aware of how these aspects may influence one's perspective and experience, as well as the perceptions and behaviours of the people one interacts with.

A reflexive approach to being culturally competent would therefore entail developing an understanding of one's own cultural location, and therefore being aware of the biases, blind spots and notions which are 'taken for granted', and how these might influence an ability to be open to, or comfortable with, the cultural differences of others. Such an understanding should allow an openness to (and welcoming of) social differences, rather than fear, suspicion or threat when confronted by unfamiliar, new, divergent, or even controversial perspectives or cultures.

Being open would therefore also entail, not wittingly or unwittingly, discriminating or devaluing cultural differences, *simply because they are different*. A reflexive approach would also therefore involve an awareness of the possibility of unwittingly 'othering' socially different people or groups, and would actively resist constructing such differences. In this sense, a reflexive approach would work to look for and understand our own and others' social differences, particularly in relation to past and present contexts.

In a post-colonial era, a reflexive approach would also be aware of how colonial forms of 'othering' may have seeped into the thinking and culture of current Asian and other non-white communities. An appreciation of post-colonialism is important in developing better cross-cultural awareness. How has colonization contributed to the historic development of complex cultural identities, particularly as they play out in present forms?

Of course, we are not denying that with a reflexive approach there is no room, or a need, for specific information about other cultures. There is a necessary place for using such information to open up a space for appreciating difference, and changing assumptions about differences, so that much less is taken for granted about other people. However, that is precisely the place for such information: it is in its ability to challenge assumptions, and unthinking devaluing of others' views or experiences, on the basis of difference alone, that it is useful, not as knowledge in and of itself. In a reflexive approach, information and knowledge about differences are mostly significant for their ability to change and challenge fixed or prejudicial mindsets, and to simulate more learning about ourselves in relation to the myriad of other people (whether they appear socially different or not) with whom we constantly mix. Good working reflexivity is therefore something which should allow us to interact more appreciatively with all sorts of people, whether they appear socially or culturally different from us or not. For this reason, a reflexive approach is essential to all good social work practice, not just the cultural aspects of it.

Reflection point 2.1

How then might a reflexive approach be attained?

Below are some questions which might help you to become more reflexive (especially in relation to cultural awareness).

- Who am I (personally, socially, culturally, historically, etc.).
- What blind spots might I have as a result of who I am?
- What types of unfamiliar situations make me uncomfortable?
- What is it about those situations which I find 'different' or which makes me uncomfortable?
- What am I assuming about those situations and the people in them (and why do I think they make me uncomfortable)?
- What is it about me that makes me hold those assumptions? Where do they come from? Is it anything to do with my own experiences or social background?
- What kinds of things about me, which I value, are perhaps being protected/ preserved by having these assumptions about other people?
- What have I become aware of from answering the above questions?
- What will I do differently as a result of these new awarenesses?

Activity 2.3

Think of an instance you experienced when you felt socially different from someone else, or other people in the situation. (For example, it might be a time when you started a new course of study at university, or a new job, or perhaps when you travelled to a country you had not been to before.) Try to answer the above questions in relation to that experience.

Reflection point 2.2

Think of a recent experience where you felt that you needed to understand more about someone else who you identified as socially different from you. How will you approach trying to understand their social difference? What have you learnt about yourself and how will this affect the way you relate to them? Do you think the way you relate can be seen as reflexive?

If you can take a reflexive approach in your work generally, it will be applicable not just to working across different cultures, but should enable you to work more inclusively with all manner of social differences, such as class, age, gender or different sexual orientations. In this sense it is applicable to several of the different domains, not just the obvious one of critical reflection. Being reflexive should enable better work with diversity, a better ability to examine and develop a value and ethical base (contributing to better professionalism), and a more refined ability to act upon human rights and social justice.

Conclusions

In this chapter we have outlined the concept of cultural competence and some of the major models for practising in a culturally competent way. We have also criticized the cultural competence approach and proposed a reflexive approach to working inclusively. We then defined and discussed the concept of reflexivity and how it can be used to inform an inclusive approach to practice. We used the concept of 'othering' to analyse how social difference can be constructed, and how a reflexive awareness of one's own self is integral to developing an inclusive approach. We ended by posing some questions and activities to enable a more reflexive understanding of oneself, and how to apply this in relating to others.

Key points

Cultural competence may:

- Provide a limited way of working with people who are socially different
- Be overly simplistic or behavioural
- Imply that knowing about the various dimensions of cultural differences will automatically make one culturally competent.

It is vital to be (reflexively) aware of one's own social/cultural self, in order to appreciate one's own biases, before being able to work in an accepting and open way with others. A reflexive approach also involves understanding why, and how, social difference can be constructed (through the process of othering), and one's own role in this.

3 Being white – feeling guilty?

Bridget Ng'andu

Chapter overview

By the end of this chapter you should have some understanding of:

- Whiteness and white privilege
- Anti-racist social work
- The dominant ideas, norms and relevance in social work practice with BME families
- Applying critical multicultural perspectives to anti-racist practice.

Introduction

This chapter examines the current debates on 'whiteness' and whiteness studies within social work, and explores what being white means for practitioners, particularly white practitioners working with Black Minority and Ethnic (BME) families.

The discussion about racial difference tends to focus on the problem with 'racial' identity and identification (Maxime 1986). It may be argued that greater attention needs to be paid to white identity in social work. Frankenberg is concerned that identity is rooted in white cultural norms, and white people are inclined to be *'the non-defined definers of other people'* (1993: 197). The emphasis on whiteness as a positive norm is largely unremarked on, while being black is closely defined and seen to be negative. Privileging white culture and identity leads to the understanding that, although difficult to define and lacking character and shape, the concept is a point of reference for all white people when appraising and evaluating others. This leads to the marginalization of BME individuals and groups.

Anti-racist social work practice requires a common understanding of words and language; however, this has proved problematic, and ongoing clarification is required on terminology such as 'black', which is used in this chapter 'to refer to all groups who, in the historical and cultural context of the UK, have been and continue to be constructed as "other" to the assumed white European norm' (G. Singh 2014: 18). BME or Black, Asian and Minority Ethnic (BAME) are equally problematic because groups are defined in relation to colour in the first instance. Although contested, the terms are commonly understood and used in policy, procedure and social work practice.

There is little doubt that white social work practitioners are challenged by the developing awareness of what it means to be white, and how this impacts on work with BME individuals and groups. This chapter seeks to develop the ideas on white privilege and how white dominant norms impact on social work practice in the UK. Examples are drawn on to demonstrate and explore knowledge and skills required in practice. The Professional Capabilities Framework (PCF, BASW 2012) domains of professionalism, values, diversity, knowledge, intervention and skills, organizational context and professional leadership apply to the key issues under discussion.

'Race', racism and ethnicity

In order to talk about 'white' and 'whiteness' in social work, the key concepts of 'race', racism and ethnicity require further discussion. Woodward (2003) notes that the term 'race' is often enclosed in inverted commas to indicate lack of validity as a descriptive and analytical tool. 'Race' is a socially constructed, rather than a biological, term (Spencer 2006). The latter rests on the assumption that humans can be divided into distinct types based on biological and phonotypical differences. Pilkington (2003) also states that 'physical markers' such as skin pigmentation, hair texture and facial features are drawn upon to attach different meanings to different 'races'. According to Woodward (2003), these meanings can involve hierarchies and lead to hostility/racism.

Racism occurs when groups of people are discriminated against on the basis of inherent group characteristics (Lavalette and Penketh 2014). Historically, the concept of 'race' has been informed by a number of developmental phases including those derived from scriptural/religious perspectives which, for example, portray 'black' people as heathens. Other 'biological' explanations, rooted in Darwinism, are used to justify 'oppression and slavery based on the supposedly evolutionary inferiority of the "black" race' (S. Singh 2014: 21). This perception of BME groups continues today, leading to discrimination based on one's ethnic background. Lavalette and Penketh (2014: ix) state that 'ethnicity is used to describe a group possessing some degree of coherence and solidarity, and who share common origins and interests'. Although contested and changing, these terms are central to discussions on whiteness and white studies.

What is 'whiteness'?

Whiteness, as a concept within the field of race and ethnicity, 'sits at an intersection between historical privilege and identity, something that has a contemporary dynamic but which is not universally shared' (Meer 2014: 152). Furthermore, experiences of segregation, for instance in South Africa, must be seen within the context of white majority conceptions of the given identity (Hague 1998 and Hewitt 2005, cited in Meer 2014).

Writings on whiteness can be traced back to African-American authors such as Morrison (1970; 1981), Baldwin (1984), and Du Bois (1999), but greater attention has been paid to whiteness studies more recently in Australia and Britain (Moreton-Robinson 2004; Garner 2007). Frankenberg (1997) explored how the lack of exploration and acknowledgement has maintained whiteness and how this relates to the development of theories on 'race'.

Proponents of anti-racist social work could also have provided a comprehensive analysis of the level and quality of social work engagement with BME service users which better incorporated the developing body of knowledge referred to as 'critical white' or whiteness studies (Jeyasingham 2012).

The focus on whiteness offers potential insights at a number of levels. First, it tends to take the focus away from the widely noted violence and oppression experienced by non-white people, allowing for the invisible and hegemonic ways in which power generally operates. Second, enabling the focus to move away from the 'preoccupation with the problems experienced by racialising others problematizes the normative practices that sustain white centrality' (Jeyasingham 2012: 672). Finally, it is important to examine whiteness within the socially complex arena which includes colour, ethnicity, difference, language/accent and regional/national identity.

Other commentators (Garrett 2012) argue that an overemphasis on whiteness risks reinforcing the black/white binary, particularly if a narrow critical analysis continues to exclude groups such as the Irish travelling communities who can experience the same racism as non-white communities (see Chapter 3). Whiteness also requires a broad, socially constructed definition within a wider political economy, as the majority of societal resources continue to be held by the white majority in most European countries.

A key area of concern for those wishing to develop anti-racist practice is how to address the fear and guilt which is generated by 'race' and racism. This is not to say that guilt should be felt by anyone, or be a prerequisite to action, but the notion of guilt requires some consideration within whiteness studies. Guilt tends to suppress critical thought and is likely to be destructive rather than positive; however, recognition and acceptance of historical facts is important (Dyer 1997). That said, some memory of past injustices is useful. The following example illustrates how a whole nation can be victimized by a set of events for generations, i.e. the Welsh, and yet those involved in the barbaric events are barely aware of it, i.e. the English. The populations of both countries are majority white, but the differences relate to supremacist ideas based on regional and national identity. In 1847 a report on education in Wales stipulated that Welsh people could improve their life chances only if English, rather than Welsh, was the language of education. This led to the near obliteration of the Welsh language, but more importantly hit the confidence of the population to such a degree that it remains part of the national psyche to this day (National Library of Wales 2015).

Whiteness, identity and privilege

The development of anti-racist practice has been led by many BME activists who have, in many ways, enabled white people to remain outside critical examination and contributed to the maintenance of whiteness as a reference point for applying prejudice against others – i.e. white people as just people, while every other group is labelled BME (Dyer 1997).

Writing from a white feminist perspective, McIntosh (1988) suggests that 'white privilege', by which she refers to the range of unearned social rights, is possessed in an invisible way by white people. White privilege is 'an invisible package' of unearned assets she counts on but which she was not 'meant' to know about. 'White privilege is like an invisible weightless knapsack of special provisions, assurances, tools, maps, codebooks, passports, visas, clothes, compass, emergency gear and blank checks (cheques)' (cited in Crofts 2013: 107). This is related to unacknowledged advantages men benefit from as compared to women. She suggests that it is good to reflect on how white people are privileged when compared to black people in similar situations (cited in Jeyasingham 2012).

Frankenberg (1997) argues that naming whiteness will lead to an open dialogue and mark its position of dominance. She states that in the same way that men and women's lives are both shaped by their gender, white people and people of colour live racially structured lives. This becomes important to social work as the profession is dominated and informed by white norms and structure. Social work operates in a world of white privilege which is encapsulated in professional standards and regulations, although the Code of Ethics (BASW 2012) is founded on universal rights and principles of social justice. The relative dominance of whiteness in social work leads to questions about services provided by white practitioners to service users from BME communities, and the level of information and training available on institutional privilege and power.

Taking the white Irish travelling community as an example raises the question of bias by practitioners dealing with any group without expert knowledge and intelligence. It may not be assumed that BME social workers have relevant communication or other skills to meet the needs of BME service users and carers, and are immune from the exploitation and oppression of others (Keating 2000). For example, it is possible to envisage a British-born BME social worker from Zimbabwe making negative assumptions about a refugee family from Somalia.

Case study 3.1

Tom Richards is a white social worker in a referral and assessment programme of a Children's Services team. He has been in this role for just over two years. Tom has predominantly worked with white service users as the area has a low population of BME groups; however, he has recently been allocated to undertake an assessment on a black African family. The referral raises allegations of children being hit by their mother with a 'wooden spoon'. Tom is clear that this is not acceptable, but finds this difficult in his initial discussions with the mother. Tom is aware of his ethnicity and gender in working with the family.

Consider the following questions in response to the above:

- Does Tom discuss the issue of whiteness and ethnicity with his supervisor/ manager?
- Why is whiteness important for Tom in informing his practice?
- Does Tom need to research chastisement and punishment further?

- What are the implications for the family?
- Would it be useful for the organization to guide and train social workers on culture and ethnicity in relation to being a white professional? If so, what would you include in the guidance and training information?

There are a number of issues for Tom to consider when working with this family. Firstly, as a white man, he carries an unacknowledged, possibly unrecognized privilege in society. He may be aware of this, but it has the potential of influencing how he sees women and their role in families. The issue of power may influence the process of assessment and engagement, so the discussion with the supervisor/manager should include Tom's understanding of his white privilege as a man representing a powerful organization and implementing comprehensive child protection laws and procedures. Family approaches to reprimand are highlighted only if risk is involved, so Tom needs to find a workable balance to ensure that he does not alienate himself from the family.

Anti-racist social work practice

The emergence of anti-racist social work perspectives in the early 1970s and 1980s sought to address issues of 'race' and 'racism' in social work practice (Dominelli 1988; Graham 2007; Bhatti-Sinclair 2011). Anti-racist social work (Dalrymple and Burke 2006) has many aims, including challenging racism, building a positive image of black people, and acting as a platform for views on their common experiences of racism in society. The move from multiculturalism and equal opportunity to directly challenging inequalities in power relations at personal and institutional levels is an essential prerequisite of anti-racist social work practice. In relation to BME service users, Healy (2001) suggests that clearer connections need to be made between radical social work approaches, racial injustice and class. Race relations in England and Wales date back to the Race Relations Act of 1968 and 1976 (amended in 2000).

Anti-racist social work is best contextualized in the substantial political and policy developments of the 1980s and 1990s. Critics suggest that advocates promoted the homogenization of different histories, cultures and migration patterns (Lorenz 1996a). The movement also failed to champion certain BME groups – for example, Jewish and Turkish communities (Lorenz 1996b; Rattansi 2005) and made invisible the discrimination faced by others – for example, Irish immigrants (Mac and Ghaill 1999; Garrett 2012). There was also little on white-on-white and black-on-black racism (Modood 1992).

The move from anti-racist to anti-oppressive practice was a positive radical shift which included 'understanding of the links between various forms and expressions of oppression' (Macey and Moxon 1996: 309). However, this shift has 'diluted' the focus on race, and critics suggest that anti-oppressive approaches are less threatening because practitioners are fearful of dealing with 'race' and racism (Williams 1999; Harrison and Burke 2014).

The rise of Thatcherism led to what is described as the denigration of anti-racist social work rooted in neo-liberalist approaches to management, privatization, cuts in essential services and income inequalities. Harvey (2005) suggests that neo-liberalism management has taken power away from professionals, and into the hands of managers, employers and private providers. The Labour government fared no better despite embracing the findings of the Macpherson Report (1999) into the racist murder of Stephen Lawrence by developing a 'general apathy towards an overtly political anti-racist project' (G. Singh 2014: 25). The growth of private service providers linked to austerity cuts to public-sector provision has increased income inequalities (Harvey 2005). G. Singh (2014) suggests that this is a direct threat to anti-racist social work as issues of 'race' remain unaddressed despite evidence that the policies enacted have a greater adverse impact on BME communities than white communities.

Researching, developing and testing race theories is critical – for example, Maxime (1986) proposed that black children should be placed with black foster carers and supported by therapeutic input. The gradual exposure to their 'racial origin' would in turn lead to them becoming black (Maxime 1986). This suggests the perpetuation rather than challenging of pathological images. However, Gilroy warned of the dangers of promoting models of the ideal black family able to support the acquisition of 'the necessary psychological skills to thrive in a racist society' (Gilroy 1990, cited in G. Singh 2014: 19–20). Gilroy further states that the assumption that social work professionals and BME service users share common experiences is likely to lead to a disconnection from the realities of the majority of BME people (cited in G. Singh 2014).

Williams (1996) noted that the lack of self-critique by activists made anti-racist practice vulnerable. The approach appeared to undermine lived experiences, influenced by a complex network of 'race', gender, class and other oppressions, and reduce the totality of black experience in response to white racism, thereby conferring a 'victim status' on black people. She also raised concerns about a 'formulaic' approach to the placement needs of BME children. This is important as children of mixed ethnicity continue to be slightly over-represented, and children of Asian ethnicity slightly under-represented in the looked-after children population (Department for Education 2015). This has significant implications for practitioners when considering appropriate placements for these children in regard to issues of 'race'.

A notable limitation in current social work debates is a lack of strong and visible anti-racist social work rhetoric which incorporates whiteness, including the discourse on anti-discrimination, anti-oppression, diversity and difference (Okitikpi and Aymer 2010, cited in G. Singh 2014).

Reflection point 3.1

- Why is anti-racist social work important to practice?
- How would a focus on whiteness support anti-racist practice?
- What are the policies and procedures on race and racism in your organization?
- Are they accessible?

Core knowledge, skills and the Professional Capabilities Framework (PCF)

The PCF sets out the professional framework detailing the expected practice for social work students and practitioners (Kennedy 2013). The PCF has nine domains: Professionalism; Values and Ethics; Diversity; Rights, Justice and Economic Well-being; Knowledge; Critical Reflection and Analysis; Intervention and Skills; Contests and Organizations; and Professional Leadership. In this section, the domains that are particularly relevant are: Diversity; Values and Ethics; and Critical Reflection and Analysis.

Case study 3.2

Salome was 15 years old and had arrived in the UK from an African country with a couple who had posed as her parents. She was then taken to a small town in England and not allowed to leave the house. One day, Salome was told that she could not continue living with the family any more. She was found by a member of the public at a bus station in a distressed state, and taken to the children's services office in the town, where an assessment was started. Salome was allocated two white social workers to complete the age assessment and determine whether she was of the appropriate age to receive support.

• What knowledge and skills do the social workers need in order to ensure they are providing culturally competent services to young people like Salome?
• What can the supervisor/manager provide to support and guide the social workers?
• Should the social workers reflect on their own identities?
• How does this assessment process impact on Salome?

Much has been written about the core knowledge and skills required of social workers (Trevithick 2012; Teater 2014). Nylund (2006) offers an alternative to whiteness which may deal with the guilt white students and practitioners may feel (G. Singh 2014). A critical multiculturalism perspective provides a radical, anti-racist conception of whiteness which examines the 'political, social, and historical situation of white ethnicities, and the hegemonic processes, which lead to universalisation and normalisation' (Nylund 2006: 28). Critical multiculturalism includes recognizing the socio-historical context of race, and how it intersects with class, gender, nation, sexuality and capitalism. The theory provides an environment in which 'otherness' can be deconstructed and explored, and makes visible historical power struggles and social construction of whiteness.

Consideration of identity, prejudices and assumptions is likely to benefit practitioners assessing Salome and other similar cases requiring culturally appropriate intervention skills.

Reflection point 3.2

- Can you think of a time when you had to rely on someone's assessment to access a particular service? How did that make you feel?
- Can you think about how Salome will be feeling knowing that the assessment is dependent on what the two white social workers decide? Would her fear be justified?
- How helpful is critical multiculturalism to the two social workers in informing their practice?

Conclusions

This chapter has sought to explore what being 'white' means for white practitioners. It has explored issues of whiteness and privilege in social work practice. Discussions on the need for a critical analysis of 'whiteness', white privilege and feelings require a great deal more attention.

Dominant norms continue to prevail in social work practice, which, if not addressed, are likely to oppress non-white communities. Neo-liberal ideologies in the 1970s and 1980s undermined and sometimes silenced developments, leading to the acceptance of what is deemed as a softer interpretation of anti-racist practice in the form of anti-discriminatory practice which has closed down discussions about white supremacist structures and systems within which social workers function.

Recognizing and identifying with being white will contribute to an appreciation of culture and ethnicity which begins with self-awareness and this is likely to benefit the practitioner and the service user he or she relates to. Critical multiculturalism offers important insights which will lead to a meaningful engagement with issues of diversity, values and ethics, and critical reflection as outlined in the PCF.

4   Social work identities: you're different too!

Jon Old

Chapter overview

By the end of this chapter you will be able to understand and critique the following concepts:

- How social workers and students understand and explore identity
- How identity relates to the PCF domain on diversity
- How language is used, defined and shapes our understanding of what we do
- How social psychology helps us to understand our values
- How our identity and practice is shaped by the people who surround us
- How we constantly experience psychological discomfort which can diminish our value base and corrupt our practice.

Introduction

The aim of the chapter is to enable you to gain an understanding of how we see ourselves (our identity), how this identity is affected by the way we communicate, how we develop and adapt our identity to fit in with others, and how we are vulnerable to external forces. We begin by examining how social workers understand themselves and the perspectives which underpin approaches, theories and models for self-reflection. How our identity is applied in practice will be discussed, with specific reference to the term 'use of self' and person-centred, relationship-based practice which can include understanding the commonalities and differences brought by service users and carers to any given situation.

Individual difference will be explored in order to discover how it is expressed in the language we use, and in so doing draw attention to the concept of social construction. The impact of the words we speak influences how we see ourselves. The discipline of social psychology will be used to inform how we, as social workers, see ourselves as diverse and socially different. We will start to recognize how our view and use of self is constantly evolving and tied up in verbal interactions.

Finally, we will see how the concept of cognitive dissonance sheds light on the idea that the more we are exposed to the social work life, the more our thoughts, values and beliefs are impacted by the psychological discomfort we feel in ethically complex day-to-day situations.

Identifying ourselves

At the very essence of human identity is the idea that we are relational beings; we have a need for interaction and communication and a sense of where we belong in relation to others. Social work has a long tradition of theorizing the use of self in practice, both on a personal and professional level. A core part of social work is about consolidating learning and discovering the personal attributes that can be applied in practice. Self-reflection is rooted in social work programmes of study and systematically enables students to examine their own thought processes, feelings, professional practice, decision-making, areas for further development, and to recognize and identify their strengths (Yip 2006; Schön 1991; Langley and Brown 2010; Chaddock et al. 2014). Reflective journals are used to look back on and critically analyse situations. Students find this a useful developmental framework which can be applied throughout their professional careers (e.g. Bassot 2013).

Other approaches include Kolb's learning cycle, a model which helps highlight the continuum we are placed on in terms of either thinking or feeling about an issue. This has been adapted for use in social work, but its primary goal was originally to help us understand how we learn. It can be coupled with the degree to which we learn through practical interaction, at one end of the scale, and learning by watching at the other. A major shortfall of this approach is that it does not help us to consider the wider and equally influential impacts of society or the role of political influences (Vince 1998).

To bridge this shortfall we might consider using Borton's (1970) apparently simplistic reflective process that asks us to question 'What?' and 'So what?', followed by 'What now?', a question which helps us to consider how others might influence our thoughts and actions and how we might consider alternative courses of action in future situations.

Alternatively, a more rigid and focused perspective is offered by Gibbs' (1988) reflective cycle. This provides a framework by which we can:

- challenge our assumptions
- consider other viewpoints
- highlight areas of strength or developmental need, and
- make clear links between theory and practice.

(Williams and Rutter 2007)

The seemingly basic approaches to reflection which enable looking back at one's self can build on Schön's (1991) ideas of reflecting both 'on action' and 'in action'. This involves being in the moment and being aware of the experience as it happens – constantly reflecting on and reacting to our present experience.

In a similar way we might consider the idea of reflexivity and how we, as actors in any given situation, have an impact and influence on those with whom we work (Taylor and White 2000). The skill here is to continually respond to and monitor our cognitions and feelings alongside being aware of the skills and theory we put into practice. As we develop understanding of self, constant review takes place, ideally leading to improved practice and better provision for service users. The danger, however, is that the workplace, as we shall examine further on, impacts on our ability to take time, not only to consider our practice and our personal relationship with it; we are also forced to practise in ways that restrict the skills we possess and (there is less attention given to this in the literature) how we may practise in ways that change us as individuals – in ways that change who we are.

In order to embrace an understanding of the practice context and incorporate the valuable aspects of the reflective processes we have seen so far, Ruch's (2007) idea of the 'holistic-reflective-practice' can be used alongside Bion's (1962 cited in Ruch 2007) theories on 'containment'. This moves away from the individual subjective viewpoint and the dyadic supervisory relationship, and incorporates practitioners, the teams they work in, and the interlinked and interdependent organizational contexts they operate in.

In some sense this accepts the current neo-liberal direction that social work is moving in while at the same time safeguarding the theoretical and value base of social work; although this, in itself, is a questionable area. Nonetheless, this is a useful way of acknowledging that social workers as individuals and as team members exist within a system and network that is both influenced and influences other aspects of the system/s they interact with. It is logical that social workers should benefit from the same systems approach used to understand the service user's world, particularly if it enables us to be situated within, and influence, the wider social and political context. A systems approach will help us understand and solidify our identity as a member of a professional group, how we identify what social work actually is and what it does, and how it develops the self.

Consideration of our wider context takes a shift in perspective when we undertake Fook's (2012) critical incident technique. Here a personally significant event is initially described through a narrative, which is then deconstructed to examine an individual's assumptions and presuppositions, with an emphasis on where these originate from and how they impact on our thoughts and practice. As a very thorough and analytical exercise, we are encouraged to identify our biases and concepts of power, as well as our understanding of the theory we aim to use. The ultimate aim of this is to consider how we might reconceptualize and develop our practice for the better in future. The 'critical' aspect of this approach to reflection and analysis is borne of a critical approach to social work. This builds on the ideas of radical social work (Rogowski 2011), underpinned by Marxist thinking – i.e. that individuals experience oppression due to a class divide and that an understanding of this oppression, coupled with an emancipation of the oppressed, is needed in order to truly free individuals from the root causes of their difficulties. Critical social work argues that class is not the only cause of oppression. Instead, viewed from a postmodern perspective, oppression is exerted from a multitude of sources and it is necessary to deconstruct our own world-view and our service users' concept of reality to fully appreciate and combat oppression. Postmodernity, deconstruction and social constructs are underlying themes.

Discovering the self through these approaches may look like a solitary experience, not least because we are usually only examining our own perspective, which is very subjective and relies on our interpretation of events. But then this, in large part, is part of our human make-up.

Applying the self in practice

How then is the self used in direct relation to service users? Perhaps most obviously this is seen in the Rogerian-based (Rogers 1950) Person-Centred Approach (PCA), prevalent in social work education and practice. Underpinning this approach is a humanist perspective, and it is this that shapes our thinking and practice. Much like a critical approach, it is a perspective or world-view that shapes the reasoning behind the practice.

Reflection point 4.1

Consider the following questions:

- What perspective do you practise from?
- How does it matter?
- How do your own beliefs/perspectives/paradigms influence you and others?

Consider a person-centred approach derived from humanism, and/or a critical social work stance borne out of postmodernism. Alternatively, you may be inclined towards radical social work, which endorses Marxism.

PCA asserts necessary conditions considered crucial in our interactions with people – for example, unconditional positive regard, empathy and congruence. This enables us to develop a deeper understanding as we begin to feel the value of understanding our assumptions, attitudes and beliefs towards, and about, others. In order to do this effectively we must take on an honest appraisal of ourselves and commit to these principles in our work. In order to fully adhere to and truly accept these propositions, we need to be courageous and brutally honest.

Reflection point 4.2

Consider the following questions:

- Can you really be yourself, experience empathy and show unconditional positive regard if/when you work with service users considered paedophiles?
- What factors would make this possible – e.g. age, cognitive ability, past experiences such as sexual abuse?
- What informs your answers?

This may result in a change of beliefs and personal values.

A psychodynamic/psychoanalytical approach also has a strong tradition with social work, not least to justify the professional nature and theoretical base underpinning the profession (Payne 2014). This is where we might begin to understand ourselves in terms of the id, ego and superego, further enhancing our practice with service users, and developing mindfulness around transference, counter-transference, our ability to cope and our defence mechanisms.

We may build on this psychodynamic base by considering others through the life course (Erikson 1982) and, with care, start to place ourselves in that framework alongside those with whom we work. Practically, however, social workers are not counsellors or psychotherapists, and do not have the time, opportunity and certainly not the expertise, to use these principles in a therapeutic way in the traditional sense. Instead, they are practically applied through relationship-based social work.

Relationship-based social work has, at its core, the belief that what you provide the service user is delivered through the relationship you have with them. As such, the relationship with the service user is central to the understanding of the complexity of both human nature and a recognition that each encounter is unique.

Service users regularly report that the crucial element to any change, work or development, or resolution of problems, is the relationship with the social worker. In order for the relationship to be effective we need an understanding of how we function and interact on a personal and professional level (Wilson et al. 2008). By examining the conscious and unconscious elements of ourselves (i.e. utilizing a psychodynamic perspective) we have a clearer understanding of the use and impact of who we are, how we relate, and the influences on this.

So far we have considered the tools we use to discover ourselves and contemporary practical applications of the use of self. What should subsequently prove beneficial is the way we communicate and shape our understanding of self, and how this is influenced by those around us. In order to do this, we will examine at a more critical level the ideas of social construction, socio-linguistics and social psychology.

Insights of language and social psychology

Language is the predominant way in which we communicate, whether through written or verbal means. But language is more than the country it relates to, and the varying dialects and colloquialisms associated with it. Vygotsky (1962) proposed that we have an inner speech to express our thoughts and feelings, and that this is integral to our spoken word. Social construction is a perspective that further asserts that it is language (spoken and written) that expresses our view of reality, but also helps to inform it – i.e. what we believe to be actual and true is said by us and informed by what we hear.

Consider Beckett's (2003) discussion of the use of military metaphor by social workers. They use terms associated with war and violence, such as 'frontline' social work, 'strategies' to deal with children, being 'on duty' as part of their role, situations 'blowing up' and children 'kicking off'. This raises the questions 'What does this say about how social workers see their environment, the service users they work with and themselves as individuals?'

The words 'diversity' and 'difference' conjure up a multitude of thoughts and feelings. In order to express these thoughts and feelings we use language. Language at its core is extremely complex, and its meaning is interpreted through the context it is spoken in and the way in which it is delivered – e.g. the tone, speed, intonation, pitch and pace. It is formed from its historic and traditional roots, and crafted depending on its audience and intended impact.

Activity 4.1

Consider the terms you use to describe:

- yourself
- the work you do
- service users.

What does this suggest about how you see:

- your identity and role
- service user identity
- the context you work in.

Approaching language in this way can help us think about our presuppositions and potential stereotypes when we consider diverse groups of people. Presup-positions are the things we believe to be true and have in our minds when we approach a subject. However, we are not necessarily consciously aware of them; nor do we always have proof that they are true. In effect, before we encounter any issue or situation we suppose certain assumptions. Stereotypes, on the other hand, are concrete thoughts and beliefs that are usually made up of generaliza-tions, usually from tacit understanding. This is particularly pertinent when we consider that social work can often hold in high esteem through tacit knowledge – also known as practice wisdom. Stereotypes can also be classified in regards to a variety of people groups. For example, we might speak of gender stereotypes (women are more emotional than men); sexual stereotypes (gay men are 'camp'); racial stereotypes (black people can't swim), etc. It is important that we address and identify our own, not least because many are ridiculous and can impact on how we view and interact with people.

Humans have a natural tendency towards categorization; we like to order our world into easily identifiable ideas and concepts. In order to express these we must use language to assign labels, terms and categories. This is what helps us make sense of the world. By doing this we are able to quickly assess information and think about how we might act/interact in a given circumstance. We take the information we have learnt, perhaps through research and textbooks (formal knowledge) and/or what we have experienced and heard (informal tacit knowledge), and draw conclusions to form an opinion (Payne 2014).

Reflection point 4.3

Consider the following questions:

- What stereotypes and presuppositions do you have when you hear the words, 'service user'?
- Where do these stereotypes and presuppositions come from, and who informs them?
- List the words commonly used to depict service users.

This is most crucial when we think about the context of statutory social work. Neo-liberalism has had a huge impact on contemporary social work, seen in a new managerial approach to almost every aspect of practice (Welbourne 2011). This business model approach controls timescales, data entry, justification of approaches and 'evidence-based practice' to achieve 'successful outcomes' which are both 'cost-effective' and 'value for money'. This 'reality' is starting to permeate the language we use – for example, we talk about goals, SMART targets, outcomes, objectives, throughput, tasks, opening and closing, clients and customers.

Yet, given more time and less pressure, students and practitioners are able to analyse and assess information based on a thoughtful assessment of the information that not only includes experience (practice wisdom), but also research-based and informed knowledge (O'Connell and Leonard 2014). This is more beneficial to decision-making with people who use services. Yet the contemporary environment undermines and contradicts the core purpose and values of social work practice.

Reflection point 4.4

- What are the values of social work?
- Are ethical principles useful in everyday practice?
- What does social work aim to achieve?

Regardless of the route we take in our analysis, it is language which informs and shapes our thinking, and it is language that we use to convey our assessments and decisions. This, it will be seen, is open to interpretation and potentially problematic due to the very nature of language itself. The process of becoming a thoughtful and critical practitioner requires us to look inwards, and question and challenge our thoughts and beliefs. Self-examination is an important communication skill for social workers who function in complex organizations where diversity and differences, both within the workplace and in service delivery, are multiple and varied.

People are often categorized into population groups – for example, gay, black, elderly, poor; but this is only one part of a wider process in establishing identity in a social context.

Social identity theory (Tajfel and Turner 1979) and self-categorization theory (Turner 1999; Abrams and Hogg 2010) propose that individuals find meaning and a sense of who they are by belonging to a certain group or groups, and that this improves self-perception and lessens uncertainty. We begin with social categorization, finding where we fit in society. When we identify with a social category we begin to internalize the relevant group's attributes. This helps to foster a sense of belonging – i.e. if we are similar to them, if we fit in – but no one person identifies with just one group.

Reflection point 4.5

- How do you categorize yourself?

What categories do you fit into? (For example, you may see yourself as white, a woman, a lesbian, a golfer and/or a student.)

Otten and Wentura (1999) suggest that when we identify with a group we very quickly, and almost without awareness, develop a strong sense of belonging, develop attitudes and feelings that are in favour of the group (i.e. develop bias), and ultimately adopt the group's social norms. Part of a group's social norm is the use of shared language; we begin to express ourselves in similar ways, and to share group-specific jargon and terminology. There is, however, a danger that we begin to develop discriminatory attitudes towards other groups and use language that 'legitimizes myths' – i.e. reinforces derogatory stereotypes. Social psychologists would have us believe that this is done in order to achieve social dominance over other groups (Sidanius and Pratto, cited in Hajek and Giles 2005).

Reflection point 4.6

Consider the following questions based on your own experience:

- How do social work teams discriminate against one another?
- Do they use language that describes other teams as inferior? For example, 'What we do is a lot more pressured/important/difficult.'

To support this, Grieve and Hogg's (1999) research highlights that in uncertain times we develop a stronger identity with group norms – effectively becoming more like the other members of a group. To facilitate this we increase our attitudes and beliefs in regard to feeling more moralistic, believing we are more effective than other groups and, rather interestingly, believe we have a higher status than other groups.

Society, and, specifically, social work, has been going through a time of uncertainty for a number of years. In the age of austerity we see evidence of its impact: job insecurity, organizational restructuring, redundancies, demotion and increased workload. Also there is an increase in public use of services, fewer resources (and more justification for accessing them), competition and an innate feeling that workers need to prove their worth. The likelihood of a strong urge to identify with the group seems very strong.

Reflection point 4.7

- How have you noticed social workers from different teams discriminating against members of other teams?
- Have social workers you know become more discriminatory towards specific categories of service users?

Further studies suggest that comparing ourselves to others has a positive psychological impact. Social Comparison Theory (Festinger 1954; Tesser and Campbell 1982) indicates that we validate our thoughts, feelings and values by comparing them to those who are important to us. This helps us to maintain a psychological balance. However, as social workers we receive training which supports critical self-reflection and relating theory to practice while maintaining a reflexive approach. Such comparison, then, may be multiple and varied; we have a lot to draw upon and have the capacity to undertake well-informed reflection.

However, not everyone has had this opportunity and privilege. Few members of the public come into contact with social services in a time of unpressured objective reflection. Instead, they are considered 'in need', sometimes 'in crisis', and at the very least looking for support from a position of inter/dependence. In short, they are at the mercy of perceived 'experts'. Who then do they compare themselves to in order to bring about a sense of balance, to validate their actions, thoughts and feelings? Perhaps they are in the midst of a potential social-psychological no man's land.

(1995) A tenuous link could be made to Medvec, Madey and Gilovich's research that proposes we *make up and down* comparisons when we view others. Upward comparison, such as considering high achievers, competitive winners and economic successors, can have a damaging effect on our self-esteem. To avoid this we often make downward comparisons. We compare ourselves to others whom we feel have not made/achieved/won/deserved their place in society. This is psychologically beneficial as it makes us feel better about ourselves.

Reflection point 4.8

Consider the questions and statements below. Would you say any (or all) of the following to a member of the public with whom you work?

- Are you on benefits?
- There is an opportunity for you to go on holiday with other looked-after children.
- Do you consider yourself disabled?
- Here is the information I told you I would give you about your local day centre that has activities for elderly people.
- I have referred you to a parenting class.

How might the public feel about being categorized in the above ways?

In reality, our identity is made up of many characteristics which interact and overlap with one another. Intersectionality is a termed coined by Crenshaw (1991) to refer to immigrant black women in the United States of America to describe how individuals and groups of people are oppressed in a multitude of ways. The individual can be at the intersection of oppressive factors such racism, sexism, poverty and so on. Crenshaw used the analogy of traffic at an intersection – i.e. a crossroads made up of multiple roads. Each road was to represent an oppressive force (e.g. sexism, rape, violence). If we can identify where the oppression comes from (e.g. white men) we can formulate ideas around what groups the oppressed belong to (e.g. black women). Further examination might help us to see deeper areas of oppression – for example, poverty, mothers and children. This then opens the door for us to consider how these individual groups might interact with one another and the language they use to do so. By doing so we can begin to understand how they describe themselves. Then we can start to think about whether we describe ourselves using similar language and, ultimately, whether or not we identify in any way with these groups.

In order to interact with these different groups or cultures, or even groups within groups (i.e. subcultures) we must communicate through language. If we are to validate our thoughts and feelings we must verbalize them in order to assess whether they are shared. In doing so we label them. We also need to know what groups people feel a sense of belonging to, in order to make sure that the language we use reflects this and does not create a barrier to our involvement. To counteract and identify discrimination we must, as social workers, be aware of how language is used to reinforce perceived social dominance.

Social dominance theory suggests a hierarchy in society where certain groups possess a higher status and power over lesser groups. This is immediately obvious in social work. Service users would like (and sometimes need) help from us, and we have the power, in theory, to help. We also have the resources. However, service users must meet certain criteria to qualify for and meet the criteria to access these resources. Consider the terms 'homeless' and 'intentionally homeless'. Both categories are ultimately without a home, for whatever reason; sometimes justified and sometimes not. But those we deem (and this is a subjective assessment, guided by criteria, which is written yet open to interpretation) the intentionally homeless as having created this situation by their own doing and, as such, should not be given housing. Some might equate this to the idea of the deserving and undeserving poor.

On a wider scope, social dominance theory postulates that some groups seek dominance over other groups. The dominating group is usually more powerful, has easier access to resources (such as food), and is more financially prosperous – i.e. has more money. These groups seek (consciously, unconsciously, or by the fact that they are more privileged) to have dominance over other groups. The dominant groups have power to decide who should qualify for housing and who should not. Such groups have a codified way of speaking and use exclusive language which, if used outside of this group, would be construed as odd and misplaced. In social psychology we speak of in-groups (those with which we identify) and out-groups (those of which we are not a part and discriminate against). The language we use to differentiate ourselves from other groups has derogatory connotations which highlight how we view ourselves and others.

Cognitive dissonance: a threat to our selves

Leon Festinger introduced the idea of cognitive dissonance which he developed from his work on social comparison theory; the idea that the way we think and our values are influenced by the groups we interact with. He believed that people inherently strive to match their behaviour to their values, beliefs and thoughts – known as cognitions. If any of these were not in harmony (conflicted with one another), we would experience psychological discomfort. The need for consistency is considered so strong that it is a major determining factor in how we think, feel and behave (Festinger 1957, cited in Cooper 2007). An example of this might occur for someone who felt they drank too much and wanted to reduce their consumption:

- Their value and belief is that they should look after their body and stay healthy
- They enjoying drinking to excess and do so in spite of the dangers.

A social worker may experience this in the following ways:

- They believe that they should work in an anti-oppressive and empowering way with the service-using public
- They are pressured in their work and focus on completing assessments quickly over spending time hearing the voice of the service users and taking time to explore their views and emotions.

Activity 4.2

- When was the last time you experienced cognitive dissonance?
- List what your conflicting beliefs and actions were (these could be simple and straightforward).

Cognitive dissonance is easy to identify, but the issue of how it is resolved gains less focus. Broadly, there are four main ways of doing this (Cooper 2007):

1. Change the way you behave to fit with your thoughts and values
2. Minimize the importance of your beliefs and assign them to certain applicable situations
3. Abandon your beliefs
4. Modify your beliefs.

Activity 4.3

Consider how you resolved the dissonance you experienced from the example you gave in Activity 4.2.

This under-valued theory helps us see that our thoughts, beliefs and actions can easily be changed when faced with external influences such as the current context of social work and the new managerial demands placed on us. Although it may initially seem awful to think that we would abandon beliefs about valuing service users and putting their needs first, or ensuring our practice is anti-discriminatory/oppressive, it is nonetheless easy to see that we might discard these when our actions are dictated by bureaucracy. If this occurs we are ultimately changing who we are – i.e. our inner selves. As such, it is crucial to consider, before the change may occur, what parts of ourselves we consider sacred and immovable. We are not static individuals; we exist as part of an evolving system and our identity is shaped by external influences in ways we often do not think about. We need to earnestly process this and examine its relevance to the ever-changing nature of the service user's identity.

Conclusions

Social work is a difficult and emotional task, driven by factors that often contradict an ethical value base. The challenge for students and practitioners is to embrace the use of self, employing a variety of concepts, tools and models, in order to fully appreciate and apply the theories that inform our practice. By doing this we relate better to those we serve and are more equipped to deal with the external factors that shape our identity, thoughts, actions and beliefs. Understanding what we do, why we do it, and how we go about it, will help us to see how we can improve. But just as importantly it will help us safeguard our identity and the ethics that underpin social work.

Key points

- Social psychology can inform how we, as social workers, see ourselves as diverse and socially different.
- Humans have an inner speech used to express our thoughts and feelings, and this is integral to the spoken word.
- A mismatch between behaviour and values/beliefs/thoughts leads to psychological discomfort.
- Language informs and shapes social work thinking, and this is used in assessments and decisions.

Part 2

Themes from contemporary practice

5 Class, inequality and social work: 'We're all in this together'?

Christopher Smethurst

'All people are equal; it is not birth, it is virtue alone that makes the difference.'

Voltaire

Chapter overview

By the end of this chapter you should be able to understand:

- The political and ideological backdrop to class and inequality
- How class is constructed in British society
- How to relate this to social work policy and practice.

Introduction

Social class is the DNA of English society. It provides a blueprint for our lives and its effects are highly visible; but how it functions is often hidden, opaque and mysterious. In short, class matters . . . or does it? Generations of authors have amassed an impressive body of empirical evidence for the advantages conferred by wealth and social status, and where and to whom one is born. Yet the impact of social class and class inequality remains contested and subject to highly politicized debate.

At both a structural and personal level, class permeates social work practice. Social work students will be familiar with class in the context of structural inequality. However, the impact of class 'difference' is surprisingly underexplored in contemporary studies of social work practice. This chapter will explore the impact of structural inequality upon the perceptions, attitudes and behaviours of social workers, and address:

- The influence of contemporary class politics upon social policy
- The impact of social class and inequality on service users
- The social construction of a stigmatized 'underclass'
- The impact of class difference on social work practice.

Activity 5.1

- How would you define your social class?
- Does your own social class have any impact upon your practice? If the answer is 'yes', give specific examples.

Background

Social work's commitment to equality, defined in the Professional Capabilities Framework (PCF), places it squarely at odds with much of the government's social agenda in 2017. Inequality has been recast within a narrative of personal responsibility and moral deviance (Scambler and Scambler 2011). Unemployment is the product of 'lifestyle choice' (Shipman 2013) or a failure to engage with the emancipating opportunities of paid work in a zero-hours economy. Perhaps unsurprisingly, the government has attempted to resolve this potential conundrum for social work practice by de-legitimizing social work's adherence to the principles of social justice. Consequently, social workers are accused of colluding with their clients and making excuses for 'wrong choices' (Gove 2013). In addition, it is argued that social work training should have less emphasis on inequality (Narey 2014); as it encourages 'idealistic students' to view individuals as 'victims of social injustice', 'explaining away substance misuse, domestic violence and personal responsibility, rather than doing away with them' (Gove 2013).

The rationale for this chapter is that, far from being an anachronism and a reincarnation of the 'politics of envy', class and inequality have contemporary relevance to practice. They should not be rendered invisible because they are ideologically inconvenient to the government of the day, whatever its political hue. However, in a hostile political climate, and against a background of societal hostility towards those stigmatized as 'chavs' (Jones 2011), it is a challenge for practitioners to ensure that the impact of class difference upon practice is not ignored.

The impact of class and inequality

In Britain, the impact of social class is experienced directly from the cradle to the grave (ONS 2014). It is beyond the scope of this chapter to provide a comprehensive analysis, so the following section will focus on some illustrative examples: specifically, the effects of inequality upon children's well-being and the impact of poverty upon children's mental and physical health.

Low socio-economic status (as defined by occupation, income, wealth, education and access to resources) correlates with increased risks of low birth weight, infant mortality and poor child health (Weightman et al. 2012; Wolfe et al. 2014). This early disadvantage strongly influences health outcomes throughout childhood and later life (DH 2010). Some of the poor child health outcomes are associated with parental behaviour: smoking and substance misuse have a higher incidence in less advantaged socio-economic groups (Salihu and Wilson 2007; Wolfe 2014). However, the impact upon child health and mortality of poor nutrition and, particularly, the consequences of the greatly increased reliance upon food banks (Wolfe et al. 2014) is of increasing concern.

Britain has the fifth largest economy in the world (IMF 2014; World Bank 2014); yet, according to the government's own figures, 28 per cent of British children live in poverty (DWP 2015). This equates to 9 children in a class of 30. Child hunger is an increasing problem: teachers and social workers are likely to see its effects on children's behaviour, but may not be aware of the root cause. For example, child malnutrition may be revealed by an increased incidence of headaches and stomach aches (Alaimo et al. 2001). In addition, hunger has a direct relationship with a number of indices of children's behaviour and physical and mental health (Weinreb et al. 2002). After controlling for parental and environmental factors, Weinreb et al. (2002) found a correlation between hunger and child anxiety, chronic ill health, depression and behavioural problems. Further research has revealed a link between child hunger and suicide ideation in adolescence (McIntyre et al. 2013); levels of aggression (Bellisle 2004); hyperactivity (Fiese et al. 2011); impaired cognitive ability (Brown and Pollit 1996; Alaimo et al. 2001) and impaired social functioning.

The extent of the problem of child hunger in the UK is particularly evident in schools. In a recent survey of 4000 teachers, 80 per cent reported that school children were lacking in concentration and energy because of hunger (NASWUT 2014). In London, 41 per cent of teachers reported instances of children fainting because of malnutrition (GLA 2013). In both studies, teachers were bringing food into school for pupils whose parents could not afford to feed them.

Reflection point 5.1

- Were you aware of the extent of hunger and malnutrition in the UK?
- Consider the extent to which hunger experienced by service users may have an impact on your own practice.

The causes of child poverty and hunger are complex and contested. However, to frame these within a narrative of bad budgeting, bad choices and bad parenting can be viewed as simplistic, particularly because there is little supporting empirical evidence (Hirsch et al. 2012; CPAG 2014). A major factor is the combination of rising prices and falling or stagnant income levels for disadvantaged socio-economic groups (Adams et al. 2014; ONS 2014). These groups spend a higher proportion of their income on food, fuel and housing. Therefore, they have been disproportionately affected by a rapid rise in the cost of food; from 2008 to 2013 there was an increase of 40 per cent, compared to the average inflation index of 20 per cent (IFS 2014). In addition, Britain has experienced significantly higher price inflation for rents and fuel compared to France, Germany or the USA

(APPG 2014). The consequence of this is that poorer socio-economic groups are spending 7 per cent more of their budget on these commodities than they were in 2002 (APPG 2014). This results in more of their income being spent on those things which are experiencing the greatest price inflation; therefore, the percentage increase of their 'cost of living' is greater than that of the wealthier population (Adams and Levell 2014). In short, the poorest socio-economic groups have been caught in a 'perfect storm' of rising prices, falling incomes and cuts to services (Haddad 2012).

The 2010 Conservative-led coalition government demonstrated an early commitment to improving child poverty. The Child Poverty Act (2010) imposed a legal duty on governments to address targets for relative, absolute and persistent poverty, plus material deprivation. Disappointingly, since the Act was introduced, the number of children living in absolute poverty has increased by 0.5 million (DWP 2015). The steady decline in relative child poverty, from 1998 onwards, has stalled since 2010 (DWP 2015). Furthermore, it is predicted that this figure will rise by a further 0.7 million to leave 4.3 million British children living in poverty by 2020 (Browne et al. 2014). Britain's international ranking for economic wealth is starkly contrasted with its position for child poverty: Britain currently ranks fourteenth out of the 29 richest economies (Martorano et al. 2014).

It is of concern that in 2016 the government distanced itself from the statutory obligations in the Child Poverty Act and has failed to produce a detailed plan to meet poverty targets (Joyce 2014). In addition, Lupton and Thomson (2015: 22) argue that there has been a declining commitment to child well-being across a range of government departments. They note:

> a narrowing of intent which was accompanied by the dropping of policies relating to wider children's well-being (notably Every Child Matters), much multi-agency and area-based working (although areas must still have multi-agency Local Safeguarding Children Boards), and a focus on marginalized groups which had developed in the former DCSF since 2007.

Whatever one's political allegiances, it is evident that there has been an ideological shift in government policy towards inequality. Arguably, this has been accompanied by an increasingly strident rhetoric which has framed poverty within a narrative of individual, behavioural causation (Cunningham and Cunningham 2014). In order to understand current social policy, and its impact upon practice, it is necessary to dissect its ideological foundations. Before proceeding to the next section please complete the following exercise.

Activity 5.2

- Note down the key features of attitudes towards poverty, social mobility and inequality for each of the main political parties.
- Outline the similarities between the parties and identify the key differences.

'We're all in this together': a new politics of class?

In 2010, the government set about tackling the economic crisis. Its predicament was shared by many Western governments which were required to borrow heavily to rescue their ailing banks and other financial institutions (Crotty 2009; Clark and Heath 2014). In the UK, the crisis was successfully rebranded as one caused by the previous government's alleged profligate spending on welfare and public services (Wolf 2014; Hills 2015). The subsequent cuts to public expenditure were presented as unavoidable sacrifices, necessary to protect the well-being of future generations (Wolf 2014). However, Chancellor George Osborne assured the public that, although hard choices needed to be made, the burden would be shared because, in a phrase that arguably defined his time in office, 'We are all in this together' (Osborne 2013).

Osborne's rhetoric appealed to a spirit of national solidarity that transcended class or other social divisions. Similarly, David Cameron's rhetorical vision of Britain was of a 'Big Society' – one bound together by mutual interest operating at the level of local communities, rather than within social classes (Cameron 2011). However, it is clear that the burden of austerity has fallen disproportionately on those on low incomes and other disadvantaged groups: the impact of spending cuts has been 13 times greater on the poorest tenth of the population than the richest tenth (Haddad 2012). According to O'Hara (2014: 166): 'What was implemented was a regime that disproportionately affected the most vulnerable people in society while leaving the well-off unscathed.' Even the former Governor of the Bank of England – a man not noted for radical sentiment – concluded that 'the price of this financial crisis is being borne by people who absolutely did not cause it' (Mervyn King quoted in the *Guardian*: King 2011).

The extent to which the government has a coherent social vision has been debated (Walker and Corbett 2013; Civil Exchange 2015). Nevertheless, its economic and social policy rhetoric contains elements of the Conservative tradition of 'One Nationism' (Seawright 2010).

The political demise of David Cameron, following the 'Brexit vote' of June 2016, his successor as Prime Minister, Theresa May, rapidly asserted her 'One Nation Tory' credentials. With its origins in the nineteenth century, this tradition can be seen as both an ethical and pragmatic means of maintaining societal cohesion during periods of economic and social volatility. Arguably, One Nation Conservatism offers a paternalistic (if well-meaning) view of society where social divisions are largely perceived as non-problematic because the privileged classes have an obligation to those below them. In essence: 'There is a duty on the part of the rich to the poor and to the needy' (Boris Johnson quoted in Brogan 2010). However, this is a qualified obligation; significant levels of redistributive taxation are viewed as punitive and a disincentive to the 'wealth creators' (Eccleshall 2002; Dorey 2010). In summary, One Nation Conservatives acknowledge a threat to social cohesion caused by rampant inequality. They similarly recognize the influence of the structural causes of poverty without rejecting the role of individualized, behavioural factors. Consequently, interventions are arguably focused at an individual level of 'helping families out of welfare dependency', rather than through wide-scale redistribution of resources.

One Nationism has existed, in the ideological soul of the Conservative Party, in tension with the social Darwinism of free market capitalism – the latter being exemplified by the Thatcher governments. Thatcherism and its adherents reject an implicit social contract between the 'haves' and the 'have nots' in favour of a competitive individualism which orders society into 'winners and losers'. Fundamentally, this philosophy contains an essentially meritocratic world-view: that the social mobility of individuals – the capacity to 'get on' – is primarily a product of personal ability and self-discipline (Littler 2013). Success or failure is largely defined as a matter of effort; the impact of structural disadvantage is diminished or dismissed as an 'excuse' for the shortcomings of the individual (Dorey 2010; Evans and Tilley 2016).

Conservative-led administrations have presented a confusing and sometimes contradictory packaging of Thatcherite social and economic policy in One Nation rhetoric. For example, the claim of 'helping individuals trapped in welfare dependency' is in stark contrast to the policy of cutting benefit entitlements and access to public services (O'Hara 2014). However, it has been argued that a central feature of successive Conservative governments has been the normalizing of inequality: reframing punitive social policy within a narrative of compassion and common sense (Norton and Aughey 1981; Dorey 2010). Within this tradition, helping people out of poverty by reducing their access to benefits possesses a perverse logic.

Arguably, although social class would appear to be a key subject for debate, it has been rendered largely invisible in party political discourse (Scambler and Scambler 2011). Both Labour and Conservative governments have attempted to appeal to the 'centre ground' in politics by portraying themselves as the champions of 'hard-working families'. This amorphous class is given form and homogeneity through its commitment to 'hard work', rather than by the defining characteristics of occupation type and income (Todd 2014). Thus, class is largely redefined in moral rather than economic terms, with the interests of hard-working families pitched in opposition to, and threatened by, the 'workless'. Chancellor George Osborne (2013) succinctly framed this binary class division:

> For too long, we've had a system where people who did the right thing – who get up in the morning and work hard – felt penalized for it, while people who did the wrong thing got rewarded for it.

Activity 5.3

- Select a recently introduced social policy with which you are familiar.
- How might its impact be experienced by different social classes?

'Strivers versus skivers'? The modern construction of class difference

The current political trend is for a narrative of class comprising binary opposites: those in work and those who are not. The public has arguably been very receptive to this brand of class politics, responding with increasingly punitive attitudes towards the poor and wide-scale support for benefit cuts (Atkinson et al. 2012; McKay 2014; Kornhauser 2015). The current binary construction of 'a them and us', 'strivers versus skivers' society will hold few revelations for those acquainted with Charles Murray's theories of 'underclass'. Murray (1990) blends fecklessness, 'illegitimacy', welfare dependency and immorality into a rationale for the durability of poverty.

A less punitive understanding of the 'underclass' was advanced by the model of social structure known as the 'two-thirds society'. This was an influential underpinning of the 'end of class and stratification' debate during the 1990s (Noll and Lemel 2003). In essence, this model holds that two-thirds of society is 'comfortably off', while a third of the population fail to benefit from rising living standards and are 'left behind'. When Labour came to power in 1997, it internalized the spirit of this debate by threading the concept of 'social exclusion' through much of its policy agenda (Levitas et al. 2007).

Social exclusion is a multifaceted means of understanding disadvantage – arguably more complex and nuanced than analyses that focus on income poverty or traditional theories of class disadvantage – which includes poor social or family circumstances and low economic/employment status.

Conceivably, the concept of social exclusion enables a more nuanced analysis of structural disadvantage – one that can incorporate other factors such as age, disability and racism. However, there are some key ideological differences in the method by which the concept is interpreted (Levitas 2005). The *redistributionist discourse* highlights the role of structural causes of disadvantage; policy responses identify the barriers caused by social and economic inequality (Cunningham and Cunningham 2014). The *moral underclass discourse* places the responsibility for exclusion upon the excluded and broadly echoes the sentiments of Murray (1990) highlighted above. Policy interventions are targeted at an individual, rather than a structural level. There is a focus on identifying and 'turning round' troubled and troubling individuals and families (Casey 2012). Finally, the *social integration discourse* primarily highlights the social and economic benefits of paid work. A common feature of Labour, Coalition and Conservative social policy is that interventions contain a combination of supportive and coercive measures to draw people into employment (Hayden and Jenkins 2014). The government's Troubled Families initiative arguably represents a combination of targeted interventions with dysfunctional families, to prepare them for reintegration into the labour force (Hayden and Jenkins 2014).

Belief in the transformational qualities of paid employment is not without its critics: Todd (2014) has cautioned against what she views as a trend to make citizenship conditional upon hard work. Not only does this legitimize the 'othering' of those who do not or cannot work, it endorses the contested belief that self-identity and 'character' are inevitably strengthened through paid employment (Verhaeghe 2014). Additionally, the pitting of workers against the workless is arguably a cynical tactic that does not reflect contemporary reality: in essence, hard work and 'doing the right thing' are insufficient to lift people out of poverty and 'welfare dependency' (Standing 2014; Todd 2014). For the first time, the majority of people living in poverty are working (MacInnes et al. 2013); yet, counter-intuitively, government policy remains committed to 'making work pay' by cutting access to benefits (DWP 2015).

Potentially, the assumed boundary between workers and workless should be redrawn to reflect those who are economically secure as opposed to those who are not. However, more recent models of class have acknowledged that it is not merely a product of income and occupation but of social and cultural capital: the advantages conferred by social connections, accent, appearance and education. Two current typologies of class are presented in Table 5.1. Savage et al. (2013) identified seven classes via the *Great British Class Survey* of 161,000 respondents. They view such class differentiation as an amalgam of indicators of economic, social and cultural capital. Standing (2009, 2011) bases his model upon employment and income insecurity.

Standing's model of class incorporates the dynamics of power and domination that will be familiar to students of Marx and Weber. However, it is his pervasive theme of 'insecurity' that is particularly powerful. Standing has extended his analysis beyond employment and income insecurity to explore what he terms *rights insecurity*:

> This is the first time in history when the state is systematically taking away rights from its own citizens . . . More and more people, not just migrants, are being converted into denizens, with a more limited range and depth of civil, cultural, social, political and economic rights. They are increasingly denied what Hannah Arendt called 'the right to have rights', the essence of proper citizenship.
>
> (Standing 2014: 4)

This denial of the 'right to have rights' resonates with the assertion that current policy makes citizenship conditional upon employment (Todd 2014). However, there may be gradations of citizenship within a 'community of worth' (Anderson 2013: 4) – 'worth' being defined by an assumed correlation of personal wealth and 'economic independence' with notions of responsibility and morality (Conboy 2006; Anderson 2013; Chase and Walker 2014). Universal rights to social security benefits – i.e. the security of having a home, the security of knowing one can feed one's children – are increasingly redefined with a gift relationship between those 'footing the bill' and the recipient. The gift is contingent upon the perceived good character of the recipient, an assessment that is underpinned by continual suspicion and by the assumed moral superiority of a taxpaying community of 'ordinary people' (Conboy 2002; Jordan 2010; Chase and Walker 2014).

Reflection point 5.2

- How might the concept of insecurity, as discussed above, be experienced by service users?
- How might this have an impact upon your own work with them?

Table 5.1 Two models of the contemporary British class structure

Savage et al. (2013)	Standing (2009, 2011)
Elite	**Plutocracy**
High economic, social and cultural capital. Inherited wealth and/or occupy the most prestigious and well-remunerated occupations.	The super rich. Able to exist and operate independently of nation states, but able to use manipulative and coercive power to ensure their interests are met.
Established middle class	**Elite**
High economic, social and cultural capital. Professionals or managers.	Usually resident and linked to a particular nation state. Constitutes, with the plutocracy, the 'ruling class'.
Technical middle class	**Salariat**
High economic capital, fewer social contacts and less cultural capital than the elite or established middle class. Scientific or technical work which provides a high income.	The traditional 'middle class'. Salaried individuals enjoying high income and employment security. A shrinking class, with many fearful of being pushed into precariat.
New affluent workers	**Proficians**
Often from working-class background; have obtained reasonably well-paid jobs without necessarily having attended university. Moderate social and cultural capital.	Contractors, and self-employed. Vulnerable; 'live on the edge of burnout and exposure to hazards' (Standing 2014: 2).
Traditional working class	**Proletariat**
Relatively poor economic social and cultural capital. Tend to be older. Some older members of this class may have relatively high potential economic capital because of high property value.	Traditional working class. A shrinking class with reduced collective political power and greater exposure to risk as welfare states contract.
Emergent service workers	**Precariat**
Young with moderately poor economic capital. Usually in rented accommodation, often in urban areas. Fairly low job security. Engagement with emerging culture and technologies (internet, music etc.) gives emerging social capital.	Insecure, casual employment, few if any employment rights. No guarantee of adequate income through paid work.
Precariat	**Underclass**
Insecure, precarious employment or unemployed. Very low economic, cultural and social capital.	'A lumpen-precariat of sad people, lingering in the streets, dying miserably' (Standing 2014: 2).

'Them and us' in social work practice

'Them and us' is a powerful and influential rhetorical device when employed by politicians and the media (Anderson 2013). For social workers, it resonates with our understanding of social identity theory and the creation of 'out-groups' (Tajfel and Turner 1979). More concerning is the empirical evidence underpinning theories of the psychology of dehumanizing 'out-groups' (Harris 2014). Dehumanization refers to the psychological process that allows us to view others as being not as human as ourselves (Haslam et al. 2008). Anger, disgust and fear all influence our creation of an 'other' from who we are psychologically and empathically disconnected (Haslam et al. 2008). This disconnection weakens our sense of moral obligation to them and legitimizes institutional and individual acts of casual cruelty (Opotow 1995).

Class relations in Britain are far from being genocidal. Nor is there a suggestion that the current political climate is creating a slippery slope to acts of barbarity. However, research into the psychosocial roots of genocide provides a rich understanding of the dynamics of dehumanization at a societal level. Key is the degree to which antagonistic attitudes towards 'out-groups' can be made normative in societies manipulated by politicians and the media. Woolf and Hulsizer (2005: 102) highlight other pervading societal conditions, these being: a perception that the 'out-group' is hostile and a threat; the institutionalization of bias and a lack of acceptance of 'difference'; an assumption of superiority by the majority group. In addition, Woolf and Hulsizer (2005) indicate how the process of dehumanization can be triggered or exacerbated by a specific crisis event: for example, an economic crisis or a high-profile news story.

Media and political responses to high-profile news 'stories' about the 'underclass' reflect many of the elements of Woolf and Hulsizer's thesis. Specific and traumatic events are generalized and threaded into a tenuous narrative of causality. Cunningham and Cunningham (2014) describe how the news story of Mick Philpott, a man who killed six of his children when he started a house fire, became for politicians and the media a parable for the evil caused by welfare dependency. Similar narratives have characterized media and political responses to the death of Peter Connelly, the kidnapping of Shannon Matthews and the murder of Jamie Bulger (Jones 2011; Cunningham and Cunningham 2014; Warner 2015).

Drawing on the work of Young (2011), Warner (2013, 2015) explores the issue of class in child protection through the lens of moral panic. Middle-class detachment from the poor and dispossessed provides a fertile ground for the generation of moral panic (Young 2011: 250). The amplification of specific events into a perceived threat to the moral order invokes in the public a desire for a punitive response against a generalized 'feral underclass' (Scambler and Scambler 2011: 25). In short, a constructed class of the 'other' becomes symbolically representative of the moral deviancy of the few (Scambler 2009; Jones 2011).

Within this context it is important to emphasize that the construction of the underclass exists at an emotional and even visceral level. Following the death of Peter Connelly, emotions of anger, disgust and shame were activated by the press and politicians, and projected against all 'underclass families', particularly mothers (Warner 2015). Similarly, social work was the target of a generalized anger for its failure to be sufficiently punitive towards the welfare-dependent and morally deficient. Tracy Connelly, Peter's mother, became the face of a shameless army of moral deviants with whom social workers colluded through naïvety and the misguided application of political correctness (Jones 2014; Warner 2015).

The accusation repeatedly levelled at social workers is that they lack 'common sense' – as if it is automatically self-evident what is the right or wrong thing to do in any given situation. This binary construction of right and wrong courses of action presupposes that there *is* a right and wrong interpretation of the evidence available to professionals – what is reported to them, what they glean from reports, and what they see and hear. Ferguson (2005, 2011) provides a convincing analysis of how the psychosocial dynamics of social work practice make this process far more complex. In addition, the manner in which common sense is applied, as a criticism, assumes that it is a static concept – one that does not vary over time and place, and one that accepts the status quo (Ladson-Billings 2015). Of course, when common sense is invoked, it is an appeal to an assumed homogenous 'common' body of knowledge, values and beliefs held by 'the majority' (Kumashiro 2015). However, even if a uniform common sense existed, individual perception, cognition, emotion and mood will introduce bias into its application. In essence, what is understood to be common sense is an evolutionary short cut, saving us the time and energy required to apply analytical thinking (Mailoo 2015).

Activity 5.4

Case study 5.1

1. Read the case study below and form a mental image of J, his parents and grandmother.
2. What do they look like? Where do they live? What do they sound like?

J has spent his early childhood largely separated from his parents, with whom he has regular but brief contact. His care has largely been shared out between his grandmother (with whom J has a strong bond) and assorted carers. On one occasion, J failed to recognize his mother when she returned to collect him. Teachers report that J has a poor attention span, finds it difficult to concentrate, and daydreams in class; although he is not disruptive and is eager to please. He spends much of his time alone, lacks self-confidence, and is described as being sensitive and easily upset. He is not popular with other children and is frequently bullied. J appears to have a difficult relationship with his father, who is irritated by J's sensitivity and lack of physical strength. J's father is very critical of him and often rebukes him in public.

The exercise draws on the branch of psychology that focuses on how, when we see and hear information, we process it as a mental image (Pinker 2005). When this exercise is conducted with students, the mental images most frequently generated are of a working-class family. Students frequently begin to create a narrative around the characters, which often contains elements of the negative stereotypes associated with the working class. Students are usually very surprised when the case study is revealed to be a distillation of publicly available information about Prince Charles's early life.

The purpose of the exercise is to illustrate the power of preconceptions. Human beings are problem solvers; they are hard-wired to scan information and look for patterns. In essence, they 'join the dots' to create a picture. However, they may join the wrong dots in the wrong order to create the wrong picture. Heuristics are the mental shortcuts that constitute intuition, common sense and educated guesses. They serve us well (Gigerenzer and Engel 2007), but are also highly vulnerable to cognitive bias. One of the aims of this chapter is to suggest that it is unlikely that social workers will be immune to the cognitive biases shaped by repeated exposure to consistent and partisan messages about 'the underclass' (Conboy 2002, 2006; Jones 2011; Scambler and Scambler 2011). One such bias is 'repetition bias', where we come to believe information if it is repeated frequently enough – for example, through media stories focusing on a particular theme. Similarly, and particularly relevant to social workers, is the functioning of 'confirmation bias': the tendency to look for, or selectively process, information that confirms our preconceptions.

In the face of the enormity of the demands placed upon them, social workers are confronted by feelings of inadequacy, shame and guilt (Gibson 2014). In addition, practitioners frequently experience considerable hostility and resistance from those with whom they work (Ferguson 2011). Self-affirmation theory (Steele 1988; Aronson et al. 1999; Sherman and Cohen 2006) demonstrates that individuals are motivated to maintain a view of themselves as good and possessing personal integrity. When this self-image is threatened, individuals may respond defensively through denial or hostility towards the evidence, or individuals, who challenge this view of the self (Sherman and Cohen 2006; Trevithick 2011). Arguably, the political and societal construction of an alien 'underclass' may provide a contextual reinforcement of the practitioner's unconscious defensive strategies. This increases the potential risk of insensitive or punitive intervention which may, in turn, elicit a response which confirms the practitioner's unconscious preconceptions. This form of 'behavioural confirmation' is summarized by Snyder and Swann (1978: 148) as follows:

> A perceiver's actions, although based upon initially erroneous beliefs about a target individual, may channel social interaction in ways that cause the behaviour of the target to confirm the perceiver's beliefs.

Reflection point 5.3

How might confirmation bias, repetition bias and self-affirmation theory influence your work with individuals from a different social class?

It is, of course, important to recognize that the impact of bias and prejudice is not confined to the professional; it is worth considering how confirmation and repetition bias may influence service users' perceptions of the social worker. Similarly, it should be acknowledged that these dynamics are not limited to a stereotypical social work relationship of middle-class social worker and working-class client. Class positions may well be reversed in the professional relationship. In addition, social workers may work with other professionals from different class backgrounds. However, the key issue is to acknowledge that social workers are not immune from the impact of class bias and prejudice. The concern is that this form of prejudice has been legitimized in public discourse and normalized in social policy (Jones 2011; Scambler and Scambler 2011; Hills 2015; Warner 2015). Therefore, there is a risk that it is less visible and more socially acceptable than other forms of discrimination.

Conclusions

The social work profession occupies an uncertain position in relation to class, simultaneously castigated for being both 'soft' and politically correct, and for being punitive and oppressive (Cohen 2002). Within this context it is difficult to understand how the government can achieve its apparent vision of social work as a skills-based profession – one which is detached from its political and moral context. There is a profound naïvety in this view since it implies a denial that social work addresses inherently complex issues, which are contested, emotive and political.

Although expected to demonstrate well-established professional values, social workers are employed by organizations which are constantly responding to ideological trends. This creates dilemmas for practitioners, who may find their professional values and training out of step with the prevailing political orthodoxy. In addition, social workers are not immune from the psychological influences that may derive from popular prejudice, the media, and their own feelings of hostility, anxiety and inadequacy. The challenge for social work practitioners and social work education is to identify how the complex impact of social class should be acknowledged in social work practice and social work training.

Key points

- There is a hostile political climate which works against those who are stigmatized.
- The moral underclass discourse places the responsibility for exclusion upon the excluded.
- 'Them and us' is an influential rhetorical device which resonates with professional understanding of social identity theory and the creation of 'out-groups'.
- Social workers, like all humans, scan information and look for patterns – i.e. they 'join the dots' to create a picture. However, they may join the wrong dots in the wrong order to create the wrong picture.

6 Islam – a 'dangerous' religion?

Kish Bhatti-Sinclair

Chapter overview

This chapter will introduce Islamophobia in relation to social work practice. By the end you will have an understanding of:

- The developments in Islamophobic thinking since the beginning of the twenty-first century
- The idea of 'dangerousness' in relation to Islam
- Professional debates on race, religion and the fear of being called racist
- The importance of laws, codes and standards on diversity and difference.

Introduction

One of the reasons for examining this topic is to explore the escalating tendency to link the social, religious and family practices of the approximately 3.3 per cent Muslim population of the UK to the laws and policies on anti-terrorism. Critics suggest that strategies such as the Prevent strategy are creating resentment among some minority groups, and fear among the general public (Foley 2016).

The argument for greater understanding of these developments is that as a social worker you follow established race relations laws and policies which protect against discrimination on the grounds of race and religion. The Health and Care Professions Council (HCPC) and the British Association of Social Workers (BASW) follow domestic and universal provisions on diversity, difference and human rights in the Standards of Proficiency and the Professional Capabilities Framework (HCPC 2012; BASW 2015). Social workers are obliged to promote equal rights in service delivery to all sections of the population, including those who may be excluded from society because of their religion, culture, diet and dress. Professionals also follow policies on immigration, asylum seeking and refugees in relation to counterterrorism strategies, such as Prevent and Contest, in public services (HM Government 2011).

The British approach to cultural and religious difference is rooted in the notion of tolerance (Law 2010) – i.e. other religions are acceptable within the boundaries set by the majority cultural traditions, which in the UK tend towards Christian Liberalism bordering on secularism. Professional ethics in social work have incorporated such ideas more inclusively, but have struggled where areas of oppression have clashed – for example, on feminism and racism. Rather than examine such phenomena further, and in a collective manner, the divisions have led to parallel theoretical positions on issues where sex and race intersect, such as Sharia law on divorce and family practices relating to arranged marriages (Law 2010). Despite this, social workers argue that core professional values are rooted in the notion of an inclusive and diverse society which has a place for different cultural and religious perspectives. Opposing positions on a woman's right to choose who and how to marry (or perhaps not marry at all or be able to live with a same-sex partner) are rarely considered.

Social work education and practice is founded on charitable and philanthropic principles which have responded incrementally to poverty and deprivation since the beginning of the twentieth century. Recognizing and dealing with oppression is a key professional aim based on the idea that the battle for equality on race, sex, disability, sexuality and (less so) age has been won. Conversely, people who follow Islamic principles have roots in societies with different historical traditions and codes of behaviour. The trajectory and pace of change on equal rights in the UK is closely related to the Industrial Revolution and the two world wars, whereas modern Islamic countries are taking very different routes to development.

Muslims have lived in European counties such as the UK for many decades, and many are born and educated in the same way as any other citizen; however, the strong links with countries of origin sustain and help to maintain religious and cultural norms. Like all immigrants, Muslims leave their home countries for reasons which include commitment to fundamental human rights such as freedom of speech and movement.

Newly arrived and established immigrants find ways to balance their old and new lives in nuanced and complicated ways, and tend to settle close to others with similar experiences. Social workers who are not from these backgrounds may struggle to understand these subtleties, even if they have a developed understanding of social inclusion. Those with similar experiences, such as Muslim social workers, can act as conduits between secular and multifaith approaches to anti-racist practice and Islamic customs and behaviours, but this can be limited because the number of Muslims in the UK is small, and the majority live in four or five areas of settlement, mostly in England. The number of social workers likely to have the relevant knowledge, experience and interest in working with such groups is very small.

The word Islamophobia was coined in the early 1990s and, like xenophobia, defined the so-called real and present threat posed by followers of Islam (Runnymede Trust 1997: 1). As the concept developed, it distinguished people perceived as visibly Muslim, mainly in relation to types of clothing, such as head scarves. Some people suggested that Muslims used these outward signs (supported by Islamic teachings) to signal religious superiority and mock other faiths. Secularism in the UK is powerfully against any overt public display of organized religion and faith.

The focus on Muslim dress, along with Sharia law, has meant that people who had previously lived in harmony with other communities and religions had, over a relatively short period, acquired the status of dangerous aliens. Increasingly, liberal-minded thinkers are openly discussing the problems with Islam, the poor treatment of women and the dated approaches to family systems used by Sharia courts (Maddox 2016).

The change in attitudes can be pinpointed to the attacks in New York (2001) and bombings in London (2005). During this period perceptions of the Asian immigrant have shifted radically from an Asian immigrant who is a Muslim, to a Muslim who is working against secular society and is, therefore, dangerous.

This chapter considers the development of dangerousness and religious belief in relation to professional practice. The premise is that these messages are powerfully pervasive and social workers will be absorbing them in relation to safeguarding Muslim children and women. Professionals need to safely engage with the notion of Islamic dangerousness without fear of being called racist.

Islam and Islamophobia

Followers of Islam are often seen as one homogenous group with common rules on how to eat, dress and relate to one another. Islam is one of the biggest religions, and Muslims live in almost every country in the world, including many which are predominantly Christian and, in the case of India, majority Hindu. Given this fact it is remarkable that such an image persists. The most significant terrorist incidents in 2001 in New York, 2005 in London and 2015 in Paris were committed by people who did not live in those countries. Resident Muslims live harmoniously with other faiths, even in Islamic countries where they are in charge. Muslims are heterogeneous, and interpret Islamic doctrine and scriptures differently, depending on nation, sect, family and mosque. In relation to social justice and equality, particularly in areas such as gender, age and sexuality, perspectives and opinions vary as much within Islam as against other faiths and beliefs.

There are approximately 1.5 billion Muslims in the world (Furness and Gilligan 2010) living in cold northern climes, sparse desert regions, as well as large metropolitan cities. The majority apply Islamic beliefs to order and structure everyday life, aware that overarching class, caste and tribal systems are maintained and incorporated in community and family systems, even in the context of rural/ urban living. This unifying approach can differ from other major religions because it arguably impacts more on social aspects of daily life. Muslims, particularly second- and third-generation immigrants, agree that family and community control may be an area which requires attention, but worry that religion continues to be the only means by which they are being defined.

Islam is one of the monotheistic religions which share a common link to the teachings of Abraham, but is seen to adhere to teachings and scriptures which have not adapted to modern-day living as have Christianity and Judaism. The argument is that the strands in Christianity have evolved, and followers may fall along the continuum from lapsed to extreme belief to fit the secular structures and systems of British society.

The focus here is on the diversity of the Muslim experience, rather than the development of Islam. The two are quite different areas for consideration. Islam can be interpreted according to cultural heritage, the strands (i.e. Shi'a or Sunni) followed, the country of residence and/or origin, social class, educational attainment, and differences in relation to age, gender and sexuality. Approaches to family systems, marriage, child care and elder care can also vary. In managing this complexity, Muslims tend to create a social order or subculture rooted in ethnic or cultural history, within the society they inhabit.

Although research on the social aspects of Islam is limited, a survey (Phillips 2016) on what Muslims think about issues such as social contact with non-Muslims, homosexuality and adultery suggests that, rather than being integrated over many decades, Muslims are increasingly segregated and are far less likely to mix, intermarry or follow civic laws in their daily lives. Sharia courts are seen as an area of particular concern as they may be making decisions which impact on safeguarding adults and children, while holding little civic responsibility and receiving limited external guidance.

Jay (2014) suggests that child protection agencies have not always challenged community practices for fear of feeding racism and have, as a result, have been slow to act on important indicators of child sexual exploitation such as repeated missing episodes, the use of inhibitors such as alcohol and drugs, and tracking devices such as mobile telephones.

The UK prides itself on the diverse nature of its cities. Critics suggest that Muslims may be jeopardizing this by living only with other Muslims, and drawing influences only from Islamic traditions and family customs (Phillips 2016). Muslims facing discrimination would argue that the need for greater privacy is the result of resentment and antagonism towards them, and denial of their experiences (Hogan and Mallott 2005). Secular society is failing to provide Muslim-friendly environs, surroundings and services.

The increase in segregation is a source of worry for liberal Muslims who follow Islamic traditions but see the world through different eyes. They maintain that variation is the norm, even in situations which appear cohesive. Justifying and explaining their faith is a daily task, even when they are among Muslims and non-Muslims. Justifying norms is a time-consuming task, and for some people requires more time, space and investment than they or others are prepared to offer.

The private nature of family life means that anyone located outside the kinship group is deemed an outsider – i.e. anyone who views Islam differently according to historical, familial or personal understanding of ideas such as permissive behaviour. Protecting and consolidating family and community space is a common pattern followed by other minority groups facing similar challenges, such as Jewish communities.

Reflection point 6.1

The aim of this exercise is for you to reflect on family influences and privacy in relation to group dynamics and kinship bonds.

- Think about the people you would include in your wider family group.
- Draw a circle within a circle.
- List the people you consider to be located in the inner circle – i.e. those who are most influential and with whom you share common values.

- List the people you consider to be located in the outer circle – i.e. those who are in your kinship group but may not be part of your inner circle of influence.
- What does this say about what you share and who you share it with?
- To what extent would you consider this an issue of privacy?

Reflecting on this exercise – how do you understand kinship and closeness? Do kinship bonds protect you and those closest to you? Where are the main family influences located? Are the people who impact on your adult life in the inner or outer circles?

According to the 2011 UK Census, Muslims number around two million, or 3.3 per cent of the British population (Hussain 2011) of whom about 50 per cent originate from Pakistan and reside mostly in the London Boroughs of Bethnal Green and Barking, and beyond in the northern English city of Bradford. Birmingham continues to house the largest number of Muslims at 14 per cent. Beyond this the population numbers are very small, particularly in the three other countries of the United Kingdom, and tend to be incorporated in the category Asian. The sparsity of the Muslim population living in semi-rural England is illustrated by the following numbers: 1.2 per cent of Asians live in the south-west; 1.48 per cent of Asians live in West Sussex, which has the largest number in Crawley (2.37 per cent). Many reports (Runnymede Trust 1997) and studies are rooted in large conurbation areas where the majority of Muslims reside. However, Islamophobia exists not necessarily towards people who live in the same area, but more because the government and media reports conflate the perceived threat from terrorism and immigration and lay it at the door of every British Muslim, wherever she or he resides.

The message coming from government sources suggests that immigration is out of control and criminal activity is rife among Muslim groups (Guru 2012). However, this is not evidenced by official statistics; the profile of established immigrant families is mainly young, and the population increasingly British by birth. Evidence suggests that young Muslims appear to be more, rather than less, traditional (Phillips 2016) in their world-views and moral positions, a defensive reaction perhaps to the growing evidence of bombings, shootings and other threats linked to young Muslim men with an obsession with mass killings (Sengupta 2016).

Activity 6.1

The exercise below is exploratory and offers you an opportunity to research the population in your area to find out how Muslims are seen and represented. The aim is to search and find the number of Muslims who live in your locality.

- Decide on your search terms (such as ethnic minority population and Asian) and input into an online search engine.

- Make a list of the categories used in statistical data, and the numbers against each one.
- Try other search terms such as 'hate crimes' and 'Muslims'.
- Compare with data found on the Office of National Statistics website.
- Relate to your contact with and experience of Muslims.

The *dangerous other*

The influence of Islamic ideas on Christian Liberal societies dates back to the Crusades (Merali and Shadjareh 2002) and the British colonial times. Muslims have lived in the UK for more than 300 years (Runnymede Trust 1997), but for decades the numbers were so small that they have been lumped into a group called Asians – i.e. people originating from the Indian subcontinent. During the 1960s, larger numbers arrived from Pakistan, Bangladesh and India, but continued to be grouped under the general umbrella of hard-working immigrant Asians who lived in clusters and ran shops and curry houses. This was the time when the notion of the *dangerous other* was applied to sets of immigrants, mostly young men, originating from Africa and the Caribbean. The stereotype in the 1970s and 1980s was that African-Caribbean men were big, black and bad, while Asians were passive and unassuming. The shift to the 'Dangerous Muslim' came about quickly after the attack on the twin towers in New York on 11 September 2001 and the bombings in London on 7 July 2005. Suddenly Muslim citizens were the enemy within, and Muslim countries were seen as net contributors to insurgency and civil disturbance. This was a surprise for many British and American Muslims, who did not automatically align themselves with terrorist activity, but rather saw themselves as law-abiding citizens with rights and responsibilities. The attackers were perceived in the same way as by any other community – i.e. as politically motivated human bombs with little regard for life.

The force with which London and New York reacted lost the cities two main advantages. First, their reputation as liberal-leaning centres with a welcome for all newcomers. Second, their reputation as safe urban areas with freedom of movement. The subsequent developments led to draconian measures at border crossings, and an increase in internal surveillance and security measures targeting terrorists seen to be motivated by religious doctrine. This process had the effect of heightening fear, and narrowed definitions of groups seen as dangerous. Subsequent law, policy and practice on counterterrorism predictably consolidated the idea of the 'Dangerous Muslim' man, a concept which was easy to understand and develop because the image was at once recognizable and fear-provoking. News media and social networks fed this by widely publicizing atrocities committed by individuals across the world.

Interestingly, Muslims themselves saw these developments in a diverse and complex way. For example, mosques became involved in the Prevent agenda in the UK, imams were offered training, and women were targeted to support greater cohesion and counter extremism (HM Government 2011). The British government recognized the need for multilayered approaches which were severe and moderate. The 2015 Counter-Terrorism and Security Act added to the 2000 Terrorism Act which defined the threat to security, and extended police, detention and deportation powers. For public services, the 2015 Act asked each local authority to set up a panel which planned, identified and supported possible recruits likely to be drawn into terrorist activity. The panel could refer the identified vulnerable person to a provider of any health or social care service (Stationery Office 2015, Chapter 6: 26). The combined powers of the laws on terrorism and the Prevent and Contest strategies conflated religious beliefs, fundamental doctrine, active recruitment by international jihadi groups, and internal mechanisms for controlling immigration and community surveillance (Guru 2012). Essentially, Islam was being used as a tool to engender fear from a group with easily defined characteristics, with some presence in a few British cities but little to fight back with. This shifted thinking on the key constituents of an open and diverse society.

The escalation of the notion of the followers of Islam as inherently dangerous has spread across the Western world (OSCE Office for Democratic Institutions and Human Rights (OSCE/ODIHR) 2011). The Muslim is motivated by religion and is culturally and morally inferior, threatening, and impossible to connect or cooperate with. The Muslim is perceived as so different that a normal British person is unable to relate to or connect with him or her.

The international backdrop to Islamophobia is rooted in terrorist attacks, but also other violent events seen to be perpetrated by Muslims such as bombings at Glasgow airport in 2007, the 2015 bombings in Paris, and various gun-related crimes in Europe in 2016. After these events, governments across the world had to justify spending on internal security, and the wars in Iraq and Syria, at a time of extreme austerity. It may be argued that Muslims became an easily identifiable target rooted in age-old religious differences by nations with crusading, colonial and imperialistic histories. The securing of internal borders was used for the 'leave' campaign in the 2016 referendum on the European Union. The NSPCC saw a rise in calls to its helplines, and advised families and professionals on its website to look for signs of bullying and radicalization in schools.

Nevertheless, the terrorist incidents in Paris, Nice and Munich in 2015 and 2016 did involve suicidal Muslim men, a fact which requires detailed examination, not least because they appeared to be young, vulnerable and suffering mental ill health.

Figure 6.1 illustrates how complex identities can be conflated into one stereotypical image which not only essentializes one group (in this case Muslim men), but excludes all others (such as Muslim women and older people). The problem illustrated is that the reconfiguration of the Asian immigrant into the religious zealot/terrorist developed into the 'Dangerous Muslim'. The concern relates to the ease with which these ideas form and grow. Where will this thinking lead?

The ideas encapsulated in Figure 6.1 are themselves a danger to civilized thinking and oppose the forward-thinking, inclusive principles set out in professional codes and the PCF domain on diversity. The 'Dangerous Muslim' is a fixed, negative entity devoid of humanity – an image which is hard to find and even harder to reconcile in daily British life.

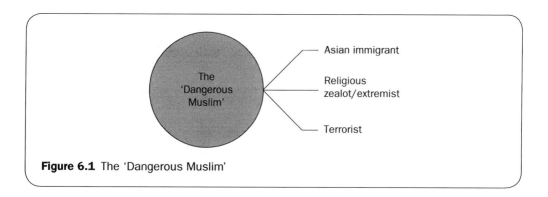

Figure 6.1 The 'Dangerous Muslim'

The Muslim penalty

Figure 6.1 further illustrates that Muslims are penalized by the simple fact of being different and Muslim. Religion can exclude Muslims from societal systems, but other factors intersect to disadvantage still further – for example, the Home Office reported that during the 2014/15 period hate crimes recorded by the police increased by 18 per cent from the previous year. Of the total number reported, 82 per cent were race hate crimes and 6 per cent were religion hate crimes (Corcoran et al. 2015). Population figures also suggest that, within the category of Asian, Muslims have larger and poorer households constructed around multiple extended families who share care responsibilities for children, adults and older persons, often with few resources and very little input from the welfare state, including social care. Coping strategies can lead to insularity, which in turn can limit the intergenerational life chances of children, parents and grandparents. Social work intervention can locate and support larger, poorer households, but there is little to suggest that professionals have the necessary set of skills or access to communication and information systems to improve services.

For social workers, the very aspects which bind Muslim families (who are often the service users) can be seen as problems for non-Muslims (who are often the professionals). Despite the need to maintain their religious identity, liberal Muslims agree that change is desirable (Phillips 2016) in areas which affect day-to-day relationships and privilege men over women, as in the case of inheritance and dowry-giving. Historically, both practices are rooted in an equal distribution of wealth among male and female children, and the idea that when newly married a woman departs with her share of the family fortune which allows her a level of independence from her husband should the marriage falter or fail. Men do not get a dowry, but are secure in the knowledge that they inherit later in life. Regrettably, not all families are wealthy and not all the distribution is equal. Strong family units share common characteristics which guide and control members. These can vary across religions, but cultural pride and honour are key to family, kinship and marriage.

Critics suggest that Islamic teachings are only as fair as those who interpret them, but supporters argue that at least Islam takes into account the need for women to have financial independence within marriage. But this raises the question of priorities – i.e. how should families resource customs which are not necessarily needed in a country such as the UK, and should social workers have a view on where family resources should be best utilized.

The ethnic penalty has now become the Muslim penalty (Alexander et al. 2013). In the war against terrorism Muslims become the new enemy (both within and without), a scapegoating method to divert the gaze away from austerity, poverty and the dismantling of the welfare state. As suggested by Vakil (in Alexander et al. 2013), the solution to the problems facing contemporary society appear to lie with Muslims – the thinking is along the following lines: if only they would stop exploiting children and women, and waging war, the world would be a safer place.

Islamophobia impacts on Muslims at a number of levels (Runnymede Trust 1997), including personal prejudice, violent abuse and assault, exclusion from active participation in society in areas such as news media, and discrimination leading to low incomes, lack of promotion and services which may lead to enhanced life chances.

Activity 6.2

The exercise below will enable you to reflect on your personal and professional situation and consider the perspective of Muslim colleagues and service users and carers.

Reflect on the idea of a penalty faced by Muslims within your:

- town, city or village
- service, and
- organization.

Do you know the religion of the people you work and provide services for? If so, make a list of the ways in which:

- Muslim staff are penalized
- Muslim service users and carers are penalized.

Social work and Islamophobia

The principles on which diversity is based include respectful acknowledgement of difference in language, accent, dress, diet and customs related to religious worship/celebration. The legal and policy initiatives developed between the 1960s and 1990s led to the idea that living well together, and interfaith dialogue, would promote community cohesion. The post-2000 focus on religious difference is superseding discussion on commonality and developmental ways to improve understanding. However, there is little research or analysis here of who is involved, and what the actual problem is (apart from a perceived national threat from terrorism).

Counterterrorism policies show little discrimination between Muslims and those seen as Muslims. Although 'Asians' as a term appears dated, the idea that all Muslims/terrorists are brown persists. Racism as an act of discrimination which results in the putting down and disempowering people who are different in relation to colour, religion, culture and region remains a concern. The link between racism and Islamophobia – i.e. anti-Muslim sentiment against people perceived to have an 'internal culture or value system' (Merali and Shadjareh 2002: 5) is in need of urgent attention.

Although Muslims as a group are not protected in law, discrimination on the grounds of religion is covered under the 1976 Race Relations Act and the 2010 Equality Act. Public employees, such as social workers, follow the 1998 Human Rights Act and the 2006 Equality Act, alongside universal and European conventions. Legal definitions are broad and cover all religions, as well as atheism and humanism, and provision is in place on religious worship, diet and language. Legal protection, however, does not take account of factors such as perceptions and experiences of Muslims.

The skills social workers need to deploy include identification and incorporation of family and religious heritage in care assessment and planning. Professionals may also look out for discriminatory behaviour affecting children who are different in image and presentation (Furness and Gilligan 2010).

Relationship-based practice suggests that organizational practice with adults and older people is better if individual needs and wishes are met. Greater scrutiny of professional bias in systems and procedures, along with improved training and support, is also likely to improve services for all groups.

The area of mental health is particularly interesting as the level of stigma is likely to be higher among minority groups more generally, and Muslims in particular. The link between diminishing mental health services and the number of young Muslim men involved in terrorism and child sexual exploitation needs to be made within disruption strategies.

Islamic cultures and family systems are inherently private, and problems are generally dealt with internally with little recourse to external intervention, which is likely to be seen as a failure to cope and manage. Social workers are likely to be seen to interfere with and change the group mechanisms which hold families together, but culturally sensitive practice should still prevail.

In researching a group of young Somali men perceived to be at risk, Mason, in Alexander et al. (2013), found that there is perpetuation of stereotypes. A situation or place can be seen to harbour risky behaviour from a group, and funding may alleviate this risk. Those under scrutiny are, for reasons linked to masculinity, shown to identify with the very characteristics which label them a problem. Often the identification is more about posturing than real, but the cycle of deprivation continues until a number move away through educational attainment. Mason's research demonstrates that young men are self-aware and knowingly contribute to masculine stereotypes. What is unclear is whether all young men would behave in a similar way, and what are the actual indicators of risk aside from the fact that these young men were Somali and Muslim. So, while these people may be like any other in society, their colour, socio-economic status and religion define them as a group at risk. Mason suggests that the risk prevention

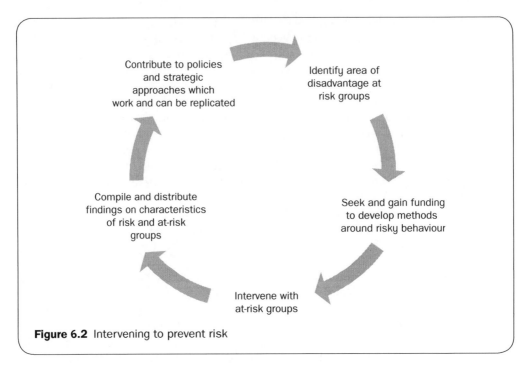

Figure 6.2 Intervening to prevent risk

agenda needs to be better informed on the long-term stigmatization of groups who may already be disadvantaged in society. For social workers, the process of intervention may involve identifying the area of disadvantage deemed at risk, locating funding, intervening appropriately, and informing others of the characteristics of at-risk groups and approaches which inform future development.

A central question about Islam is the desire of followers to choose to believe in it. Merali and Shadjarah (2002) suggest that the right to choose is a problem for liberal-thinking, tolerant Britain, particularly followers of the liberation movements. For example, feminists worked over decades to enable women and minority groups to be what they want to be, and yet Muslim women appear subservient to religious dictate seen as written and led by men. Terrorism policy suggests many such men are violent and subversive. No right-thinking feminist is going to challenge this possibility. Social work values derive from movements which fought for fundamental human rights, and students are rightly taught the importance of self-determination and respect for diversity, but only if it meets the standards set by the majority.

Social workers align with the English middle classes, who appear to be struggling to see how the battle against racism can be won in the context of terrorism, Sharia law and the rights of women originating from Muslim countries. The struggle to remain broad-minded, while facing media and political concern about the rise in the numbers of refugees fleeing the wars in the Middle East, and the internalization of the threat from extreme ideology, has became a challenge for many people. The growth in the media coverage of racist organizations have confronted conventions of polite society and added to questions about the enemy within.

Table 6.1 Closed and open views of Islam

Distinctions	Closed views	Open views	Social work: diversity and difference
Monolithic or diverse	Islam is monolithic and unresponsive.	Islam is diverse and progressive.	Muslims live in all countries of the world and incorporate their own cultures and traditions with those of the host communities. This makes them responsive to learning about other religions and cultures.
Separate or interacting	Islam runs parallel with other religions and cultures and is not influenced or affected by others.	Islam shares common foundations with other religions and cultures.	Islam, Christianity and Judaism share common ideas and principles. Muslims acknowledge this openly and interact respectfully in interfaith initiatives.
Inferior or different	Islam is underdeveloped, barbaric and sexist.	Islamic teachings have a great deal to contribute to society.	Islamic scholars argue that religious texts promote progressive ideas on equal rights – for example, for women in marriage – but agree that interpretations can vary. Muslim families have strong bonds and ties within and across countries of residence and origin. This enables a cross-fertilization of ideas on care which can add to the thinking on child protection and safeguarding.
Enemy or partner	Islam seen as violent, aggressive, threatening, supportive of terrorism, engaged in a clash of civilizations.	Islam seen as an actual or potential partner in joint cooperative enterprises and in the solution of shared problems.	Muslim scholars, social workers and service users have a great deal to contribute to the development of social welfare, and should be consulted on the development of law, policy and practice.
Manipulative or sincere	Islam seen as a political ideology, used for political or military advantage.	Islam seen as a genuine religious faith, practised sincerely by its adherents.	Islam is an established religion with historical roots, customs and norms which are well used and tested. All religions have political undercurrents and, like all religions, Islam has followers who misrepresent and use the faith for their own gains.

(Continued)

Table 6.1 (continued)

Distinctions	Closed views	Open views	Social work: diversity and difference
Criticism of the West rejected or considered	Criticisms by Islam of the West rejected out of hand.	Criticisms of the West and other cultures are considered and debated.	As a secular profession, social work requires confidence in debating religious differences. This includes critical consideration of how Islam is seen by the West, and vice versa.
Discrimination defended or criticized	Hostility towards Islam used to justify discriminatory practices towards Muslims and exclusion of Muslims from mainstream society.	Debates and disagreements with Islam do not diminish efforts to combat discrimination and exclusion.	Debating key questions which relate to the welfare of vulnerable adults and children is a critical part of social work practice. Open and active dialogue which critiques approaches to discrimination, racism and social cohesion should be encouraged across faiths, cultures and traditions.
Islamophobia seen as natural or problematic	Anti-Muslim hostility accepted as natural and normal.	Critical views of Islam are themselves subjected to critique, lest they be inaccurate or unfair.	Critiquing religious ideology respectfully is a key task for social work professionals and academics. Developing for a where common ideas, ways of observing, and applying rules to everyday living, should offer a way forward for developing knowledge and understanding.

The Runnymede Trust produced an important report in 1997 which provided detailed guidance on Islamophobia, synthesized in a table, which set out closed and open public perceptions of Islam by the general public. Table 6.1 has been adapted to include a fourth column on how social workers may view both perspectives. Given that many of these views are sweeping generalizations it is likely that social workers will see Muslims in relation to lifestyles, cultural customs and personal morality – i.e. in a critical, reflective way. The focus is likely to be on commonalities, rather than differences and weaknesses.

Social workers are also left unarmed in some contexts – for example, the child sexual exploitation (CSE) scandals in British cities with large Pakistani communities. The locality reports offer important insights into professional failings, but little in the way of guidance on investigative and post-investigative skills on diversity and difference. Martin et al. (2014) focus on social workers' confidence in working on CSE cases in multifaith, diverse communities, and recommend annual auditing and training needs analysis. The Professional Capabilities Framework and the BASW Code of Ethics offer little to inform such dilemmas. Social work research and literature focuses more on racism and less on religious discrimination, but has the potential to find and analyse information on political thinking and its impact on professional attitudes and behaviour towards Islamic traditions and customs.

Conclusions

Social interaction is rooted in the idea that humans share ideas, exchange views and engage with one another in a manner which takes account of customs, habits, systems and structures. Islam is founded on the same doctrine as Christianity and Judaism, and shares the key rules on human behaviour. The assumption that codes of conduct conflict substantially with societal laws and policies is not borne out, even in Sharia courts, which tend to act as go-betweens deploying methods of conciliation. Muslims always have recourse to civil systems, and many use divorce and family courts. British Muslims hold multiple identities and are part of wider society, which they value rather than threaten (Alexander et al. 2013).

Understanding perspectives means that people can disagree with different ways of living. This does not mean that you are actively discriminating, but that you are aware that disagreement is important in engaging with the issues – for example, in relation to children's or women's rights. Muslims themselves will disagree on fundamental questions across gender and age divides. There is little doubt that social workers will view religion and faith in a range of ways, but most will see this as adding to, rather than taking away from, diversity.

The challenge for social work academics is how to reclaim equality and difference in a robust, rather than lukewarm, way in a manner which does not compromise cohesion, but emphasizes social justice on the grounds of difference.

Key points

- Islamophobia is a homogenous term manufactured to demonize Muslims.
- Like all forms of discrimination, Islamophobia prevents the human development of young Muslims and curtails their life chances.
- Muslims are like any other minority group, they follow the rules of the country in which they live, and should be allowed to contribute fully to wealth creation.
- Research on the contribution of Muslims to civil society is required.
- Social workers are aware of, and can inform, the debate on Islamophobia without fear of being called racist.

7 Roma people: are discriminatory attitudes natural?

Dan Allen

Chapter overview

In order to reduce the risk of social work practice colluding with this prejudice, this chapter will explain why a sustained effort must be made to critically reflect on the absurdities that might be believed, including how these belief systems might determine poor social work practice. Therefore, by the end of this chapter you should be able to understand:

- The impact of cultural determinism, evolutionary psychology and memetics on professional social work practice with Roma people
- The possible relationship between memetics, biological determinism, human growth and the epigenetic impact on Roma communities
- The transferability of psychological knowledge between and across other service user groups
- The way in which phenomenological theories must be used as first-order knowledge to develop the values and skills needed to promote anti-discriminatory behaviour and practice when working to engage all people.

Introduction

The famous French philosopher Voltaire once wrote that 'those who can make you believe absurdities can make you commit atrocities', and it is in the context of this quote that this chapter is written.

Throughout history, we have witnessed the various ways in which hate speech and prejudice have been used to justify atrocious acts. While, for some, a misguided belief means that these outrages are contained in the pages of history, it is important for students and early career social workers to acknowledge the fact that society continues to believe absurdities, and that these belief systems can be reflected in the various ways that some think, feel and behave.

In order to advance an understanding of the relationship between absurd belief systems and the opportunity for atrocious acts further, this chapter focuses specifically on the position of Roma people. As a much maligned and misunderstood community, they remain victims of hate speech, racism and the most extreme forms of hostility.

Background

The word 'discrimination' has legal status in British law, particularly in relation to gender, race, disability, sexual orientation and age. Students and early career social workers routinely apply equality laws and duties, such as the 2010 Equality Act, but in doing so also have to critically consider the impact of discrimination through theoretical lenses provided by disciplines in psychology, sociology and the medical sciences.

Discrimination may be defined as categorizing or distinguishing between factors or variables in a positive, negative or neutral way, but also as a means by which an 'in-group' can justify the inclusion or exclusion of others. Not only does it have clear implications for contemporary society, it can also impact significantly on the 'sense-making' activity that is social work. Central to achieving effective anti-discriminatory practice, therefore, is the ability of students and early career social workers to explore ideas related to discriminatory attitudes and behaviour and, most importantly, the capacity for personal and professional change.

The methods needed to inform and underpin anti-discriminatory practice have been pursued in a diverse range of applications (Dominelli 2002; Thoburn et al. 2005; Parrott 2010; Payne 2012; Thompson 2012). Until recently, however, the specific knowledge values and skills needed to work with Roma people have received limited attention in social work practice and educational systems. For example, the curriculum guides which were produced by the College of Social Work, a now redundant organization, focused on general issues rather than specific service user groups.

This chapter considers the ways in which we, as human beings, might come to believe absurdities, and practise in discriminatory or oppressive ways. By introducing the paradigms of cultural determinism, evolutionary psychology and memetics, this chapter will consider how these social pressures might shape and inform the way that students and early career social workers might think, feel and behave when working with Roma people. Extending this discussion to consider the impact of absurd social beliefs on Roma people themselves, we will also consider the possible relationship between memetics, biological determinism, human growth, and the epigenetic impact that this all might have on the individuals, families and communities who social work seeks to support.

Finally, this chapter will provide a fundamental introduction to the theoretical assumptions of phenomenology. It will argue that critical reflection must be used as first-order knowledge so as to evidence the values and skills needed to promote anti-discriminatory behaviour and support understanding of the impact of own values on professional practice. In order to commence this learning opportunity, you are invited to complete the following activity.

Activity 7.1

Identifying presupposition

Imagine that you have been asked to visit a Roma family to conduct an initial assessment. On a sheet of paper, list the words or phrases that you are aware of to describe Roma people. Then, use critical reflection to summarize and describe how you might be feeling and what you might be thinking about carrying out this visit. Once you have completed this activity, put the paper to one side.

What are the concerns?

Social work practice with Roma people is often reported to be driven by pathologizing or culturally relativist reactions (Roth and Toma 2014; Allen 2015). Here individuals, families and communities are made responsible for their own living conditions and completely separated from the influence of social pathologies and structural inequalities. As a group subject to the label 'hard to reach', Roma have become doubly marginalized. For social work, this is a clear paradox. On the one hand, due to their experiences of multidimensional and trans-generational discrimination, Roma people might need more support from social workers; on the other hand, they are considered a marginal group, thus implying that the profession might exclude them. For these reasons, the theories and methods developed in this chapter will focus on social work with Roma people.

In the following pages this paradox will be problematized to establish the need to resist the risk of practising in a pathologizing or culturally relative way, not only with Roma people, but in all aspects of social work practice. As social work is a 'sense-making' activity, this chapter assumes that students and early career social workers will be required to draw upon the things that they see, smell, hear, touch, and in some cases taste, to make sense of complex social situations. Given the prevalence of culturally determined stereotypes and perceptions, phenomenology will be used to explain why it is absolutely essential, when working with all people, that social workers ensure that they understand how the senses being deployed to gather and assess information may be biased by discrimination.

Who are Roma?

The term 'Roma', first chosen at the inaugural World Romani Congress held in London in 1971, is a widely accepted name to describe a diverse range of communities who live across Europe. Across the European Union (European Commission 2011), 'Roma' refers to Roma, Sinti, Kale and related groups, including Travellers and the Eastern groups (Dom and Lom), and people who identify themselves as Travellers or Gypsies. In this chapter, however, the word 'Roma' is more specifically used to refer to the populations of people who have migrated to the UK from Central and Eastern Europe.

Consistent with the local parlance, this chapter recognizes that, in the UK, the word 'Roma' is used separately from the European definition. It is not used to describe other indigenous ethnic 'Gypsy', 'Traveller' or other occupational travelling groups. Although a fuller exploration of the fascinating differences between

'Gypsy', 'Roma' and 'Traveller' groups living in the UK might be useful, any additional detail is beyond the scope of this chapter. For readers new to this discussion, the book *Social Work with Gypsy, Roma and Traveller Children* (Allen and Adams 2013) is recommended as an accessible foundation text from which to better understand the diversity that exists within a much broader context. Before we do move on, however, it is crucial to understand that the terms 'Gypsy' 'Roma' or 'Traveller' do not describe the heterogeneity which exists, and are, in some applications, examples of the ways in which social constructivism has shaped a discriminatory public perception that could be applied to discriminatory attitudes towards other groups.

Roma in the UK

There are thought to be approximately 225,000 migrant Roma individuals living in the UK (Brown et al. 2014). Discriminatory discourses place in the foreground their 'big families', 'high social assistance levels', involvement in organized crime, and 'negative attitudes to general social values' (Urh 2011: 473). According to populist views, these characteristics are deemed strange and deviant against a notion of dominant social ideals (Ryder et al. 2012). As a result, and similar to many other migrant communities living in the UK, Roma people are excluded as either being 'troublemakers' blamed for not wanting to engage with the rest of society (Roth and Toma 2014), or as being 'troubled' (Brown et al. 2013). This oscillating discrimination represents a paradox which is shaping the contemporary situation of Roma in the UK, and throughout the world (Stewart 2012).

For students and early career social workers seeking to engage and support Roma people, it is clear that examples of such oscillating discrimination can often result in examples of oscillating practice. Where Roma individuals, families and communities are publicly perceived as 'troublemakers', there arguably follows a pathologizing response and the implementation of punitive practices. It is here that any perception of 'risk', heightened by stereotypical presupposition, is then used to justify various projects of social control, including the systematic removal of Roma children from their families and communities (European Roma Rights Centre 2011; Allen 2015). In addition to increased use of statutory intervention, there follows the use of defensive neo-liberal or neo-conservative procedures based on a deficit, rather than a strengths-based model of practice (Roth and Toma 2014). It is on these occasions that wider perspectives, including those related to structural inequality and social pathology, are lost to narrow populist assumptions which reinforce perceptions of Roma people as 'troublemakers'.

The alternative view, that Roma individuals, families and communities are 'troubled', is equally problematic. In contrast to a pathologizing reaction is the phenomenon of 'cultural relativism' (Healy 2007). Conceivably determined by an uncritical orientation towards anti-discrimination, obligation and duty, cultural relativism becomes manifest in a practitioner's reticence towards establishing the basis for intervention – even when intervention might be necessary. Similar to the tragic outcomes reported in those serious case reviews which pepper social work history, including those published after the death of Victoria

Climbié in 2000 and the death of Daniel Pelka in 2012, assessing individuals, families and communities through a culturally relativist lens can lead to the 'rule of optimism' (Dingwall et al. 1983) and exacerbated risk caused by positive discrimination.

In order to reduce the risks associated with pathologizing or cultural relativist reactions, anti-discriminatory practice requires social workers to ensure that any decision to act, or not, is based, as far as possible, upon verifiable fact, rather than on discriminatory judgement. Yet, while the evidence base used to guide anti-discriminatory practice exists in theoretical principle and in social policy concordats, it is arguable that, with the clear exception of Allen and Adams (2013) and Roth and Toma (2014), there is a clear shortage of evidence to inform the achievement of this with Roma people in practice.

Before moving on to consider a method for anti-discriminatory practice further, it is first important to establish a rudimentary understanding of how examples of discrimination towards Roma people have come to pass so that we can consider how they might come to impact on the social work assessment. In doing so, this chapter will consider, fairly briefly whether discriminatory attitudes are natural, before establishing the basis for a phenomenological approach to social work activity.

The roots of discrimination

Discrimination towards Roma people is prevalent and extremely damaging (O'Nions 2011). It has been increasing in recent years in the UK, but has roots that stretch across the entire world. For more than a thousand years, Roma people have been stigmatized, abused, misunderstood, misjudged and excluded from society (Kuhelj 2014). Understanding why this treatment continues, however, is complicated. Within this chapter, we will begin this process of understanding by considering the impact of cultural determinism.

Consistent with social learning theories, which integrate behavioural and cognitive theories, cultural determinism is an ideational perspective which advances the assumption that a majority culture is able to determine and control the behaviour and functioning of individuals, communities and societies (Spiro 2001). In contrast to biological determinism, the belief that human behaviour is controlled by an individual's genes (Waggoner and Uller 2015), cultural determinism, in its most basic form, argues that human behaviour is determined by systems of shared social ideals, concepts and rules that are all communicated by memes (Keesing 1981: 74). The discussion will return to biological determinism shortly; but first, it is important to consider the various ways that cultural determinism uses memes to transmit discrimination and discriminatory behaviour.

Socially constructed memes

According to Brendtro and Mitchell (2013), memes are the cultural analogues to genes. While genes have a biological function and contribute to each person's unique physical features, memes self-replicate, mutate, and respond to social

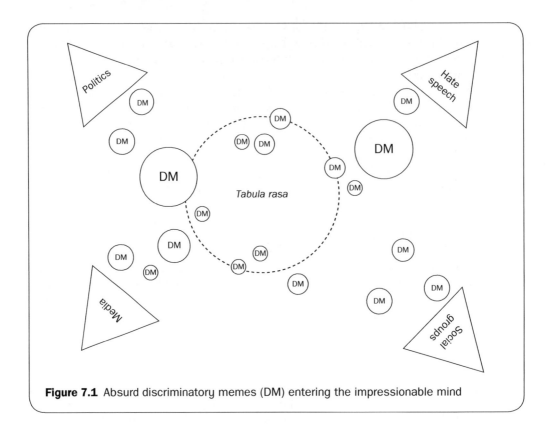

Figure 7.1 Absurd discriminatory memes (DM) entering the impressionable mind

pressures to form the basis of a belief or accepted norm in the minds of individuals across a culture. If John Locke's paradigm of *tabula rasa* is acknowledged – the epistemological idea that individuals are born without 'built-in psychological content' – a meme comes to represent the way by which the mind is filled by those discriminatory beliefs which are created and passed from one person to another (see Figure 7.1).

Of course, positive memes exist too; but for the purpose of this chapter, negative memes are significant. For example, in the context of child protection and adult safeguarding in England and Wales, commentators on serious case reviews (see, for example, Brandon et al. 2013) observe that social work practice can succumb to various external expectations as it fails to apply strengths-based models or ensure that the value is given to the individual context of an individual, family or community. As all memes are able to determine the way in which people might think, feel and behave towards others, it could be argued that negative memes have also led to pathologizing reactions, as seen in the development of the Prevent strategy and the recent decision by Mr Justice Anthony Hayden to remove a child from her family for reasons related to emotional abuse inflicted by an exposure to a judgement of religious extremism. Conversely, as shown during the inquiries into the murders of Victoria Climbié and Daniel Pelka, information given by parents and carers can also create false memes which can lead to cultural relativism, the rule of optimism, and a reticence or failure to act.

Transcending both examples is the suggestion that pathologizing and culturally relativist reactions are transported via memes. They represent culturally determined discrimination, and can be identified as an absurd commitment to ignorance which is fed by negative emotions such as hate, despair, doubt and fear. Some negative memes reflect long-established, historical stereotypes based on perceived biological or physical differences (such as sexism, ageism or disablism), whereas others are more situational (such as Islamophobia). The time and place in which memes circulate show, therefore, that discrimination is socially constructed. They reflect the different types of perceived threats which correspond to different levels of fear, and vary depending on specific social circumstances. Unlike genes, memes have no biological basis and can determine the cause and effect of discrimination in society. If Voltaire's quote is recalled once more – 'those who can make you believe absurdities can make you commit atrocities' – negative memes become the internalized schemas or belief systems which can fill up the mind and be used to justify atrocious acts. It is for this reason that discriminatory behaviour does not operate as a biological function; it has to be learnt and reinforced by those absurdities and status quos which become uncritically accepted as universal truths.

To understand this line of reasoning further, it could be argued that a discriminatory meme was created, like a virus, when David Blunkett, a former British Labour Party politician, warned in 2013 that the influx of Roma migrants into the UK would create untold social trouble, including increased criminal activity and riots (Bowers 2013). By identifying Roma people in this way, Blunkett created a discriminatory meme, which became manifest as a collective social physiology, and led to social polarization and the separation between the majority 'in-group' ('us') and a Roma 'out-group' ('them'). As Figure 7.2 shows, these absurd discriminatory memes became internalized, and accepted as truisms, leading to atrocious behaviours which deepened and justified societal divisions, causing further stigmatization of Roma communities and the social unrest which Blunkett predicted.

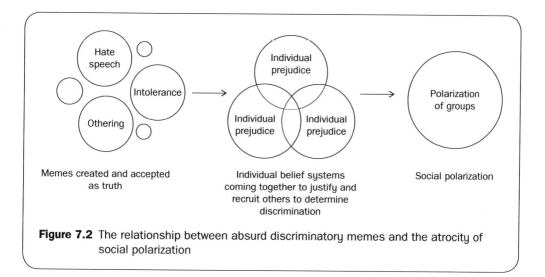

Figure 7.2 The relationship between absurd discriminatory memes and the atrocity of social polarization

Using Figure 7.2, together with the Blunkett example, it is possible to see the way in which memes can be used to unite individuals and justify social intolerance. This shows, therefore, that discrimination is not a natural or biological function because it only exists and survives as an accepted or reinforced socially determined construct. Instead, discrimination provides the basis of human 'sense-making' to establish the difference between a positive and a negative. This notion is further supported by Waggoner and Uller (2015), who use genetic research to prove that human brains do not have an inborn 'hate circuit'. Hate, and discrimination, like the notion that Roma people are 'troubled' or 'troublemakers', has to be learnt, but once learnt can become established at a deep unconscious level of emotional conditioning (Rutstein 2001).

The fact that discrimination is a social construct presents a concrete threat to anti-discriminatory social work practice. As discriminatory memes spread, and become accepted, it is arguable that some social workers might accept demeaning labels, blame and a rather Orwellian concept of groupthink. Here the risk of pathologizing or culturally relativist reactions could become manifest as individuals and organizations become desensitized to absurdities about Roma criminality, unworthiness and inferiority, perpetuated by policymakers and supported by mass media and right-wing political organizations and actors. These stereotypical rumours and examples of oscillating discrimination could then create bias, thus compromising the verifiability of the assessment and subsequent intervention. The challenge for safe and effective practice is to seek to critically reflect on what has been advanced, so as to identify and reduce the impact that discriminatory emotional conditioning might have on the social work activity, and the possibility for atrocious acts.

Discriminatory memes, epigenetics and biological determinism

In an earlier section, the term 'biological determinism' was introduced. As stated, that theory, a little like the 'nature' element of the nature–nurture debate, implies an idea that most human characteristics, physical and emotional, are determined at conception and largely unaffected by environmental factors. Social work paradigms are critical of such a rigid causation. Instead, by importing key themes from epigenetics (Meaney 2001) – the science of how the social and physical environment can shape and alter human genes – social work respects the belief that lived experiences can determine the way in which people respond to, or adapt to, social environments (Perry and Szalavitz 2011).

A large corpus of social work knowledge draws on biological and psychological research to recognize that when people live in safe, stable and supportive environments, certain genes are activated which help those individuals build resilient brain pathways. Consistent with attachment theories, Brendtro and Mitchell (2013) explain how nurturing and caring environments turn on genes in the brain's hippocampus, thus regulating individual responses to stress and increasing confidence and emotional intelligence. Conversely, when individuals experience discrimination, social work understands that they might become anxious, fearful individuals who are fretful and overwhelmed by stress. When safety is replaced by insecurity, genes are activated to determine how the amygdala can respond

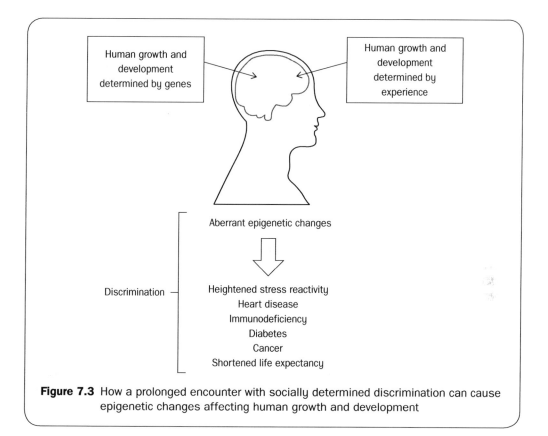

Figure 7.3 How a prolonged encounter with socially determined discrimination can cause epigenetic changes affecting human growth and development

and redesign the body for defensive survival reactions. It is here that epigenetics, and the model of plasticity, show that while discrimination is not natural, the social determinants of it can have a measurable impact on the human growth and development of individuals, families and entire communities (Waggoner and Uller 2015) as shown in Figure 7.3.

Although the impact of epigenetics on Roma people has not been fully researched, Maier and Meaney (2001), Kuzawa and Sweet (2009), and Carey (2012) show that discrimination may lead to epigenetic changes which can create chronic insecurity, helplessness and social defeat. Here, negative social memes, created through oscillating discrimination, can cause those people who experience oppression to retreat from challenge instead of learning new ways to cope (Brendtro and Mitchell 2013). Given the impact that discrimination can have on human growth and development, it is argued that temporary emotional states, such as distress and anxiety, can become enduring traits.

While Kuzawa and Sweet (2009) found that some enduring traits, caused by epigenetic changes, can be reset by experiences of security and inclusion, genetic research carried out by Meaney (2001) and Carey (2012) has shown that significant epigenetic changes may be passed on for up to four generations. Considering the impact of discrimination on people living in America, both authors found that the prolonged exposure to the discrimination of a great-grandparent may be passed down to a great-grandchild. If we consider the task presented to professionals working in initiatives such as 'Troubled Families', which is trying to break the cycle of deprivation steeped in kinship and cross-generational culture, this understanding becomes crucial. Here, symptoms such as heightened stress reactivity and other chronic health problems, such as heart disease, immuno-deficiency, diabetes, cancer and a shortened life expectancy, were reported. It is important to note here that all of these concerns are also reported in Roma communities living throughout the world (O'Nions 2011).

Case study 7.1

The family you have been asked to visit in Activity 7.1 are aware of anti-Roma memes spread by government actors. Use your sociological imagination to consider how the impact of these memes (spread in the last few years) might impact on community psychology and the epigenetics of individual Roma people.

'For [Roma] the age of criminal responsibility should be the moment of birth because being born is, in fact, their biggest crime.'
Miroslav Sladek, politician, Czech Republican Party

'A significant part of the Roma are unfit for coexistence. They are not fit to live among people ... These animals shouldn't be allowed to exist. In any form. That needs to be solved – immediately, and regardless of the method.'
Zsolt Bayer, co-founder of the Fidesz Party, Hungary

'Gypsies are grouped around well-known criminals ... there are gypsies who are born criminals [who] do not know how to do anything other than to commit criminal acts.'
General Mircea Bot, Chief of the Bucharest Police

'We've got to be tough and robust in saying to [Roma] people you are not in a downtrodden village or woodland, because many of them don't even live in areas where there are toilets or refuse collection facilities. You are not there anymore, you are here – and you've got to adhere to our standards, and to our way of behaving, and if you do then you'll get a welcome and people will support you.'
David Blunkett, politician, UK Labour Party

While resilience is an important factor in any biopsychosocial debate, epigenetics shows us the importance of challenging discrimination in all of its manifestations. In light of what is now known, not only should students and early career practitioners recognize and reject public discourse that perpetuates stereotypical, racist, hateful or discriminatory views, they must also engage individuals, organizations and structures to take effective action against them.

Social work as a sense-making activity

Social work is a sense-making activity. It requires individuals to apply their senses to 'make sense' of the situations they encounter, to arrive at safe and effective assessments. However, Logie et al. (2015) suggest that many students and early career social workers believe that practice can be determined by existing value judgements and non-reflected personal opinions. The clear risk here is that an uncritical acceptance of cultural determinism, and the memes which can transport it, can lead to pathologizing or culturally relativist reactions. When visiting Roma families, for example, some students and early career social workers might call on those internalized negative memes which have created social polarization and the separation between the majority 'in-group' (us) and an 'out-group' ('them'), and develop a sense of being a 'cultural stranger' (Fuhse 2012). When confronted with their own 'culture shock', Fuhse (2012) implies that some practitioners might perceive the presence of risk through a discriminatory lens. As some social workers might feel 'out of place' while visiting a Roma individual, family or community, their non-reflected personal values and value judgements might become a measure of risk that is often used to justify the need for formal social work involvement, or not. Rather than working to understand the challenges that were being faced by individuals, families and communities, each individual social worker could (albeit unwittingly) represent a further layer of structural discrimination.

Avoiding discrimination requires students and early career social workers to understand what they might be bringing to the working relationship in terms of attitudes and beliefs, and to what extent these simply reflect culturally determined discriminatory memes. Here, ethical and effective practice demands specific efforts to isolate presuppositions to consider how these may influence professional judgements and undermine the legitimacy of any assessment. One way that this can be achieved is through the application of some fundamental phenomenological assumptions.

Isolating discriminatory memes

Phenomenology began with the work of Edmund Husserl, and was subsequently developed by Martin Heidegger, Maurice Merleau-Ponty, Jean-Paul Sartre, and others. Described as the foundation of all first-order knowledge (Giorgi 2008), phenomenology is an important theoretical framework which can be used to understand the various ways in which discriminatory memes can interfere with the 'sense-making' activity of social work.

The specific theory used to isolate or 'bracket' discriminatory views, so that they do not impact on social work practice, is known as the epochè, the theoretical moment where discriminatory judgements are suspended. Thus, the core aim of epochè is doubt – not a complete doubt about everything that is in the world, but a doubt about the memes that may influence everyday knowledge (Giorgi 2008). Although a common misconception, it is important to appreciate that the epochè does not mean that all learnt knowledge and cultural transmissions must be abandoned. Instead, the epochè should enable the assessing social worker to be as objective as possible. Consistent with phenomenological assumptions, identifying presupposition and discriminatory memes is a core requirement in any preparation or readiness for direct practice.

Activity 7.2

Achieving the epochè

In the first activity you were invited to consider the way you might be feeling about carrying out an initial assessment with a Roma family. The aim of this activity was to help you identify and externalize any presupposition. The activity was located at the beginning of the chapter so that the information subsequently presented did not affect your response. In this second activity, you are invited to go back to the list of words that you completed in the first activity. Reading back the words, use critical reflection to consider:

- How these words and feelings might impact on the social work assessment, and
- What steps you could take to ensure that these words and feelings do not impact on the social work assessment.

Applying phenomenological skills in practice

The need to identify, accept and then bracket potential discriminatory memes is the first stage in effective anti-discriminatory practice. The next stage, according to phenomenological assumptions, requires individual practitioners to acknowledge the fact that any relationship with Roma people – and all other groups, in fact – is fixed within the historical, social and political dynamics which have served to construct boundary distinctions such as fear and mistrust. As a result, relationships between social workers and Roma families may, at least initially, be characterized by suspicion and fear, and this can only be dealt with if it is first acknowledged. In some attempt to reduce this risk, Ferguson (2011) suggests the use of comments like:

- I appreciate that you do not want me to interfere in your life. It must be very hard for you to accept me being involved in your family, given that you do not like it.

  Or . . .

- It is very important that I work with you and your family. How can we work together in a productive way so that I do not need to be involved in your family any more?

By acknowledging such historical, social and political dynamics, it must also be made obvious that social work involvement is not being instigated on the grounds that the family are from a particular ethnic and cultural group, but more accurately because there are real and tangible concerns about an individual's welfare. In terms of child protection and adult safeguarding, it is important that social workers are very clear about this, emphasizing that the welfare of the individual is paramount. Families will need to understand that where there is a criticism of them, this relates to the impact of their 'care' (or lack of it) and is not a criticism of their culture or community lifestyle. Social workers should also make clear that any formal processes, including court action, will be used only if there is evidence that an individual is experiencing harm. It is equally important to be clear about what needs to change in order for the local authority to be less concerned and to be able to reduce or change the focus of their intervention. At all times, the social worker might do well to apply the reflective activities presented within this chapter to ensure that discriminatory memes are actively considered and applied in social work interventions.

Activity 7.3

Reflecting on the lived experiences of others

Reflecting on the learning that you have achieved so far, consider the thoughts and feelings that Roma individuals, families and communities might have towards social workers and social work intervention. Once done, use critical reflection to consider:

- How the thoughts and feelings of Roma people might impact on the social work assessment, and
- What steps you could take to ensure that these thoughts and feelings do not impact on the work that you might have to do.

Listen, engage, and form relationships

The next phase of phenomenology proposes that social workers need to gain a fuller understanding of the situation by engaging with, and listening to, the individual's, family's or community's own reported experience. In principle, this theory is known as *Dasein* (Heidegger 2005), and it refers to the intersectionality of experiences and behaviours which are shaped by and inform the world in which we live. By focusing on the lived experience of Roma people, phenomenology suggests that social workers might do well to communicate a sense of genuine interest and a determination to form an alliance in working together to achieve mutually satisfactory solutions.

Making sense of 'Dasein' in practice

Phenomenology suggests that the social work assessment would do well to focus on physical perception, motivation for power, and identity. A range of questions could be used by social workers to achieve this, and I have listed some here which can be used to communicate with individuals as part of the assessment process. Can you think of any others?

- How do you define yourself, and what words do you use?
- What does being Roma mean to you?
- What does being a Roma (child/parent/adult and so on) mean to you?
- What are the main differences between your culture and my culture?
- In what way do your family and community support you?
- What is the hardest thing about being a Roma (child/parent/adult and so on) and how do you cope with this?
- If you could change anything about your current situation, what would you change and why?

By seeking to achieve an understanding of individual Dasein, the family's own understanding of what it means to be Roma could be explored by those involved in the assessment process. Similar to motivational or strengths-based interviewing (see Payne 2014), this process is also likely to establish a picture of Roma culture in relation to the specific individual or family in question – what being Roma means in their lived experience, and what the practical and emotional features of being Roma entail. Although the social workers may believe that they know some of the answers, epochè requires that presupposition, or learnt discrimination, is put to one side so that room can be made to communicate clear messages to the family that no judgements are being made about their unique lives or circumstances. As shown by Allen and Adams (2013), the use of phenomenology in social work with Roma people is likely to engender a sense of trust and start to provide more clarity about the present situation. It is not, however, without its risks and limitations in practice.

Understand cultural aspects of communication

A number of theories described by Payne (2014) reason that proposing generalized or hypothetical questions, such as those outlined above, can create an opportunity to reduce conflict and lessen the likelihood of attempts to undermine social work involvement by transferring the power, or expertise in problem resolution, to the family. As a useful method in the social work assessment, this style of questioning can prove invaluable when applied strategically in a carefully considered conversation. However, using generalized or hypothetical questions as a strategy in any assessment raises some concerns regarding the need to exercise a degree of sensitivity to cultural expectations.

As shown by Currer (1986), some people may perceive generalized or hypothetical questions with suspicion as they require a degree of social or emotional imagination that may otherwise be seen as unusual, and some people may respond by protecting against or circumnavigating the topic being discussed. Meaningful attempts should also be made to verify responses through more direct and deliberate forms of inquiry. For phenomenology, this approach should always focus on lived experience and seek to engage individuals, families and communities so as to allow them to discuss their strengths, weaknesses, opportunities and threats. In this sense, social workers may be in a stronger position to help families and communities understand social work processes, and demonstrate that intervention can be more equal, inclusive and based on respect.

Language can create huge barriers in engagement between Roma and social workers, and in most cases social services frequently need to use interpreting services in order to communicate effectively. On many occasions, however, an interpreter who is able to speak one of the Romany dialects might not be available, so the only choice is to use an interpreter who speaks the language spoken in the country the family came from. Usually, English is a second language for Roma, but often their vocabulary in this language is limited. For this reason it is really important that social workers understand that some English words do not easily translate into those languages used by Roma people.

Case study 7.2

Allen and Adams (2013) describe the work of an independent agency working to support one Roma family who was struggling with the care of their child, and the social worker asked them if they thought that they would benefit from parenting classes. Allen and Adams (2013) explain that once the interpreter had translated this, the family thought the social worker was offering them sex education and became embarrassed. As a result, it appeared that the family was reluctant to cooperate. The social worker had the insight to check with the parents what they thought parenting classes were, and once this had been clarified the family was happy and grateful for the opportunity to learn how to look after their child.

The case study above shows why clarifying the potential variability on the meaning of words, particularly social work terminology, is so important when working with Roma people. Of course, the development of these values and skills is not specific to social work with Roma people. There is a great deal of evidence which suggests that culturally sensitive practice requires complex verbal and non-verbal communication skills, alongside the use of plain English (Fook 2012; Healy 2012; Thompson 2012). Most importantly, social workers must avoid assumptions. Social workers must trust, but they must also validate and confirm understanding.

Helping families and communities understand social work processes

Roma families, like many others who come into contact with statutory services, are unlikely to understand the various social work processes. If any assessment is being undertaken, it is crucial that families understand what this entails, what is being judged, and what changes are necessary to reduce concerns. As the assessment is a culturally specific process, based on Westernized notions of welfare and devised by political actors and professionals to ease or inform service delivery and outcome measures, it should not be a surprise that the people social workers work to support do not always understand why and how an assessment is delivered. For example, if there is to be a safeguarding assessment, then the individuals or family involved will need to understand how this works in order to prepare and participate to the best of their ability. Where appropriate, a family group conference could also be used. Again, none of this is different to any other family, but the situation might feel particularly alien to members of Roma communities if they have had very little contact with formal government structures, and in any case feel under threat from them. In this context, it is particularly important that families have information about their rights, including sources of independent support and the relevant complaints procedures. However, at the same time as working effectively with families, good practice demands that the needs of the person receiving social work intervention are placed at the centre of all decision-making.

Being part of the solution

Critical and radical social work theories (Fook 2012; Healy 2012) recognize discriminatory social work in relation to minoritized groups. As we have begun to establish in this chapter, the existence of discriminatory memes in social work can impact on the social worker and the cultures and organizations within which they work. It is here, according to Urh (2011: 465), in the maintenance of discrimination and inequality, that individual social workers can 'fail to challenge structural barriers which exist in certain social contexts'. Avoiding such complicity in practice requires individual social workers to advocate for Roma families with various service providers, including with their own local authority.

Working both 'for' and 'with' Roma communities requires social workers to challenge the status quo and be proactive in the development of policy and practice that recognizes the impact of oppression and discrimination. Where social workers choose to highlight structural inequality in this way, they can also begin to challenge the potential idea that social work practice is inevitably on behalf of an oppressive agency. By proving that social work is ready to work with Roma families and communities in matters of social justice, as well as in matters pertaining to support and protection, students and early career social workers might begin to reverse the damaging effects of cultural determinism, and promote the core social work traditions of empathy, genuine positive regard and meaningful support. In order to achieve this, students and early career social workers must first be willing and able to understand how the sense-making activity of social work might be prejudiced by those culturally determined personal belief systems which might have never been critically considered.

The Professional Capabilities Framework (BASW 2015) requires all social workers to adhere to a series of minimum standards of proficiency. In regards to behaviour and anti-discrimination, it states that professionals should learn about identity and understand the key characteristics of groups likely to be discriminated against. Social workers must be committed to reflecting on and dealing with ethical dilemmas within the frameworks of social justice, inclusion and equality. In relation to daily practice, there is a stipulation for developing approaches which support the person-in-the environment and family composition, life experiences and characteristics.

Activity 7.4

Consolidating learning

Arguably, the hardest application of anti-discriminatory social work can be found on those occasions where the behaviour of others challenges our ability to demonstrate genuine positive regard. These circumstances are likely to be personal and might differ from person to person. In order to consider this ethical dilemma further, you are invited to test phenomenological approaches by critically reflecting on an example of practice which might challenge your ability to work in an anti-discriminatory way. In order to achieve this, I would like to invite you to imagine working with an individual, family or community in a situation which might test your ability to demonstrate genuine positive regard: once done, try to complete the following six steps.

Step 1: Start by writing a list of those words or phrases which best describe how you might be feeling, and what you might be thinking about working with this individual/family/community.

Step 2: Read over the list of words or phrases and reflect on how these thoughts and feelings might impact on your social work practice.

Step 3: Devise a strategy which enables you to put these thoughts and feelings to one side so that they do not impact on your professional behaviour.

Step 4: Using your sociological imagination, write a list of words or phrases to describe how the individual/family/community might be feeling, and what they might be thinking about you.

Step 5: Read over this second list of words or phrases and reflect on how these thoughts and feelings might impact on your social work practice.

Step 6: Using all of this information, reflect on the theories, methods and layers of support that you might need in order to form an alliance in working together to achieve mutually satisfactory solutions.

Conclusions

This chapter argues that social work with Roma people is inevitably complex and challenging, taking place as it does in a context of conflict and discrimination. A casework approach which does not recognize this context is destined to be ineffective unless it is influenced by phenomenological and other theories, including cultural and biological determinism, memes and social polarization. When working with Roma people, social workers must be prepared to understand the potential tension which might be caused by elements of their involvement. Social workers should first aim to achieve a critical but balanced view of their personal and professional values, and then proceed to identify and then epochè presupposition in order to minimize risk. Critical reflection on the influence of discriminatory memes on roles and responsibilities is likely to lead to the challenging of professional judgements and the legitimacy of an assessment based on the sense-making activity that is social work.

Roma communities require a high level of cultural sensitivity when engaging with professional services, but the same laws, methods and approaches used to safeguard children and adults are applicable. Social workers who communicate well, and understand diversity as a positive form, as well as one which may polarize and separate the professional from the service user, are more likely to engage and intervene in a meaningful manner.

Key points

- The fact that discrimination is not natural and only exists as a long-established or situational social construct.
- The ways in which social polarization and discrimination can be passed, as a contagion, from one person to another through memes.
- The ways in which cultural determinism, which presents a view of Roma people as living in contrast to the norms of the majority population, can become manifest in social work practice if accepted without critical reflection.
- The way in which phenomenology could be used to bracket discriminatory memes and understand the impact of populism on social work practice.

8 Reclaiming and embracing spirituality as a legitimate facet of social work

Gerry Skelton

'Physical strength is measured by what we can carry; spiritual by what we can bear.'

Source unknown

Chapter overview

After reading this chapter, you should be able to:

- Explain what spirituality is, and why it is important in social work and related disciplines
- Understand the concept and experience of spirituality
- Begin to reflect on your own spirituality and that of carers, service users, colleagues and others
- Identify core qualities, values, principles and ethics, skills and sources of information to help you address spirituality from a more informed perspective
- Apply your understanding of spirituality to social work practice in a way which makes sense to others
- Analyse and evaluate the impact of spirituality on yourself and those you work with.

Activity 8.1

Before you read this chapter, please write your responses to the following questions.

- What do you understand by the word spirituality?
- Why should social workers be interested in spirituality?
- Have you ever had a conversation about spirituality, and how did that feel?

Introduction

In terms of life and all its manifestations, mysteries and muddles, I have developed what Einstein referred to as a *'holy curiosity'*. As a result, I have been on a most interesting, challenging, frustrating and rewarding journey for a number of years, that has galvanized me to change the discourse and attempt to establish spirituality as an important facet of our lives and those we serve. As a social work student, practitioner, trainer and educator in Northern Ireland, I can truly state I was never introduced to this concept in any of these roles, but found it emerging in myself and resonating in my work. My ignorance was, I argue, fairly typical of many social work practitioners, managers, commissioners and regulators, given the absence of it in their primary and subsequent training. This has a number of immediate and longer-term implications which I will return to later.

But let me start by relating the following verbal exchange between me and a social work student in a recent lecture addressing assessment and its various forms and functions:

Gerry: 'When assessing, we need to view the person holistically, taking into account their emotional, physical, psychological, social, spiritual needs'

SW student: 'Did you say spiritual?'

Gerry: 'Absolutely . . . it's as important as any of the other categories I just mentioned . . . what is it about spirituality that prompted your question?'

SW student: 'I didn't think we were allowed to mention this in class or ask about a person's religious beliefs . . . isn't that private and a bit dangerous to ask people?'

Gerry: 'Dangerous . . . because?'

SW student: 'Well it's their business, and people in Northern Ireland are sensitive and don't want others to know their religion!'

Activity 8.2

Before reading on, please reflect and ask yourself:

- Was I surprised to see/hear spirituality emphasized in a social work lecture?
- Do I identify with the student's or lecturer's viewpoint initially?
- Was the student right about spirituality being 'religious'; 'private'; 'dangerous'; 'sensitive'?

The above exchange is typical and reflective of the general challenges I experience with students, colleagues and professionals of any discipline I have worked with (in Northern Ireland or the UK more generally) in attempting to raise this remarkable, but apparently fundamentally challenging, concept of spirituality.

Several points emerge from this honest and telling exchange:

- The apparent misunderstanding of spirituality and an insistent conflation of spirituality and religion
- The centrality of spirituality to social work involvement/intervention: seeing the person (carer, service user and practitioner) holistically along a lifespan continuum

- The need to establish and embed spirituality as a legitimate theme in social work education, training and practice, and equip students and practitioners to respond, rather than react to, the needs of those we serve
- The evident resistance to addressing spirituality, which may be personally, professionally or contextually based, or a combination of these.

The remainder of this chapter will address each of these points, related questions and subsequent implications. It is my fervent hope that what follows will be an encouragement to the reader of whatever status, role and circumstance to explore spirituality openly and be inspired to embrace its teaching and practice insights.

Background

Historically, there is a general dearth of attention within the professional literature on spirituality (e.g. Richards and Bergin 1997; McLeod 2001), although this is changing. Perhaps recent legislative requirements, and the resultant thrust towards holistic engagement with consumers, has increased the attention afforded to spirituality (e.g. Miller 1999; Mansager 2000), alongside more 'traditional' considerations of health and well-being.

A brief, contextualized, historical overview

Although a comprehensive discussion of the religious, philosophical, social and cultural evolution of society is clearly beyond the remit of this chapter, it is, nonetheless, instructive to offer an epigrammatic overview in order to better grasp spirituality's history.

Traditionally, spirituality was generally understood as a religious concept and experience. Religion dominated world-views and situated itself as an authority on individual and collective lives (Slife et al. 1999; Mursell 2001; Reamer 2015). Indeed, for many civilizations, religion was the unquestioned basis of legislative and social order. As societies (particularly Western) developed, a more modernist perspective emerged, challenging and often relegating the role of religious authority (e.g. Jones 1994) in favour of rationality, calculability and scientific certainty (Capra 1982; Morrall 2008). This, in turn, gave rise to a host of increasingly psychological, sociological and humanistic orientations and resultant freedoms. Indeed, it could be argued that the initial reliance on a theistic disposition gave way to the elevation of science, professions and individuality, leading to a gradual secularization (Moore 2003; Webster 2005).

This culminated in the centralization of the individual who exercises personal freedoms (Giddens 1991), as evidenced by increased rights, citizenship, consumerism, and a proliferation of participatory mechanisms. Thus, individuals could increasingly defer to an internal rather than external authority (Gray 2008). Arguably, this emphasis on 'self' was initially embodied in the emergent work of humanistic psychologists, including Maslow and Rogers (Cushway 2009).

Conversely, this has also produced a more risk-adverse culture, as people report increased insecurity, fear, uneasiness, alienation, estrangement and depersonalization, experienced at an individual and collective level (Bauman 2006; Gray 2008). Perhaps this is an inevitable corollary of societies in transition: declining pillars of authority, lack of consensus on various societal issues, increased globalization and resultant challenges (including pluralism, diversity, consumerism, propagation of knowledge, competing ideologies, migration, terrorism). Ironically, this emphasis on individualism (Willows and Swinton 2000; Morrall 2008) has also produced a range of helping professions, particularly in Western societies.

The decline of religious authority was commensurate with the rise in sociological and psychological perspectives that were often antagonistic to religion and spirituality (Hunt 2002; Moore 2003). In terms of the helping professions, this became very significant.

The twentieth century witnessed a philosophical transformation as changes occurred in the social order. The work of Marx and Durkheim entered the mainstream and opposed religion's dominant role, believing it was often inimical to people's well-being (Hunt 2002). This was also supported by Freud, who viewed religion as 'a universal neurosis' (Freud 1959; Bocock 1977; Webster 2005); consequently, a predisposition to pathologize spirituality became apparent in Western models of psychiatry (Capra 1982).

Such developments led Bauman (2006) to characterize the post-millennium epoch as 'an age of uncertainty', with people confronted by constant changes, choices and demands. This is exacerbated by the decline of traditional anchor points for individuals, including former bastions of power and expertise, with Bauman (2006) concluding that such 'endemic uncertainty' has culminated in fragmented ways of living.

In postmodernist terms, the promise of increased rationality, knowledge, understanding and control remains unfulfilled, and fundamentally disputes any attempt to produce 'grand narratives' that purport to offer universal explanations (Parton and O'Byrne 2000). On the contrary, the postmodernist stance emphasizes the plurality of truth and how 'reality' is often socially constructed. In essence, there is no one truth but many, and perhaps people have to embrace living without certainty and attendant insecurity (Smart 1999). Thus, the pursuit of truth places greater emphasis on personal agency, rather than believing it to be the preserve of privileged authority, and spirituality may offer a conduit to a more meaningful existence. Heelas and Woodhead (2005) argue that America and Britain are undergoing a 'spiritual revolution' and, as institutional religion declines, people are attracted to more personalized, holistic spiritual practices.

What is spirituality?

Activity 8.3

Before reading on, please return to Activity 8.1 and reflect on what *you* understand spirituality to be (or not).

Having established a broad historical overview, please journey with me as *we* grapple with defining spirituality, attempting to 'part the Red Sea' between a purely religious and secular understanding (George et al. 2000; Miller and Thoresen 2003) and contextualizing it contemporarily (Cornah 2006, Rowson 2014).

Although not as well researched nor commented upon, there is a growing body of literature addressing spirituality in social work, championed by a relatively small but significant number of writers and practitioners, including Moss (2002); Crisp (2008, 2010); Holloway and Moss (2010); and Skelton (2012) – among others.

The term 'spirituality' is a notoriously vague, elusive and ambiguous one (e.g. LaPierre 1994; Furness and Gilligan 2010), yet widely used, leaving Cobb (2001: 4) to rightly conclude that 'much weight . . . has to be borne repeatedly by a single word'. The literature revealed a surfeit of competing definitions, meanings, interpretations and descriptions of spirituality (Gall et al. 2005), coupled with an often obscure 'vocabulary of approximation' (Cobb 2001) that commonly results in bewilderment and confusion.

Spirituality is often primarily (though not exclusively) subsumed within a religious understanding (Pargament 1997; Emmons 1999), and these terms are used interchangeably (Hall and Edwards 2002). Spirituality is derived from the Latin word 'spiritus', meaning breath of life (Capra 1982; Gregoire and Jungers 2007) and the religious argument is that life is the gift bestowed from a divine being(s). However, spirituality is not confined to any one religion (Fairholm 1997).

Lines (2006) chronicles various efforts to define spirituality – from Bucke's (1923) cosmic consciousness, Ouspensky's (1934) perception of the miraculous, Maslow's (1970) cognition, Assagioli's (1991) claim that 'all development is spiritual', to Ffomm's (1986) 'to be rather than to have'. The author found greater resonance in Elkins et al.'s (1988) more pluralistic definition – namely 'a way of being and experiencing', encapsulating humanistic and religious facets; albeit claims regarding quantifying 'spiritual variables' are somewhat contentious. Jones et al. (2000) concede, making no attempt to systematically define spirituality, but offer various characteristics, including prayer, wholeness and search for meaning. While partially illuminating, these views constitute descriptions rather than definitions, are clearly imprecise, and often predicated upon religious perspectives. However, many do prefer to conceptualize religion and spirituality as overlapping, albeit distinguishable, constructs (Thoresen et al. 2001; Miller and Thoresen 2003).

Reflection point 8.1

At this point, how does *your* definition of spirituality compare to the above information?

Some researchers argue there are often clear distinctions between religion and spirituality (Zinnbauer et al. 1997), although these are often blurred (Cornah 2006). Religion can be understood as institutional, ritualistic expressions of belief in an ontological deity that exercises authority over its membership and adheres to generally accepted interpretations of existence (Smith 1995). While a legitimate expression of religion (Hill et al. 2000), spirituality is not necessarily religious, and attempts to separate it into religious and secular terms represent a false dichotomy, as people can be spiritual believers but not religious followers (Josephen et al. 2000). This challenges the assumed relationship between religion and spirituality, which are not synonymous (Canda and Furman 1999; Myers and Williard 2003; Thompson 2010).

Furthermore, many can highlight the damage perpetrated in the name of religion, ranging from wars to more recent ecclesiastical abuses. While it is reasonable to argue that religion may well have been misrepresented, the reality of religiously fuelled conflict (including Africa, the Middle East and Northern Ireland) is painfully apparent. Therefore, religion and, by implication, spirituality, may not be terms easily embraced. It is also noticeable that much of the literature assumes a Christian orientation, which is obviously restrictive and arguably culturally insensitive (e.g. Sue 2006; Barrott 2008; Stirling et al. 2009).

Reflection point 8.2

- Are spirituality and religion the same for you?
- Is your understanding of spirituality dependent on how and where you were raised?
- Is this equally true for carers and service users?
- How does this potentially help or hinder good social work practice?

An equally valid understanding constructs spirituality within non-religious paradigms (Crisp 2008; Harris 2014): viewing it as a distinctly human phenomenon. From a secular perspective, spirituality is understood as an innate, animating life force (Swinton 2001), reflecting basic life orientations (Nelson-Jones 1992), assisting self-transcendence (Helminiak 1998) or 'potentialisation' (Emmons 1999): the human spirit galvanizing personal resilience with which to negotiate life's vicissitudes. However, Whitehead (2003) criticizes the propensity for research to ignore a more existential understanding of spirituality, preferring a traditional theistic perspective. Tacey (2004) echoes this tendency, claiming that helping professions often ignore the spiritual dimension due to their secular training.

Reflection point 8.3

- What do you understand by secularism?
- Can you detect an equal welcome for secularism and religion in your workplace discussions, supervision and management activity?

The literature also revealed a plethora of 'spiritualities' that are often referred to (perhaps pejoratively) as 'New Age' (West 2000; Cobb 2001). Within this broad kaleidoscope, a diverse collection of spiritualities exists (religious, philosophical, humanistic) as well as a popular vocabulary ('self'; potential; realization; fulfilment) and a rich tapestry of spiritual practices. These include a host of self-help (yoga, reiki, meditation, retreats) and caring enterprises inspired by a religious or humanistic spirituality (Fairholm 1997), including Alcoholics Anonymous, the Samaritans, Cruse, Relate, professional social work, counselling and so on.

The common and contrasting themes emerging from the literature follow three distinct, but potentially overlapping, strands: spirituality can be understood in strictly religious terms; be informed by religion and related wisdom; or be a secular disposition. Interestingly, a number of studies reported respondents declaring themselves spiritual, but not religious (Mahoney and Graci 1999). It is also noteworthy that transcendence is viewed as a core characteristic, even if there is disagreement as to what this constitutes. Zappone (1991) rightly challenges the narrow conceptualization that focuses on 'self' and sees spirituality as a catalyst for communal interconnectedness. Therefore, it comes as no surprise that spirituality, as a term, tends to elude tight operational definitions (Miller and Thoresen 2003: 27).

Spirituality: characteristics and concepts

Plainly, commentators differ in how they understand spirituality, ranging from existentialism to a manifestation of the divine. This is further complicated by the vocabulary that accompanies discussion on the origins (and expression) of spirituality, including God; 'soul' (Elkins 1998); 'real' (Hick 2001); 'numinous' (Lines 2006); 'life force' (Swinton 2001) – but most concur that 'mystery' encapsulates it best! Still, there is a need to clarify the associated helping emphasis, including 'spiritual practices' (Assagioli 1991); 'presence' (Rogers 1980); 'spiritual healing' and 'unfolding' (West 1997, 2000); 'spiritual orientation' (Corey 2005); 'spiritual centredness' (Lines 2006); coupled with what practitioners believe these entail. Several (Thorne 2000, 2002; Lines 2006) seek to assist the helpee in connecting to the immanent or transcendent divine; Lynch (2002) is concerned with 'the good life'; Pattison (2002) prefers 'human flourishing'; while less theistic-orientated conceptualizations may focus on self-development.

Theists and secularists may diverge at various junctures, but there is tacit agreement that spirituality, however defined, is often important. It involves insight, transcendence and a quest for meaning (Cascio 1998; Peterson and Seligman 2004); belief in something better (whether a celestial being, self-actualization, enhanced existence); and is concerned with accessing a dynamic, revitalizing energy and resultant growth. It also accentuates the primacy of personal experience and any resultant meaning ascribed (Mahoney and Graci 1999). Sinclair et al. (2006), Holloway and Moss (2010), and Furness and Gilligan (2010) cite a number of concepts related to spirituality, including: integrity, wholeness, hope, meaning, journey, compassion, forgiveness and kindness. In facing adversity, it can serve as an overarching construct (Brenner et al. 2009)

that assists personal resiliency and identity (Koenig et al. 2001). It is also fundamentally relational (Hamilton and Jackson 1998; Sinclair et al. 2006), whether
connecting to the numinous, other people or nature (Cobb 2001); and being
inspired accordingly.

Clearly, spirituality is a potent, multidimensional term that eschews standard
definitions or interpretations. It is often paradoxical: an abstract concept yet, for
many, concrete experience; its parameters are narrow or porous; it exists, but is
difficult to test; can be religious yet transcend such affiliation; and is also secular.
Ultimately, spirituality rests along a secular, humanist and metaphysical continuum,
and any understanding of it has to be contextualized accordingly (Thompson 2010;
Furness and Gilligan 2014). Perhaps one needs to be wary of being too eager to
define such a multifaceted, dynamic and ineffable term (Cornah 2006; Rowson
2014), leading to oversimplification and misrepresentation (Miller and Thoresen
2003). Conversely, given its subjective nature, there is a danger spirituality can
become too malleable and relativized (Gray 2008); its meaning dependent upon its
proprietor. Conceivably, in postmodernist terms, this is an acceptable dispensation.

While accepting that spirituality is a difficult, multilayered and, for many,
intangible term to define, I cannot resist adding to the range of attempted
conceptualizations in an effort to more readily grasp, and then articulate, my
understanding of it. As a starter, my non-technical definition of spirituality can be
summarized as 'a struggle between *Inspiration* and *Perspiration*' (Skelton 2014).
Moving beyond this, and bearing in mind the sheer challenge of defining it,
I humbly offer the following, and hope you find it helpful.

Spirituality refers to a collection of contextualized aspirations, beliefs, preferences and practices that are primarily focused on accessing an inspiring and
sustaining spirit: human, divine, or a combination. Consequently, it rests on a
broad, existentialist, secular–theocentric continuum, is unformulary, and is fundamentally an evocative, transcendent, resurrection experience helping one to
galvanize one's spirit of resilience in a desire to purposefully respond to life's
vicissitudes. It is not so much an answer to one's struggles, but a way of adopting
a meaningful disposition in order to make sense out of such trials, garner determination, foster optimism or acceptance, and enable the person to resist helplessness in the face of pain or suffering. Conversely, it is also a resource that enables
the expression of deep gratitude for life, a wider appreciation for one's role in the
universe, and offers opportunities to enjoy a more contemplative experience. My
contention, therefore, is that we possess a spiritual self, which acts as an integrating filter through which all experience is processed. At its best, a healthy, well-an-
chored spirituality can represent a dynamic, animating elixir in the hands of the
alchemist, providing inspiration, faith, meaning, purpose, vitality, hope, optimism
and spiritual fortitude in the face of potential concern, distress and despair. It also
acts as a catalyst to moderating the effects of pain, illness, loneliness, alienation,
etc., and a return to equilibrium and/or well-being. Indeed, our spirit, however
conceived or understood, is one of our most important strengths and, when mobi-
lized, can be a positively pulsating, irresistible, irrepressible and indispensable
resource. At its worst, an uninformed and unchallenged spirituality can leave
people at the mercy of charlatans, unfulfilled promise, ignorance, discourage-
ment and self-doubt. It can culminate in a dispiriting, fragmented experience that

exacerbates alarm, fear, ill health, and so on, and impedes proper perspective, acceptance or healing.

I am convinced that spirituality is a legitimate window to contextually view many of life's issues, and gain a helpful, discerning perspective, along with resulting recourse to inherent strengths located within our spiritual immune system. In the hierarchy of people's struggles, spirituality may be a pressing or modest issue; but addressing it should routinely be part of the helper's agenda for skilled and sensitive exploration, though never imposed nor prioritized over more urgent concerns. All helping encounters are most effective when the concern of the helper is genuinely apparent, and an attentive readiness is offered in responding to whatever the person brings.

Spirituality and the helping professions

Reflection point 8.4

- Where and when have you heard the word spirituality?
- Is it in social work law, policy, procedures?
- In the average person's vocabulary, how many words or phrases can you think of that have 'spirit' in them?

Undoubtedly, the antecedents of the helping professions were originally religious and spiritual (e.g. Sawatzky and Pesut 2005). Intriguingly, 'psyche' is Greek for soul (Capra 1982; Moore 2003; West 2004; Webster 2005), and psychology (and psychotherapy) has its spiritual roots in the earlier practice of witches, priests and shamans (West 2000).

Spirituality is recognized as an essential part of children's development (e.g. Hay 2006; Hyde 2008), and the UN Convention on the Rights of the Child (1989) and the Children Act (1989) and Order in Northern Ireland (1995) address spirituality, albeit within a religious/cultural context. These are complemented by additional legislative Acts (educational, human rights, and supporting practice standards, codes and protocols). There is also growing recognition that elders need to have their spiritual needs catered for (MacKinlay 2006); they are increasingly woven into the fabric of palliative care, although not always consistently or insightfully. It is interesting to note the earlier and later life emphasis reflected here, while the middle is predominantly unaddressed, and to speculate as to whether these are perhaps 'safer groups' for professionals to engage with in this sensitive area? Conceivably, spirituality becomes more of a concern for theorists, practitioners, carers and service users alike in our later years (West 2004).

Within the therapeutic field there is an increasing, if inconsistent, inclination to address spirituality (Cornah 2006; Gale et al. 2007). The internationally employed American Psychiatric Association's diagnostic manual of mental illness (DSM: IV) incorporated spiritual 'disorder' for the first time in 1994. By implication, this also drew attention to spiritual 'order' – namely health and well-being.

Furman et al. (2004) and Furness and Gilligan (2010, 2014), among others, have identified a resurgence of interest in spirituality within social work publications, and Man Ng and Chan (2005) argue it should be a consideration when intervening. Interestingly, Sperry (2000) and Gray (2008) attribute this renewed interest to the rise of individualism yet, oxymoronically, increased meaninglessness and isolation, particularly in the West. They equate spirituality with an individual and communitarian search for purpose and belonging, which may also be explained by a developing pluralism, multiculturalism and diversity, now increasingly apparent.

The medical model has also been traditionally unwelcoming of the exploration of spirituality (Moore 2003; Cornah 2006). A typical configuration of health was predicated upon physical, mental and emotional components, and even the more recent biopsychosocial model tends to relegate spirituality. In many ways, the predominant proclivity of the medical and psychological professions is to pathologize spirituality (Dein 2004; Turbott 2004).

Spirituality and intelligence

Recent developments have also expanded the traditional emphasis on intelligence quotient (IQ) to include Goleman's (1996) emotional intelligence (EQ), and this has been complemented by what Zohar et al. and Zohar and Marshall (2000, 2001) call spiritual intelligence (SQ). The premise is that SQ underpins IQ and EQ, and helps people access enhanced values, principles, creativity and purpose in an effort to serve self and others in a more enriched and inspiring way.

Alexander et al. (2003) note the presence of 'intelligent spirituality' in education, which involves exploring the various wisdom traditions, extrapolating learning and cascading it accordingly. These processes encourage learners to become attuned to the rich source of available learning and corresponding attribute development, resulting in more responsive practitioners. This readily parallels with similar emphasis on 'learning communities', 'intelligent organizations' and 'spiritually intelligent leadership' (Fairholm 1997; Miller 2008; Myatt 2014). However, commentators argue EQ is not well researched (Petrides et al. 2004) and caution against potentially conflicting claims (Fineman 2000). This may also be levelled against SQ, as an informed critique is still outstanding.

Irrespective of a theistic or secular spiritual orientation, many who present to social services may not (initially) characterize their issues as spiritual in nature. However, the vast majority of typical (and atypical) concerns posed (including anxiety, despair, abuse, illness, ageing, addictions, self-efficacy, loss) may well contain a spiritual thread.

Furness and Gilligan (2010) and Skelton (2012) believe that much of the usual province of social work is amenable to spiritual discussion and, along with others (Emmons 1999; Seligman 1999; Cox et al. 2007), assert that spirituality helps individuals transcend their present predicaments, establish meaning, perspective and resolve, and assists in self-acceptance, problem resolution and enhanced well-being.

Spirituality, health and well-being

Indeed, there appears to be a growing awareness of the interconnectedness of one's body, mind, emotion and spirit (e.g. Man Ng and Chan 2005; Thompson 2010), although arguably this was often acknowledged outside of the Western helping approach. Thus, increasing calls for practitioners to meaningfully engage with spirituality are evident (e.g. Miller and Thoresen 2003; Skelton 2012).

Interestingly – and the parallels are obvious for social work – Grey (1994), Burke et al. (1999) and Waite et al. (1999) (among others) suggest addressing spirituality contributes positively to counsellees' well-being. Incorporating spirituality into a wellness paradigm would, argue Myers and Williard (2003), help counsellors to view spirituality as integral to people's optimum functioning. This is increasingly recognized by governments, who insist counsellors are part of primary response teams in emergency situations (Brenner et al. 2009), with West (2000) speculating that this is another illustration of the counsellor as secular priest.

Johnston (1995), in a cross-cultural comparative study of 15 families, found spirituality (interpreted religiously and humanistically) was a resiliency mechanism. Hamilton and Jackson (1998) concluded that often the impact of adversity on individuals brings spiritual issues to the fore – a similar conclusion was reached by Angell et al. (1998). These authors also interpreted spirituality as a resiliency factor when embracing the challenges of trauma. This has also been echoed in Meisenhelder (2002), Peterson and Seligman (2003), post-9/11 research in America and Brenner et al. (2009) finding spirituality a helpful factor in the midst of such traumatic events.

Religion

The literature recognizes people do seek help for unresolved religious questions (Crisp 2010). Carers/service users may have concerns approaching 'secular' social workers, fearing their spiritual perspectives will be ignored, denigrated or pathologicalized (Cornah 2006; Gilligan 2009). Thorne (1998) identifies a range of phenomena that may require a spiritual discussion, including spiritual experiences, premonitions, despair, evil, etc. Thus, some may seek pastoral support from within their own 'household of faith' (Lyall 1995), although Lyall is overly restrictive when focusing on the person's faith tradition, as some may well benefit from a more pluralistic spirituality (West 2004; Lines 2006).

Social work responses to addressing spirituality

Another broad issue to emerge from the literature concerns the willingness of social workers to address spirituality. While some commentators highlight its use in practice (Crisp 2010; Rowson 2013), the author is persuaded that a degree of professional resistance and defensiveness exists, which may well extend to social work educators (e.g. Gilligan 2003; Furness and Gilligan 2014). In mitigation, Lines (2006) cites several compelling reasons including: spirituality being a value-imbued concept; lack of practitioner experience; and potential ethical conflict with own or employer belief systems. It is important to be conversant with, and informed by, relevant ethical and regulatory requirements in addressing spirituality, and practitioners must be wary of improperly incorporating spiritual dimensions and influencing carers/service users.

It may also be accounted for by the apparent taboo (West 2000; Coyte et al. 2007) associated with spirituality. Cobb (2001) explores several reasons for this, citing personal and professional preferences for keeping spirituality a private concern (as my opening exchange with the student epitomized), its religious implications, prevalence of more scientific claims, and its inevitable link with death and dying. It is a reasonable supposition that people can feel embarrassed, inadequate and insecure when addressing spirituality, and cultural norms can often reinforce this. Additionally, this can be exacerbated by social, political and religious conflicts, especially those experienced in Northern Ireland or the Middle East. However, predicating their approach upon the assumption of privacy is arguably tenuous and contradictory, as many 'private areas' (including sexuality, abuse) are habitually addressed by social workers. Similarly, West (2000) argues that counsellees are often reluctant to discuss spirituality due to counsellors' apparent disinclination to broach it. Schreurs (2002) supports this broad contention, claiming many studies report psychotherapist resistance to addressing religion and spirituality. Again, this may well be indicative of the persuasive influence of overly critical theorists (including Freud, Ellis) who equated 'religiosity' with mental illness. Indeed, Coyte et al. (2007) challenge this perceived stigmatizing relationship between mental health and spirituality, and encourage practitioners to meaningfully engage with spirituality at a policy, procedural and practice level.

Reflection point 8.5

Factors mitigating against addressing spirituality in the social work encounter include:

- The obvious need for caution in the face of increased litigation and a perceived censorious professional culture
- Social workers may not want to, nor feel free enough, to disclose their own spirituality
- Legitimate reservations about personal and professional boundaries
- Practitioner confidence and competence
- Many supervisors are untrained to address or support social workers in their area
- It is a difficult concept to grasp and raise, even in conversational terms
- There is always a danger of social workers projecting/displacing their own spirituality, existential struggles, joy, etc.
- Many are fearful of violating ethical codes of practice
- The practice setting, role or context-specific issues may inhibit any meaningful discussion of spirituality
- Fearing accusations of proselytizing.

Spirituality and training

A recurring thread emanating from the literature was the lack of practitioner training in spirituality (e.g. Matthews 1998; Coyte et al. 2007; Furness and Gilligan 2010), whether in nursing (Thompson 2010), medicine (Cobb 2001), social work (Furman et al. 2004; Gray 2008) or counselling (Schreurs 2002; Myers and Williard 2003). The resulting implications include an impression that spirituality is not considered an academic, professional discipline, and practitioners are unprepared, therefore lacking competence or confidence to address it. Additionally, many may not appreciate spirituality's relevance for the carer/service user, or misunderstand its expression.

Nevertheless, there is growing insistence (e.g. Furman et al. 2004; Crisp 2008, 2010) to have spiritual competence and sensitivity (and related policy, curricula and practice models) explicitly addressed as a professional requirement. This could include multicultural spirituality (Henley and Schott 1999; Purnell and Paulanka 2003; Gray et al. 2008) like Afrocentric and Native American to complement the Judaeo-Christian, Eurocentric and Caucasian emphasis. Inevitably, this would better prepare practitioners to embrace spirituality more willingly and skilfully. Indeed, ignoring it could constitute not only a disservice to the counsellee (Koenig et al. 2001) but 'an omission of care' (Grey 1994: 219).

Spirituality interventions

In terms of intervention, the literature reflects a range of models, strategies and techniques, but no universal agreement as to what constitutes best practice. However, there is a broad consensus that spirituality should be addressed within a holistic, integrative approach. Many of the aforementioned commentators (including Furness 2003; Corey 2005; Furness and Gilligan 2010) argue that practitioners should have a working definition of spirituality, be prepared to explore their own, and exercise caution regarding their ignorance in this area. They posit various practitioner attributes including: openness, increased self-disclosure (sharing own spiritual experiences), sensitive regard, ethical accountability, risk-taking, informed understanding, and adopting a position of 'intuitive enabler' and 'fellow traveller', rather than expert. Watts (2001) suggests the use of 'reflective questioning' and adopting the postmodernist stance of 'not knowing': encouraging people to enter into spiritual exploration and discovery. Yalom (2008) exhorts practitioners towards 'reciprocal self-revelation' and 'deep' self-awareness, while honestly embracing the challenges of mortality. It is this process that enables practitioners to be authentically present and meaningfully connected to those in distress.

Borrowing from more recent developments in counselling practice, among many others, Hinterkopf (1998) and Jesse et al. (2007) advocate taking a 'spiritual history' as part of the usual assessment process, to establish the importance (or otherwise) of spirituality to carers/service users. These commentators consider spirituality a rich resource that needs to be utilized, even if it is time-consuming, requires additional training and can be uncomfortable (Cornah 2006).

Imaginatively, Pargament (1997) suggests adopting Lazarus and Folkman's (1984) transactional model for coping with stress in addressing spiritual issues, and using it to research how people generally cope with spirituality. Gall et al. (2005) extended Pargament's idea in offering their 'spiritual framework of coping'. Wilber (1979) provided a rather complex ten-fold human (spiritual) development model that received some acclaim (West 2004), but also criticism for its arguably cumbersome construction, assumptive base, and linear and hierarchical emphasis (Heron 1998; West 2004).

A recent development is 'Souldrama', a therapeutic, psychospiritual group action model, leading participants through seven sequential stages of spiritual development (Miller 2006). However, this is primarily American-based and has yet to be critiqued broadly. One approach that has is the 'sanctuary model', developed by Bloom in America, which offers a trauma-sensitive caring environment for those service users most troubled, feeling unsafe or exhibiting risky behaviours. This model has been introduced into Northern Ireland (2007), and part of it facilitates the exploration of the cultural, religious and spiritual motivations that underpin such behaviours, thinking and feeling, and finding successful self-management resolutions for the child/adolescent in care.

White (2006) presents a more generic framework within which healthcare practitioners can discuss and cogitate on the impact of spirituality (on themselves and service users). She argues that spirituality must be construed as integral to a holistic approach to caring. Several commentators (Tacey 2004; Corey et al. 2007) echo this, asserting that spirituality needs to be addressed alongside the usual counselling issues, rather than relegated to more specialist interventions.

Furness and Gilligan (2010) developed a framework for assessing the significance of religion, belief and spirituality in social work. Their realized aim was to help social workers develop a more attuned, highly developed reflective approach to cultural competence across the spectrum of social work practice arenas. This has been generally well received, and is one of the core resources to follow up after reading this chapter.

Skelton (2012) has been advocating the adoption of a biopsychosocialspiritual model for the helping professions generally, including social work. He argues that, through this more ecological prism, the practitioner will inevitably develop a more meaningful and rounded appreciation of the respective carer/service user. This, in turn, will help identify core strengths within the person and situation that the worker can help build and/or rely upon. In addition, other areas can be identified that, with the right attention and resourcing, can be subsequently nourished in the child, adolescent, adult, elder, and used to increase the person's capacity for self-reliance, resilience, learnt helpfulness (Seligman 1990) and so forth.

It must also be appreciated that not every social worker, carer or service user will want or need to explore their spirituality. Indeed, some service users may well be compelled to have social work involvement in their lives and only reluctantly, but often defensively, engage with the social worker. This does not preclude the raising of spirituality, but does demand additional caution regarding purpose, timing, pacing and so on.

In undertaking this work, it is incumbent upon the practitioner to have a level of spiritual fitness – so what might this mean?

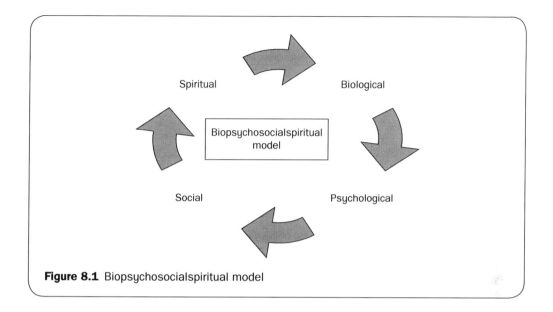

Figure 8.1 Biopsychosocialspiritual model

What does 'spiritual fitness' look like?

Spiritual fitness is, in essence, ensuring that the greatest resource available to you is cared for – **you**! This is often as true for the carer/service user as the social worker (commissioner, director, inspector, manager, practitioner). It will, therefore, require a number of things to feed one's resilience, including (what follows is not prescriptive or exhaustive – each person must exercise personal agency in choosing wisely) the following.

- Meaningful and protected **'time-in'** and **'time-out'** for self. For example, you need to have time for you to 'be' and not always 'do' (human being vs human doing!); time to be with people that contribute to your positivity and help replenish your 'well of being' (well-being) and are more tonic than toxic! You need time away from the often unrelenting demands of life (whether as a social worker, carer or, on occasion, service user – we all need real breaks). This is why holidays, respite breaks, etc. are so important for everyone.
- It is also useful to parallel and extrapolate lessons from other 'fitness' regimes. Were one struggling physically, many would recommend undertaking some physical exercise in an effort to increase fitness and capacity. In turn, spiritual fitness (like emotional fitness, which is much less talked about) will necessitate undertaking some disciplines to get those flabby spiritual muscles into better shape. For example, undertaking healthy relaxation, meditation, increasing your non-work-based reading, feeding creativity and imagination, reducing alcohol and caffeine intake, spending time with others, nature and self (monitoring and transforming negative 'self-talk'), and ensuring self-soothing is always drawing upon healthy and nourishing practices.

- Supervision can also provide a supportive platform to safely and confidently explore your own, and others', spirituality – for example, discussing how to plan to raise this with carers and service users, possible resources that could be made available to them, etc. But this is also dependent on the supervisor being open to addressing spirituality.
- It is also important to know when to ask for help, who to ask, and where it can be sought. It is my long-held contention that those who offer so much help, willingly and often self-sacrificingly, are the worst at either asking for help themselves, or accepting it. Hopefully, as you reflect on this, you can take this as an encouragement to change your ways – interdependence is the healthiest way forward for one and all!

Relevance to students and practitioners

Students and social workers should be encouraged to do the following.

- Reflect on their upbringing and consequent influence of religious/secular factors in shaping their current understanding and openness/resistance to spirituality.
- Explore why spirituality may be an important resource to realize in the helping encounter for carers and service users.
- Identify where spirituality can be readily incorporated into the usual repertoire of social work intervention (interviewing, information gathering, assessment, skills, knowledge and theoretical considerations, etc.) and therefore become a normative consideration.
- Reflect on what signals social work education and training send out generally – and students/practitioners specifically – that would encourage/discourage carers and service users from feeling confident about raising spirituality as a legitimate theme for exploration.

Interestingly, in recent times in Northern Ireland, students have begun to request the inclusion of spirituality in their initial training. Wilson and Kelly (2010), Skelton (2012) and Coulter (2014) have highlighted an apparent reluctance of colleagues, yet the simultaneous increased interest from social work and counselling students, culminating in Skelton delivering the inaugural spirituality workshops in the universities of Ulster, Queens, Belfast Met and Bradford.

So why should helping practitioners' address spirituality?

- It is deeply respectful of personhood.
- People have a right.
- Presenting concerns may have antecedents in spiritually related issues!
- Addressing spirituality can contribute positively to people's well-being.
- Much of the usual province of social work, counselling (and related fields) is amenable to spiritual discussion: whether religious, humanist or existentialist . . .

and spirituality assists individuals in transcending present predicaments and gaining greater perspectives and resolve.
- It is a rich area of potential carer and service user resource.
- Professional ethical codes require practitioners to be au fait with current developments. It's incumbent upon them to be conversant with all approaches, including spirituality!

Activity 8.4

Attempt to identify any of the following that you believe are core to meaning-ful social work interventions:

- Carer/service user encounter addressing spirituality
- Core qualities, values, principles, ethics and professional skills.

Some suggestions . . . core practitioner attributes in addressing spirituality include the usual social work:

- Qualities (including love, sensitive regard, genuineness, warmth, compassion, openness, understanding, patience, faith, hope, enthusiasm, courage)
- Values (respect for personhood; acceptance of the person and their starting point; trust in self and the other's inherent ability and capacity; honesty in owning our own spirituality and being prepared to share this, as and when appropriate; truth in acknowledging our personal and professional competence in the face of this multilayered and challenging theme)
- Principles (including personal and professional integrity, responsibility, accountability, assurance around appropriate levels of confidentiality; upholding own and others' dignity, privacy and ensuring informed choice, and so on)
- Ethics (including beneficence, non-maleficence, informed consent, justice and so on)
- Professional skills (including establishing rapport, observing, listening, assessment, analysing, evaluating, reflecting, recording). An often overlooked skill is flexibility: a necessary prerequisite for the effective practitioner, bearing in mind that it is more often the quality of the given and received relationship that appears to impact the helping encounter than any particular stance, theory or model adopted by the social worker. This also needs to take account of service users' hopes, expectations and external influences (Hubble et al. 1999)
- Resourcing (including sharing your starting point and hearing the other person's, providing additional material, information on theories, models, approaches, techniques that others have found helpful).

Spirituality and abuse

Definitions and discussions about spirituality often assume positive and life-affirming stances, but there can also be a more Newtonian counterpoint. The literature alerts many to the dangers inherent in addressing it (e.g. Gilligan 2008, 2009; Morrall 2008), whether secular or faith-based.

Within the broad spectrum of the helping professions, various commentators (including Feltham 1999, West 2000, Mearns and Thorne 2002 and Gall et al. 2005) candidly acknowledge the potential for abuse of those seeking help, and that great care must be taken to ensure responsible practice. Sloan and Bagiella (2000) dispute claims about the success of integrating spiritual issues into helping encounters, citing this tendency for spiritual abuse. There is ample evidence to support this concern, including historical pogroms and contemporary examples (Jonestown and Wako massacres) and clerical exploitation. For West (2000), unhealthy spirituality can also include 'demonic possession', while spiritual abuse can result from the imposition of (often distorted) religious beliefs (Heron 2001). Clearly there are instances where spiritual abuse can prosper, particularly within ecstatic experiences which may render people vulnerable and diminish equilibrium. Moreover, practitioners may coerce or proselytize, attempting to impose their spirituality on others (Sloan and Bagiella 2000; Faiver et al. 2001). Masson's (1989) censorious critique of psychotherapy serves as an overarching caution in this area. Nonetheless, unhealthy spirituality is a value-laden term, and practitioners need to remain open to the possibility that individuals are free to choose their 'devils' or 'gods'.

Spirituality and anti-oppressive practice

The author is cognisant that, historically, social work theory and practice have often been predicated upon white, patriarchal, Westernized, Judaeo-Christian presuppositions, with a tendency to assume universal applicability (e.g. Palmer and Laungani 1999; Lago and Smith 2003). Indeed, social workers must ensure they are conversant with legislative and ethical demands for pluralism, and avoid the obvious dangers of cultural countertransference or imperialism (Owusu-Bempah and Howitt 2000; Corey et al. 2007). The need to inculcate more culturally competent and sensitive practice has already been established, and this will increasingly involve practitioners having to embrace spirituality as a regular feature of good practice. Such developments have to be placed within (and scrutinized by) wider legislative developments, including the inexorable demands for rights, litigation and a 'new transparency of professional behaviour' (*Observer* Editorial 2002).

Spirituality and ethical responsibility

Furthermore, various commentators (e.g. Etherington 2004; Robinson 2007) and codes (BASW 2012) are replete with exhortations ensuring social work is predicated upon ethical standards. Practitioners are cautioned to adhere to core principles, contracts and boundaries, and the importance of recognizing the limits of their own and others' competence and experience. These also acknowledge the dangers of social workers imposing their own spiritual values, and caution against transference or assuming 'cultural homogeneity' (Turner 2000).

This ethical stance has to be contextualized within legislative requirements emphasizing the centrality of the 'consumer', and reducing the obvious power differentials between service providers and recipients. Thus, people are insisting on being treated holistically (Purtilo and Haddad 2002; Geist-Martin et al. 2003), representing a more empowering engagement (Heron 2001). An emergent implication is that addressing spirituality may potentially reduce such differentials within the helping encounter (Skelton 2012). Simply stated, opening up spirituality necessitates a more reciprocal helper and helped exchange, within which the role of 'expert' may well be shared.

Spirituality and supervision

Various commentators (including Howell 1982 and Shohet 2007) accentuate the need for quality supervision. This is also an ethical requirement and necessary mechanism for practitioners to garner support, remain focused, seek respite from the incessant pressures encountered, develop good practitioner habits and (hopefully) avoid exhaustion. Supervision is also fertile ground for discussing apposite spiritual interventions, and encouraging critical reflection, insight and reflexivity (Etherington 2004; White et al. 2006; Thompson and Thompson 2008).

Nevertheless, supervision is not a panacea, and has obvious limitations, including time constraints, overreliance on supervisee self-reporting, willingness and motivation to change ineffective practice, and lack of supervisor expertise (or interest). Moreover, there is reported supervisor resistance in addressing spirituality within supervision (West 2004; Furness and Gilligan 2010); while others (Pritchard 2000; Feltham 2002) note that good supervisor training is uncommon.

Conclusions

A number of recurring themes were identified, including a resurgence of interest in spirituality, despite its conceptual and operational ambiguity. The literature also revealed a predominantly individualistic and theistic inclination regarding spirituality (Pargament 1997; Sperry 2000; Cobb 2001), with occasional evidence of a more communitarian, pluralistic and secular interpretation and application (Zappone 1991; Hanson 1997). While there are divergent voices, spirituality is often perceived as important to people (e.g. Sinclair et al. 2006; Holloway and Moss 2010), and provides a non-pathologizing explanation for experiences (e.g. Turbott 2004; Skelton 2012). It was also interpreted as a significant moderating factor (increasing resiliency, optimism, meaning, while simultaneously lowering distress, isolation) and contributed positively to well-being (e.g. Peterson and Seligman 2003; Corey 2005).

Concern was expressed that social workers are often poorly equipped and resourced to intervene meaningfully (Moss 2005; Crisp 2010), and those that broach spirituality often fear professional censure (Schreurs 2002; Skelton 2012). Models, frameworks and matrices are emerging to assist history-taking, assessing and intervening, but these must be viewed in the context of the modern tendency to be over-instrumental.

The need to exercise ethical diligence is paramount, ensuring none intrudes upon people's spirituality unsolicited. It was also evident that little exists in the way of policy for spiritual intervention or care, which carries a range of practice implications for users, carers, providers and practitioners, even in terms of quality assurance mechanisms (Furman et al. 2004; Spalek and Imtoual 2008).

The author argues that spirituality remains relatively under-researched and commented upon, particularly in Northern Ireland/Britain, and this chapter will contribute to the wider corpus of academic and professional knowledge, understanding, and resultant practitioner competence, and support the author's career goal of increasing professional responsiveness within his practice.

It is my contention that spirituality is as central to one's life as the very air we need and breathe, and it often serves to inspire one to better – whether overcoming life's vicissitudes, or revelling in one's achievements and/or resilience. Spirituality is embedded in all of the world religions and some of the great philosophies of life, essentially celebrating the human or divine spirit located within each person, and representing a source of considerable strength when fully engaged with and realized.

The learning on spirituality across the helping professions has regenerated interest (Tacey 2004) along with the population more generally (including Celtic spirituality). This may be correlated to an increased existentialist search for meaning (Tacey 2004; Wagler-Martin 2005; Gray 2008) that may well provide a counterpoint to Bauman's (2006) 'endemic uncertainty'.

Professionals are looking for purpose and meaning, while ensuring that they communicate, assess and intervene appropriately. Many are aware that philosophical approaches may provide important transferable messages which can, and should, be used to enhance roles and responsibilities in any organizational context.

I began this chapter declaring I was on a journey, and my primary assumption that spirituality is an increasingly important issue is valid, particularly in our postmodernist age. I believe that helping is fundamentally a spiritual activity, echoing the 'wounded healer' (Nouwen 1972; Holloway 2007) whose disciplined contribution involves turning their 'pain to gain', and serving others (and self) holistically. Such practitioners know that social work should not only have a duty of care, but duty to care and, in addressing spirituality, might find it best to adopt the position of intuitive enabler, fellow traveller – *never* expert.

I feel I'm something of a 'mid-husband', trying to breathe life into an often taboo subject which is as essential to life and living as breath itself. Notice I don't claim to be giving birth . . . it is already alive, just awaiting liberation as the zeitgeist for the twenty-first century.

Activity 8.5

While remaining mindful of not succumbing to the temptation of elevating spirituality in a hierarchical struggle with, and against, other more pressing concerns, how could an understanding of spirituality, and a willingness to address it, help in the following social work openings? And what spiritual resources can be potentially identified and realized in these helping encounters?

Adolescent:

'I don't care, you don't care – no one cares about me . . . it's like I'm always being punished!'

Adult:

'I've no control – I feel like we're all just puppets on a string.'
'I hear voices . . . God/Devil made me do it.'
'My culture gives me permission to hit my child and does not allow you to talk to my wife – just me.'
'My child is dying and I don't know what to do, to think . . . where to turn.'

Elder:

'I have nothing to live for.'
'I think about, you know, what comes after this . . . is it the end? Will I be punished . . . I have made mistakes, you know.'

Activity 8.6

- Are you interested in spirituality?
- In attempting to define or describe spirituality, what words, phrases and terms would you, or others, use?
- What are your sources of support when things are difficult?
- In terms of your support network, what resources would you describe as spiritual?
- How would you characterize/describe/define *your* spirituality?
- In what ways is spirituality important for carers, service users, colleagues, etc.?
- Why does social work (and related professions) not explicitly address spirituality in education, training, research and practice?

- Would you feel confident raising spirituality as a question, theme, experience in your social work classes with the lecturer, peers, etc.?
- How would you feel if a carer or service user asked if it was ok to talk about their spirituality?
- Is it important that academics, practice teachers, trainers and others in similar roles take the responsibility for raising apparent taboo issues within the relatively safe environment of education, training and supervision? Or should the practitioner wait on the carer/service user to bear the weight of raising the issue and hope that the practitioner is open to it?
- What are some of the key signals that would **encourage** or **discourage** you to raise spirituality as a theme and aspect of your life?
- Would similar signals encourage or discourage carers/service users likewise?
- What do you understand by the term 'cultural competence'?
- How does addressing spirituality nourish your self-care and that of others?

Key points

- Spirituality is embedded in all of the world religions, and some of the great philosophies of life, but is under-researched and commented upon in social work.
- Spirituality is as central to one's life as the very air we need and breathe.
- Spirituality inspires one to overcome life's vicissitudes and revel in one's achievements and/or resilience.
- Professional knowledge, understanding and competence will increase responsiveness.

9 Service user involvement in social work education: avoiding the spectre of tokenism

Lisa Armstrong and Angela Etherington

Chapter overview

By the end of this chapter you will be able to:

- Understand the relevance of service user and carer involvement in social work education
- Appreciate the importance of working with service users and carer co-educators to increase knowledge and skills
- Critically appraise hazards and risks
- Apply models and types of participation to social work practice
- Inform the development of policies and procedures on service users and carers.

Introduction

Service user and carer involvement has been acknowledged as a transformative catalyst within social work education by students, staff and service users. Beresford (2014) states that:

> User involvement is seen as a driver for cultural change, challenging paternalism and improving mutual understanding. Students repeatedly highlight the value of seeing service users and carers as active and helpful contributors to their learning, offering real life insights, instead of only encountering them in crisis moments in their life.

An applied profession such as social work requires a knowledge base which draws upon numerous sources in order to develop good practice. The classification of these sources is not always straightforward; nor is it conventionally recorded. One key source of insight may be derived from knowledge which is based on first-hand experiences of social work interventions (Pawson et al. 2003; Humphreys 2005). This body of knowledge may not always be formally captured and published, but nevertheless it forms a vital resource for students and practitioners.

In statutory social work, professionals are called on to implement legislation which can have life-changing consequences for an individual and/or their families. These interactions frequently take place at times when the individual may be potentially at his/her most vulnerable and in greatest need of assistance or protection. Furthermore, it has to be considered that social work interventions are not always based on free choice, but a necessity that arises through the administering of a statutory instrument by social services (Forbes and Sashidharan 1997).

This chapter will offer an exploration of the contribution of service users and carers to the education and training of students, who may eventually be called upon to implement statutes such as the Mental Health Act (1983, amended 2007). The chapter will examine the hazards and risks which must be accounted for in the delivery of effective and meaningful involvement. A case study will be used to describe and examine the powerful role that service users and carer co-educators have to play in providing alternate perspectives on statutory social work functions.

Background

In order to understand the development of service user and carer involvement in social work education and training, it is advisable to briefly consider its origins.

Service user and carer involvement is a required element of all undergraduate and postgraduate social work programmes in the UK (DH 2002; HCPC 2014a, 2014b). The importance of the role of service user and carer involvement was further emphasized within the recommendations of the Social Work Reform Board (SWRB 2010a, 2010b) and appeared as a cross-cutting theme in the Professional Capabilities Framework (PCF), specifically the domains of Critical Reflection and Analysis and Professional Leadership. In relation to social work education, the SWRB reiterated that 'service users and carers should be consistently and substantially involved in the design and delivery of courses' (SWRB 2010b: 3).

The history of service users and carer involvement in social work education pre-dates the passing of the Care Standards Act (2000), a legislative framework which underpinned the 'Requirements for Social Work Training' (DH 2002) and led to the formation of the General Social Care Council (regulatory predecessor to the Health and Care Professions Council). Sections 61 and 63 of this Act set in legislation the protection of the profession of social work in the UK.

Developments can be crudely cast into two different paths of ascent. First, the shift in government policy to accommodate the service user and carer perspectives is ascribed to the consumerist model of service provision championed by the Conservative governments of the 1980s (Butler and Drakeford 2001), and rebranded by New Labour during the 2000s as personalization (Leadbeater 2004; Ferguson 2007). Second, as a result of service user activism, a mobilizing movement where like-minded communities came together (sometimes in association with social workers) to critique and develop bottom-up services. Arguably, community activism pre-dates the implementation of the consumerist model (Beresford 2000) and it may be that the marketization of social care over time led to an increase in the demand for consumer-led services which in turn resulted in a greater voice in the training and development of its workforce.

Arnstein (1969: 217) classified the types of participation and presented a model that evaluated the spectrum of degrees of participation. Arnstein's Ladder of Citizen Participation has been modified and adapted to a number of settings, including in mental health training (Tew et al. 2004: 53–4) and service user involvement in research (MacKay 2002, cited in Ager et al. 2005a: 474; Sweeney and Morgan 2009: 27). Whereas these works may not directly offer models of how to promote service user and carer involvement, what they do offer is methods by which the nature of the involvement can be assessed and reviewed.

During the 1980s and 1990s, the development of social models of disability, a burgeoning disability rights movement, and a consumerist model of social care created an environment where service users were able to empower themselves (Beresford and Campbell 1994). This led to the emergence of self-identified, self-organized and self-run groups campaigning for rights and representation at local and national levels.

During the 1990s, a series of publications appeared from the Central Council for Education and Training in Social Work (CCETSW) and the National Health Service Training Directorate promoting the need for service users' involvement in social work training, sometimes with reference to particular services such as mental health (NHSTD 1992; Beresford et al. 1994; Crepaz-Keay et al. 1997). Few peer-reviewed academic papers exist prior to 2002 outlining the role of service users and carers in social work education, with the notable exception of Manthorpe (2000), Reynolds and Read (1999), and Croft and Beresford (1990).

Subsequent to the passing of the Care Standards Act (2000) and the formalization of the social work degree pathway, a range of authors have discussed and presented service user accounts and perspectives in a range of settings – for example, families' experience of poverty (Gupta and Blewett 2008); palliative care social work (Agnew and Duffy 2010); small-group interdisciplinary training with a focus on mental health (Tew et al. 2012), and collectives of service users who refuse to be labelled (Citizens as Trainers et al. 2004).

Molyneux and Irvine (2004) and Robinson and Webber (2013) examine the origins and diversity of service user involvement in UK social work education alongside a range of guidance and advisory documents (Levin 2004; Tew et al. 2004; Ager et al. 2005a; Branfield et al. 2007). However, more recent publications have questioned the benefits and measurable outcomes of service user involvement in social work education (Robinson and Webber 2013; Irvine et al. 2015).

Current requirements stipulate that service user and carer roles should be evident across the design, recruitment, delivery and assessment of qualifying and post-qualifying awards. However, visibility to students is still mostly confined to the recruitment and readiness to practice processes, and service users and carers are mainly presenting through the lens of personal experiences (Sadd 2011; Wallcraft et al. 2012).

Hazards, risks, potential pitfalls and ethical concerns

Since the publication of Requirements for Social Work Training (DH 2002), service user involvement in social work courses has become integral, albeit patchy, across courses and modules. At this juncture, education providers are committed to furthering service user involvement in course delivery as a response to the requirements of course accreditation. The effective practical delivery of meaningful service user involvement is a challenge as it requires structural adjustment at the teaching, departmental and institutional levels, while remaining true to social work values.

The key stakeholders in social work education include the student body, service users and carers, the educational institution and the employer organizations. It may be assumed that each grouping has the same end goals – i.e. to provide a safe, effective and efficient service which equally meets the needs of all stakeholders. However, the primary consumers of educational processes are the students in the first instance, although employers benefit in the long run as graduates are recruited and introduced to the workforce. It may be, therefore, that students and future employers have more to gain from the contribution made by an individual service user or carer, and the latter may be disempowered or further alienated from the experience (see Table 9.1). This power imbalance is frequently discussed from polarized viewpoints within literature (Beresford 2005; Webber and Robinson 2012). Less frequently explored is the potentially large emotional toll on the service user who may or may not have the emotional or practical resources to deal with it. Service users and carers are rightly concerned about the impact of their involvement, knowing that the ultimate goal is to offer future social workers opportunities to improve their knowledge and skills. Many service users and carers are aware that they are contributing to an altruistic endeavour which is likely to benefit others in the long term, rather than seeking short-term gains for themselves (Webber and Robinson 2012).

Ethical concerns are central to the debate, and social workers follow codes of conduct (HCPC 2012) and the Code of Ethics (BASW 2012) which state that social workers are committed to the principles of human rights and social justice. The British Association of Social Workers (BASW) also stipulates that social work organizations and individuals seek to empower individuals and contribute to the continuous improvement of professional practice.

Tokenism

Tokenism, or tokenistic involvement, is perhaps the biggest hazard of the service user and carer involvement process. Tokenism has been defined variably as a lack of positive outcomes, or the insincere fulfilling of policy priorities (Beresford and Croft 2001; Molyneux and Irvine 2004; Webber and Robinson 2012).

Classroom teaching based on personal testimonies or narratives is routine and welcomed by the student body; however, this approach has been dismissed as tokenistic and potentially perceived as reducing service users to the status of an exhibit (Armstrong and Etherington 2010). At this time it is clear that further work is required by social work educators in the design of programmes that enable the development of service user contributions which evolve at the same rate that the student body's level of knowledge increases, perhaps accepting that the service user narratives are an intrinsic early step in a student year group's path to qualification. Within this scenario the needs of the students are unlikely to be

Table 9.1 A summary table of the hazards/pitfalls, risks and ethical concerns arising from service user or carer involvement in the education process

	Hazard/Pitfall	Risk	Ethical concerns
Power	Within current social work education there exists a complex interplay between a number of stakeholders. The service user's voice may not always be given fair representation.	That individual service users or carers and their representative organizations will withdraw from the education process and/or feel that their participation in the process is exploitative on the part of the educational institution and its staff.	We recognize service users as experts by experience, but do not necessarily reward them on an equal standing with other external consultants.
Tokenism	That service user and carer involvement in an education programme lacks positive outcomes, or is merely viewed as a compliance exercise.	Reduces the service user to a teaching aid, and there are limited positive outcomes for the service user or carer.	That there is no empowerment of the service user or carer, and that any information conveyed has little or no impact on practice development.
Welfare	That the service user or the carer's physical, mental and emotional needs are not adequately provided for.	That a service user or carer's health is negatively affected due to involvement in the teaching process.	The staff and the institution have a duty of care to the service users or carers, as well as the students and other staff.
Representation	That the service user and carer experience brought to the teaching environment is individualized and not adequately representative of the wider service user community.	Students receive a narrow view and potentially polarized view depending on the service user standpoint.	Through social work values, there is a responsibility to encourage the empowerment of the individual. However, there is also a responsibility to represent the larger community and ensure that improvements in practice are made.

immediately compatible with the expectations of the service user (Irvine et al. 2015) as the understanding of the first-year, first-term student may be relatively simplistic when compared to that of the same student in the final year. It is therefore advisable to introduce students to models such as Arnstein's Ladder of Citizen Participation (and its derivatives), where some of the necessary transfer of service user and carer knowledge and experiences would be classified as being in the 'degree of tokenism' range (Arnstein 1969, Figure 2: 217; MacKay 2002, cited in Ager et al. 2005b).

An open demonstration of poor inclusion as a result of paying lip service and ticking boxes is hard to defend in social work education, as such practices breach core professional values. Students are more likely to learn poor, rather than good, ways to consult and collaborate, and service users and carers are less likely to participate.

In order to avoid tokenistic input, social work lecturers are best placed to introduce and actively involve service users in planning and preparing for the interaction with students. This would ensure fuller, more confident participation and greater sharing of experiences and expert knowledge.

Although tokenism remains a spectre which haunts all service user and carer contributions, eradication requires human and financial resources, alongside a holistic understanding of the relevance and importance of those receiving care services. Educational providers function as institutional hierarchies, and even if students and lecturers are committed to integration the likelihood of service users being on an equal footing is a desired aim, but may not be achievable (Webber and Robinson 2012).

Reducing the service user to a teaching aid

Although personal testimonies or narratives make an important contribution to developing understanding of service user perspectives, such input has been critiqued as overly individual and often focused on poor or inadequate social work practice. However, although narratives can be utilized appropriately to make a vertically integrated contribution to the entirety of the programme, there remains a risk that these may become somewhat voyeuristic on the part of the student(s). Here the academic must, in consultation with the service user or carer, establish rules, boundaries and ethical principles such as respect for the individual, choice and client self-determination to enable the application of core professional values in a classroom context. The challenge remains to make the interaction a two-way process from which all the directly involved stakeholders benefit. To this end, feedback from the student body and staff to the service user, explaining the impact of a narrative, is a possible avenue to explore.

Labelling

It is a basic facet of the human condition that people, animals and goods are simplified, classified and grouped. For example, it may be argued that the term 'service user' is problematic and inaccurate, as well as patronizing (Beresford 2003;

McLaughlin 2009). However, like many similar phrases used in social work, it remains a term entrenched within the current academic literature (Robinson and Webber 2013). In a professional context, social workers divide statutory functions into sections which roughly reflect law, policy and practice. Implementation may be based on approaches such as the medical model and the perceived needs of a particular group, both of which may seem benign, but can have a stigmatizing long-term effect. It could be suggested that continued labelling in social work education is a by-product of teaching in the absence of service user contributions and direction.

Labels propagate stigma via the removal of an individual's identity – for example, in the case of mental illnesses they can lead to a diverse range of individuals with differing lifestyles, backgrounds, experiences, presentations and aspirations being lumped together under one stigmatizing label. This grouping of individuals with disparate needs and experiences also increases the unrealistic and inflammatory notion of the identikit service user.

Representation

Finding a representative voice is problematic in relation to any group or subject, and like the general population the service user and carer community is no exception in its heterogeneous composition. It would, therefore, be foolhardy and naïve to entertain the notion that any service user and carer involved in the design and delivery of a course will be representative of the entire community and able to provide 'one service user voice' (Molyneux and Irvine 2004). Could it be that social work educators need to acknowledge, from the outset, that input from service users, particularly into classroom teaching, is almost always based on their personal experiences, expertise and opinions, even when they are acting on behalf of a wider organization? This facet of service user and carer representation has been documented as a concern of both staff and students alike (Robinson and Webber 2013; Irvine et al. 2015).

Increasingly, social work education providers are linked to organized service user and carer educator groups who may be attached to programmes or modules, but there is limited literature on the collusive nature and dynamics of close collaboration developed and sustained over many years.

Service user and carer welfare

Many service users are in receipt of direct medical and/or social care, and many carers are responsible for those with extreme health, or related, needs. However, those seeking input into any consultative or collaborative process must ensure that their welfare and physical needs are given due consideration, particularly in relation to communication, access, diet, aids and an open and welcome approach to hospitality. This may include ensuring that the teaching spaces and IT have the required access, through to considerations of the physical, emotional and mental impact that the teaching experience may have upon the service user or carer. It may also require briefing time before and after the teaching or other activity.

Planning and preparation

The integration of service users and carers into social work education teams means a number of practicalities must be addressed. There is a need for the service user and carers to receive a robust induction and training which supports their needs and enables them to further develop their own skills and confidence (Levin 2004). It is essential that any teaching interface is conceived and scheduled in an empathic and timely fashion. Conversely, there is little consideration in literature, or in guidance, about the importance of the training and development of social work academics on working with service users and carers (Levin 2004).

The question of power

From the outset, there is an uneven distribution of power within social work education (Robinson and Webber 2013). If the positions of the stakeholders may be crudely refined and characterized as: the **student body**, which is in essence a consumer paying for a product; the **employer organization** of future social workers, who require a fundamental knowledge of social work theory and safe and effective practice; the **education provider**, usually a large organization

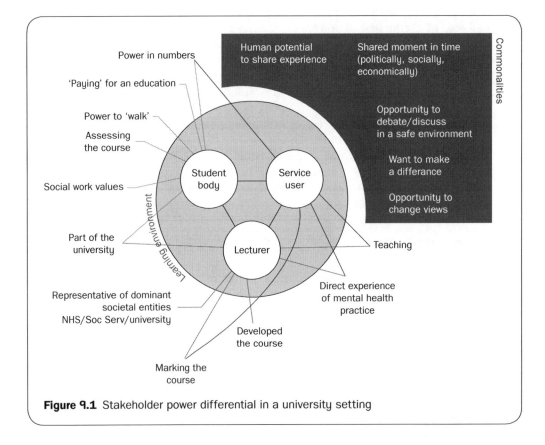

Figure 9.1 Stakeholder power differential in a university setting

which runs numerous courses across many disciplines, **academic tutors** and **service users and carers**. The question of who holds most power in an institutional setting, such as a university, is debatable, but there is little doubt that service users are likely to be in the position of least power. The dilemma of how to resolve the distribution of power, while meeting the statutory requirement for service user and carer involvement, continues. Sustained work endorsed by the student body, the institution and future employers (Forrest et al. 2000) to further historical advances, alongside greater statutory and policy support, is a possible way forward. Figure 9.1 demonstrates the power differential, commonalities and differences between the face-to-face stakeholders within the learning environment.

Perhaps ironically, part of the solution in addressing the power differential in the case of the service user and the educational institution lies in labelling. Whereas it might be argued that individual service users being referred to as consultants or co-educators is just semantics, in some cases this can directly influence the rate at which contributors are reimbursed and, importantly, initially perceived by the student body.

Case study 9.1 Squaring the circle

This case study presents a vehicle by which the application of the Mental Health Act (1983) is explored from the perspectives of a service user and a social work practitioner, based upon the personal experiences of the two authors, a service user educator and a university lecturer/Approved Mental Health Professional, when working with undergraduate social work students.

Mental Health and Mental Health Act (1983) Assessments

Social work in the context of mental health is one of the most challenging areas for students, mainly because of the models of care being used – for example, medicalization of mental illness can be broken down into lists of symptoms and behaviours, but ultimately a diagnosis can leave an individual with a label which is likely to be questioned by students taught to utilize social models of care. The impact of a mental illness on a person's life is as unique an experience as the individual themselves.

Mental health social workers in the legally defined Approved Mental Health Professional (AMHP) role are expected to administer one of the most powerful statutory functions of any professional. Under the Mental Health Act (1983, 2007), an AMHP can detain an individual against their will and compel the person to undergo treatment, thus potentially opening them to stigmatization and social exclusion.

In keeping with the BASW Code of Ethics, social workers will strive for the 'least restrictive means' in the application of the Mental Health Act. One of the challenges of social work education in mental health is enabling the student to gain the perspective of the service user. This is particularly pertinent in the case of Mental Health Act assessments. Therefore, service user and/or carer co-educators have a particularly important role to play in social work education (Beresford and Boxall 2012). In the case study that follows, the service user's role is that of a co-educator who is providing a narrative with which they will challenge the students in the following areas of knowledge:

1. Mental health
2. Mental health legislation
3. Mental health assessment processes
4. Personal levels – prejudice, sympathy and empathy.

Power balances within the teaching environment

This case study is based on an undergraduate mental health programme led by two co-educators – a lecturer and a service user – both of whom have extensive experience of the Mental Health Act. The process of engagement followed a number of stages set out below. Ethical practice suggests that those involved should disclose relevant facts to one another and the employer institution, so it is important to note that the lecturer and the service user were only known to each other through the co-education process.

Prior to the execution of the course and the co-presented session, extensive discussions took place to establish what the course was trying to achieve, and the terms of engagement. So the service user educator's role within the module was as a co-presenter in the session exploring the Mental Health Act, and as an assessor of the students' group presentations. The feedback generated was returned to the students via the student mark sheets.

Key elements examined in the course using co-educators were:

• The nature of mental illness
• Addressing the stigma of mental illness
• Exploring the Mental Health Act and associated acts
• Presenting contrasting perspectives of the application of the Mental Health Act
• Facilitating 'real life' feedback on social work practice in mental health settings
• Highlighting the individual nature of mental illness and the impact of that illness on the individual's recognition in society.

Personal narratives were seen to be a powerful means by which to explore mental illness, as they can challenge stigma and pre-existing prejudice, provide insight into living with severe and enduring mental illness, and potentially empower the service user/carer educator. However, on Arnstein's Ladder of Citizen Participation, the service user narrative is considered highly tokenistic (Arnstein 1969). The co-educators discussed this perception extensively and considered methods by which the presentation of the narrative would not be perceived as the service user co-educator being used as a visual aid or an exhibit to be examined, but instead as part of an empowering exercise. Within the teaching process the method utilized was essentially one of initial non-disclosure – i.e. the service user co-educator was introduced to the student group as a mental health consultant and not as a service user. This strategy of non-disclosure of status was used to avoid the stereotyping of a mental health service user as requiring help, or sympathy, or even being a person to be fearful of, so that the knowledge and expertise of the mental health consultant could be conveyed without prejudice. The hope was that the class would see before them a person who was capable, knowledgeable and an expert, through experience, in mental health law.

In the formal lecture part of the mental health law session, the service user and the lecturer shared the presentation duties equally, and each gave responses to the students' questions based upon their individual perspectives. The service user educator went on to reveal that they were a service user only in the second half of the session, when the focus shifted to personalizing and exploring the implications of the legislation for both service users and practitioners. The impact of a mental health act assessment was then explored from the lived experience of a service user and a mental health practitioner.

Of the elements explored, the 'squaring the circle' exercise (see Figure 9.1) had the greatest impact on the academic co-educator and the student body, as the meeting of narratives describing contrasting perspectives of the same action added a depth to the teaching experience unattainable without a service user co-educator. In essence, the service user narrative added a third dimension to the two-dimensional mechanical assessment process which tends to be the nature of the Mental Health Act assessment. The way in which this was presented to the student group was as a sequence of events encountered through the process of conducting a Mental Health Act assessment, which started with the worker looking at the service user's background, and concluded with a hospital admission. The entire sequence of events is illustrated in Table 9.2.

Conclusions

The authors believe that service user and carer knowledge is based on first-hand experiences of social work interventions, and should be valued as such. Personal narratives are a powerful means by which mental illness may be explored. An open and honest exchange will enable change, challenge stigma and prejudice, and provide insight into severe and enduring mental illness. The power differential between the service user and the educational institution can reinforce stereotypes, so the aim should be to enable and empower all the key stakeholders.

Educators committed to ethical principles – such as respect for the individual, choice and client self-determination – are more likely to demonstrate social work values in a classroom context.

'The squaring the circle' exercise is a useful approach, and was well received by the students, who felt privileged to share very personal information. The session challenged their preconceived prejudices, and provided a real opportunity to promote open and frank discussion around the Mental Health Act and its application.

Mental health service user narratives are powerful, interactive tools which are valued by students. However, their use is not without hazards and risks (Figure 9.2). The academic educator must be aware that the accusation of tokenism

Table 9.2 Differing perspectives of the mental health assessment process; the contrasting viewpoints of the assessed and the assessor

Sequence of events	Process in assessment	Social worker professional perspective	Service user perspective	Learning point
1	Background research into the individual's records.	'The notes show that, when unwell, the client experiences . . .'	They are 'listening' to the notes, more than to what I am telling them now.	It is important to consider the individual's history, but the notes are not the whole story and they are a professional's perspective. You have the primary source in front of you. Listen to the person.
2	Arrive at the home and introductions.	Set the client at ease. Use first names.	'I don't know these people' – first names are disrespectful.	You are engaging in a very formal and serious process. Perhaps consider asking the person who is the focus of the assessment how they would like to be addressed?
		Stand up until asked to sit.	Standing in my home is threatening.	Assess the environment and try to put yourself in the assessed individual's position. Everyone has the right to be safe in their own home. Do you like it when your boss stands above you when you are sitting down? Consider that the power differential of the situation is in your favour; try to readdress this if it is safe to do so.
3	The assessment interview.	Use of technical language to ease communication between professionals.	All this jargon is used to misinform and trick.	All professionals have a tendency to regress into jargon. How can the assessed individual hope to follow the process when the language used is unclear and, at times, opaque? To be able to translate technical language into plain English is illustrative that you, as a professional, fully understand what you are doing.

Table 9.2 (continued)

Sequence of events	Process in assessment	Social worker professional perspective	Service user perspective	Learning point
		Time is of the essence – 'must get on to the next call'.	This is my life and my liberty. I want to take the time necessary for the best decision for me.	This may just be one of several assessments you have to make as a professional on a particular day. You will have time constraints in your role. However, the decision to detain an individual under the Mental Health Act (1983) is a life-changing event for that person and their family.
4	Decision made that an admission is needed.	If we achieve this within a brisk timescale it will limit 'suffering and distress'.	This is too quick! I need to take care of a few things and pack my things.	Consider that if someone were going into hospital for treatment of a physical illness you would ensure that they had time to pick up a few essential items and allow them to tell you what needs to be taken care of domestically. This is not always the experience of individuals being detained under the Mental Health Act (1983).
5	Leave home and transportation.	The transportation to the hospital must be professional and safe. Use a police vehicle or an ambulance.	This is my home; I have to return here. All my neighbours can see the police vehicle/ambulance.	Consider how much stigma is still attached to mental illness in modern British society. Utmost care should be taken to try to make transportation from the place of assessment to the place of admission as dignified as possible.

Strengths:
- 360° problem solving
- Experiential learning/ primary source
- Chance for primary source to respond in the 'here and now'

Weaknesses:
- Relies on the students engaging with the process
- Power imbalances

Opportunities:
- Cultural depth
- See the individual not the diagnosis
- Opens dialogue

Threats:
- Bureaucratic barriers
- Time restraints
- **TOKENISM**

Figure 9.2 Strengths, weaknesses, opportunities and threats (SWOT) analysis of the squaring the circle case study

can be levelled at the use of narratives, and there is an onus upon them to devise strategies that enable their service user co-educator partners to address content and the levels of disclosure, to ensure that the involvement is empowering and not confined to the 'Exhibit X' scenario. Students must be made aware that the service user account is a personal one, and that the experience conveyed is unique to that individual.

Finally, all welfare professionals require the active participation of service users and carers in the development of policy and practice. The principles apply across all sectors and can be used to inform existing knowledge, skills and values, as well as new ways of working.

Key points
- Service user and carer knowledge is based on first-hand experiences of social work interventions.
- Personal narratives may be a powerful means by which to share experiences of mental illness.
- Service user and carer input can challenge stigma and prejudice, and provide insight into living with severe and enduring mental illness.
- Service user contributions can potentially empower the service user/carer educator.
- Educators committed to ethical principles – such as respect for the individual, choice and client self-determination – are more likely to demonstrate social work values in a classroom context.

10 Deaf-blind law and policy

Lucy Jacques and Rebecca Long

Chapter overview

By the end of this chapter you will have a greater understanding of:

- How to work respectfully with deaf-blind people
- How deaf-blind people experience services
- The narratives and motivations of deaf-blind people
- Relevant laws and policies
- The overlap between service users, carers and practitioners
- Key messages which can be applied to other groups.

Introduction

This chapter aims to look at the ways in which social workers can use legislation and policy frameworks to improve practice. Developing a respectful way of working with people, and understanding the difference between the role of the practitioner and the person receiving the intervention, is crucial to building relationships. Social workers who are aware of underpinning frameworks, both legislative and theoretical, are able to be more effective, inclusive, and work collaboratively to facilitate effective solutions and appropriate outcomes. The overarching purpose is to explore and explain legislative processes and statutory instruments as they are used in practice (Clements and Thompson 2011). A key aim is to inform social work practice and raise awareness about the restrictions set out in the messages, guidance and instructions that practitioners receive from their employers. Discussion will also take place on the dilemmas and tensions which can come about when social worker and service user roles and identities overlap.

The underlying principles are that as people we are all of equal value and equal vulnerabilities, and as such are both potential receivers and providers of services.

Since one of the authors is deaf-blind, and the other, as well as having a social work practice background, is a qualified deaf-blind manual sign interpreter, this chapter will use the experiences of deaf-blind, deaf and blind people to frame the discussion. In our experience, deaf-blind people are often as marginalized in practice as they are in society, having a dual or combined sensory loss and therefore fitting into neither the hearing world nor the deaf-signing world very comfortably.

This insight allows us to question the distance between professionals themselves and the people they work with. The contention is that there may be a need for, and perhaps an important benefit to, practitioners to see themselves as distant from the people they work with to enable an objective stance which allows a sense of 'I wouldn't' or 'I'm not' when judging, assessing and planning interventions. We would argue that, while this may be an important practice approach which assists clear thinking in emotionally charged situations, it can also reduce the understanding that social workers have of both themselves and the people they are engaging with. We propose that active involvement, greater flexibility and seeing the situation from a range of perspectives, along with the need to leave as small a footprint as possible in people's lives, is likely to result in best and efficient social work practice. Openness to other people's experiences, narratives and motivations will lead to more empathetic and humanistic approaches (Ferguson 2011).

The debate around the terms 'service user', 'client' and 'customer' is based on the history of each. Although 'client' is not generally used in social work, it is widely accepted by legal professionals and therapeutic providers, who do not perceive it negatively. Social workers in hospital settings find themselves working in situations where the rest of their multidisciplinary colleagues use the term 'patient' routinely, and may struggle with alternatives such as 'customer'. 'Service user' remains popular in the context of social work education, but in learning disability it may hint at user/misuser (as in substance misuse).

It is probable that none of these terms is desirable in describing the people needing or receiving services; the use of 'client' feels more personal and real. Whatever term is used, professionals must balance the risks which relate to professional thinking on expertise and power. The key message is that the client is likely to be 'the expert' on their situation and knows their situation best.

Relevant deaf-blind law and policy

Social care legislation has historically been made up of many different statutory instruments and guidance enacted over several decades as a result of greater social/political awareness. Critics suggest that the NHS and Community Care Act 1990, and the NHS and Community Care (Direct Payments) Act 1996, are based on conservative marketplace ideals, perhaps even the start of the privatization of social care (Pearson 2006; Riddell et al. 2006). These laws are wide-ranging and have benefited disabled people, particularly in relation to opportunities for greater choice and control (Riddell et al. 2006; Glasby and Littlechild 2009).

The growth of legislation, often rooted in political ideology, or perhaps global and local events, and supporting procedure and guidance, has confused practitioners and people requiring services. This has led to situations where it may be difficult for disabled people to access the services they require from the local authority because of interpretation, local custom and practice (Sense 2015).

Listed below are some of the legal frameworks relating to community care for adults and disabled children in general, and deaf-blind people in particular:

- The National Assistance Act 1948
- The National Health Service Act 1977

- The Chronically Sick and Disabled Person's Act 1970
- The National Health Service and Community Care Act 1990
- The National Health Service and Community Care (Direct Payments) Act 1996
- The Carers and Disabled Children Act 2005
- The Equality Act 2010 (incorporates the Disability Discrimination Acts 1995 and 2005)
- The Local Authority Circular (DH) (2009) 6 – Social Care for Deaf-blind Children and Adults
- The Mental Capacity Act 2005
- The Mental Health Act 2007.

The move appears to be away from giving to and doing to, and towards enabling people. The outcome has been more or less successful because resources, along with political will, have been limited. The Equality Act 2010 brought together all the anti-discriminatory laws, including the Disability Discrimination Act 1995. However, the need for new legislation to bring together all of the older legislation into a single legislative framework has been argued for by many disabled people, disability charities and relevant policymakers.

Although consultation on a combined law did take place, the response was that research mindedness and an openness to practice knowledge should lead to the identification of gaps and ways to build professional capacity. In relation to deaf-blind services, social workers may need to use their professional curiosity through approaches such as asking questions of themselves and others about the situations they encounter. For example, when confronted with a new situation it may be worth considering the following questions.

- How do I carry out a best interests assessment, or mental capacity assessment, if there are communication support needs?
- What do other people do to communicate with this person?
- Does it work?
- What is their preferred method of communication?
- How can I build rapport?
- What does the procedure and guidance tell me that can help?
- Which theories and models seem most appropriate?

An audit of professional knowledge and experience provides a practice perspective which assumes that situations where deaf-blind people are involved require a willingness to look for and use new skills in practice. Asking questions and looking for inconsistencies are rooted in methods which are evaluative and do not over-rely on one way to 'do' social work. Social workers who are open to these approaches are likely to be experienced, confident and open to self-reflection (Postle 2002).

Policy on deaf-blind service users, including in the area of learning disability, includes the Local Authority Circular (2009) Social Care for Deaf-blind Children and Adults, which is known as the Deaf-blind Guidance. This was originally issued in 2001 and reissued in 2009, introduced after Putting People First (2007) as a way of trying to redress the balance of services, service perspectives and expectations for deaf-blind people.

The Guidance expects local authorities to:

- Ensure that social care assessments are carried out by someone with a specialist qualification, and deaf-blind services are the responsibility of a 'senior' manager
- Provide appropriate services for deaf-blind people, as they may be different from services for deaf or blind people
- Offer access to one-to-one specifically trained support workers, such as communicator guides
- Produce accessible information in suitable formats.

The Deaf-blind Guidance supports the Care Act (2014), which gives additional strength and weight to the need for deaf-blind people to have a specialist assessment which is now included in the primary legislation. It could seem that, given the relatively small number of deaf-blind people, this is relevant to the practice of social workers in sensory services teams. However, taking into account that the largest group of deaf-blind people are those who have acquired a dual sensory loss, the relevance to practice in hospital teams and community adult services teams is clear.

Implications of deaf-blind law and policy for social work practice

There is a need for practitioners to be aware of the Equality Act (2010) within their practice, and indeed with their colleagues and students on placement, to ensure everyone, including those people with a 'protected' characteristic', has equal rights and equal access to everyday life. Equal rights and equal access does not mean having the same, or being the same, as people without a 'protected characteristic', but rather having 'reasonable adjustments' and support to enable them to achieve a similar final outcome.

Research mindedness is vital, not only to ensure that practitioners remain up to date with changes in thinking, models of practice and theory, but also because there is an expectation in the professional standards (HCPC 2012 and BASW 2012) that evidence-based practice is the way to build a strong professional value-base and framework for practice.

The main purpose of care legislation is to enable social workers to argue for their clients' needs – for example, in the case of social and leisure activities when this may well be considered 'something we don't provide'. Legal backup offers practitioners a better chance of getting the desired service outcomes. The dangers relate to the perception of professionals seen to advocate overzealously. They may be seen as 'difficult', not part of the team, and lacking understanding and commitment to the wider organization. This may lead to feelings of vulnerability, marginalization, and perhaps fear of losing professional credibility (Postle 2002; Smith 2005).

Legal responsibilities are supported by regulatory bodies and policies, such as those on 'whistle blowing'. Safeguarding procedures require that professionals are accountable for ensuring that their knowledge is heard and responded to (Ferguson 2011).

Good communication

Much of the social work role is around direct contact with people, be that face-to-face or in writing. How we address and are addressed as participants in any everyday interaction affects our engagement with service users and/or carers.

A number of models may be used to promote good practice, but essentially it important to engage in a two-way co-production (Hunter and Ritchie 2007) and an anti-discriminatory relationship (Thompson 2012). Both the professional and client should ideally be as equal (or made to feel as equal) as is possible. Obviously the process creates limitations to the equality of relationship, but the way in which practitioners think about practice approaches is paramount to ensuring as equal a relationship as is possible.

One of the areas that is often experienced and described in the informal narratives of people receiving services is the impact of the way that everyday contact is managed. Social workers and other practitioners work in a world of reviews, assessments and reassessments. They may see numerous people over a week, and engage in similar conversations in the knowledge that they know what is happening with the information and the parameters of the decision-making. Service users or clients, on the other hand, place a much greater weight on reviewing, assessing, or just being talked to. They feel the difference between independence and dependence.

It is important to be aware of the impact of a letter, email or phone call as it can cause anxiety which may require time for reassurance or assimilation. Good practice requires sensitivity and good person-centred communication skills. It may be a relief to get it off a to-do list last thing on a Friday, but the person receiving it may have all weekend before being able to respond. Think about whether the person you have contacted will be able to get hold of you if they need to discuss or respond to the email or letter they have received, or are going to have days where, even if they send a response, they will not get a response from you (if there is holiday/leave booked), nor be able to discuss it with you.

Overlapping roles and identities

At the beginning of this chapter we talked about overlapping roles and identities. The acknowledgement that roles and identities may cross over relates to multiple responsibilities – for example, while we may be in a practitioner role, our life outside this may involve being a carer, being in receipt of support, or any number of life circumstances which mean that this division is not always as clear as might be comfortable. Good practice may well involve acknowledging how it would feel to be the receiver of contact in this case, considering the impact that being in this position would have on your emotional well-being, and altering practice to take this into account.

Those receiving contact from social workers may be aware that they have heavy caseloads, juggle multiple expectations around tight timescales, deal with cumbersome technology, and function within different work spaces and domains (Ferguson 2009). Professionals are not expected to be perfect, but sensitive acknowledgement of the multiple layers of difference relayed in an honest and open manner may be received more credibly.

Well-informed professionals understand the importance of available care/ communication services and access issues. Those who lack planning skills tend to avoid pertinent issues, or put in place solutions which may be 'too much' and may not actually meet particular and specific needs. Assumptions are equally difficult for people who are deaf – for example, written communi- cations are not always useful. People who have British Sign Language, rather than English, as their first language, need interpreters with specialist linguistic training.

The two examples below describe common deaf-blind scenarios for practice, where two fairly simple impairments are causing stress for both the social worker and the person being assessed. The examples illustrate the ways in which solu- tions can be found using common-sense approaches.

Case studies which illustrate deaf-blind issues and concerns

Case study 10.1

Malcolm was born with retinitis pigmentosa. He had tunnel vision until the age of 12, and then lost his residual vision to light perception only. He is now totally blind. Malcolm reads on his laptop at home using electronic Braille and software to access text. He is having difficulties accessing the paperwork and forms he needs to read as part of his supported assessment as the forms contain a lot of tables and text boxes that are difficult to navigate using a screen reader and Braille display. This is increasingly frustrating him, and the process of complet- ing his assessment and support plan for assistance is overrunning the time the local authority says it should take, creating additional pressure for his social worker.

Malcolm has said that he does not want the information read to him as he wants a copy to keep.

Making paperwork and forms more accessible in a plainer format, without tables or text boxes, is a straightforward, although possibly time-consuming, option (involving copy and paste for the practitioner) if documentation and systems are not in a plain text format. This would also make it easier for someone who has a milder visual impairment and uses a screen magnifier. As with the next professional practice example, Malcolm will probably know exactly what he needs, and asking him is the first step. Practitioners can be overwhelmed with feeling they have to have all the solutions, or produce all documents finished in accessible formats. However, using collaboration and working in partnership ensures that practice is complying with the legislation, and that a solution is appropriate to the disabled person.

If someone has a milder visual impairment, then things like making text bigger and different colour paper for printing may help. The best contrast is large, black, bold, clean lettering on yellow paper or a yellow background (American Federation for the Blind 2015), but different colours will help different people. Also, large text is usually considered to be 18 point, and giant print can be 20 to 38 point. Different people with different eye conditions will need different sizes of font. It is important to check with people what they need, rather than making assumptions.

Case study 10.2

Naomi is profoundly deaf. Her first language is British Sign Language, and she struggles to gather the information needed for communication in English. She has recently started a new role in a generic adult social care team as a qualified practitioner.

Naomi is able to lip-read to some extent, has some speech, a hearing dog and also support from a communication support worker who works with her on a regular basis. She has British Sign Language interpreters for all meetings and training courses, and uses a text phone and text direct service where an operator joins the telephone call and interprets the call between speech to text and text to speech, so that both parties in the call can understand what is being said, for short telephone calls.

Although she needed some adjustments when completing her degree, her experience during placements was mainly positive. However, in this new role there have been some difficulties with her being aware that some of her colleagues and managers have not been comfortable having communication support workers and interpreters around the office, and they also have concerns about confidentiality. This has led to her feeling frustrated, and has also meant that some colleagues are reluctant to talk to her because they are uncomfortable about it being interpreted, and worry about managing information. Naomi feels increasingly isolated and not part of the team.

Her manager has indicated that there has also been some feedback from her colleagues not being happy about her using the text direct service, and there has also been a complaint from someone she called, being concerned that it is not confidential.

When out on visits, Naomi has sensed some negative attitudes from people she is working with, and their families, particularly around having an interpreter present. However, she has dealt with this at the time and feels this has not been too much of a problem as she is used to explaining the role of her human support. Naomi is also aware there have been some comments about her speech not being clear enough, and about other people not being able to always understand what she is saying.

The situation has recently become highlighted for two reasons: first, she recently misunderstood an email from a manager because the English in the email was not accessible; and secondly, the health and safety advisor in this situation is concerned as Naomi cannot hear the fire alarm.

Increased awareness in the team and wider department about deafness and hearing impairment, including its different syntax and grammar – particularly that British Sign Language (BSL) is a first language, and written or spoken English is different – would help ensure that communication is more accessible (Sutton-Spence and Woll 1998).

Working with interpreters is initially quite uncomfortable for people when they are not used to it. There are, however, some basic actions that can make it work well, including speaking one at a time, and understanding that there will need to be acceptance of the need to clarify more complex information and concepts.

Lip-reading is not able to allow a hearing impaired person to gather all of the information spoken by someone else. Some sounds look the same on the lips, and it requires a high level of concentration. It can be made easier: making sure you are looking towards the person lip-reading, you have nothing obstructing your mouth, and you are not over-exaggerating words. All help – as does ensuring that you have the light on your face.

Hearing aids are not like glasses and will not make everything better. They will muffle and distort sound, and make it difficult to pick out speech from background noise.

Naomi's hearing dog can be trained to alert her to the fire alarm. She will be aware of this, so including people in finding solutions to the areas causing concern, as well as increased awareness, will resolve many of these issues and, as with working in practice, co-production as a model can and should be used.

Conclusions

This chapter has attempted to explore the often unacknowledged similarities between the identities of social workers and the people they work with – ways of strengthening practice by increasing practitioners' knowledge of both themselves, and the value that working collaboratively and sensitively with people can bring to the social work relationship and the outcomes of the intervention.

The principles applied here can generally be transferred to other practice areas – for example, being aware of the implications of impairment. Also, approaches which combine awareness of legislation, communication access and the ability to ask people what they need, are key to successful social work relationships. Good communication means treating people as individuals with values, skills and knowledge of their own.

Key points

- Deaf-blind people have a dual or combined sensory loss, and do not fit into the hearing world, nor the deaf-signing world.
- Deaf-blind people are often as marginalized in social work as they are in society.
- Deaf-blind guidance supports the 2014 Care Act, which gives additional strength and weight to the need for deaf-blind people to have specialist assessments.
- Safeguarding procedures require that social workers are accountable for deaf-blind services.

11 Concluding chapter

Kish Bhatti-Sinclair and Christopher Smethurst

This book was written during 2015–16. In the summer of 2016, as we completed the final edit, it was difficult not to feel a sense of foreboding. The economic, cultural and political uncertainties of Brexit were being played out against the backdrop of a referendum campaign where overt racism seemed to have been re-legitimized within the cultural and political mainstream. As the Rio Olympics began, Britain seemed a very different place to the country celebrated in the opening ceremony of London 2012. For many of us, even the most cynical, the London Games provided a glimpse of a diverse and inclusive Britain that we could at least aspire to. We believe that the positive spirit of 2012 was not an illusion – that it truly represented the Best of British. But, perhaps, that many of us underestimated its fragility.

It is a truism that 'doing the right thing' can be difficult, not least when it is unclear what 'the right thing' is. We began this book by saying that we were not producing a 'How to . . .' guide. Yet, we hope that within these pages you have found information that will help you to do the right thing. However, we understand this may be a struggle; that practitioners may find themselves swimming against the tide of organizational expectation and the spirit of the times. Therefore, we hope the book has acknowledged the frailties and fallibilities of all of us, as ordinary human beings, trying to be better people than perhaps we are, or are able to be.

Social workers face ethical dilemmas on a daily basis and, in general, navigate complexity with courage and confidence. However, there are areas of practice which test their personal positions and fundamental truths, particularly with those disadvantaged in ways which are multiple, overlapping and enduring. Most social workers expect their input to make a difference, even if only in the short term. However, the danger is that placing 'sticking plasters' on deep-rooted problems (on a regular basis) will stifle their ability to recognize inequality and treat people fairly. Social workers are aware of their roles as agents of the state, but probably baulk at the idea that they may be acting on behalf of organizations acting in ways which can seem oppressive and discriminatory, particularly to those who may be different and diverse in experience.

The threats facing social work are many, varied and constant. They include the vagaries of austerity measures, inspection regimes, and public/political/ideological trends. Experienced professionals who deal with multiple factors in complex ways are criticized as 'soft' and politically correct, as well as punitive and oppressive. Chapters 2 and 3 propose that some of the dilemmas facing social workers are created by ill-conceived policy and poorly resourced practice, but also that they are working with people who are seen as outsiders, unable to live normal lives and, therefore, a challenge to majority interests. Social workers are part of institutions which support standards deemed to be normal (and perhaps superior), and may be part of the problem. They should instead be seeking out holistic, solution-based responses which look for the right ideas in the right places.

Chapter authors offer compelling ways to improve professional knowledge and skills, and suggest that dilemmas arise when there is a mismatch if social workers are asked to agree with views or tasks that work against their personal values and beliefs. Dan Allen (Chapter 7) suggests that people in safe and stable environments are better able to develop brain functioning and, therefore, more likely to be resilient; also that discrimination is not natural and only exists as a long-established or situational social construct, but that it can be passed, as a contagion, from one person to another.

Bridget Ng'andu and Gerry Skelton consider two overlapping areas of difference which propose that whiteness will mark its position of dominance because white people and black people live racially structured lives (Chapter 3), and spirituality is as central as the air we breathe (Chapter 8). They confirm that whiteness studies and spirituality (as it is embedded in all of the world religions and some of the great philosophies of life) are undervalued in social work practice and academic research. Spirituality can support people in facing challenges, but also enable skills such as resilience.

The case for reflexivity is made by Vida Douglas and Jan Fook (Chapter 2), who believe that social workers who understand their own social and cultural biases are likely to have open and accepting engagements with service users and carers. Professionals participate in the process of 'othering', rooted in social difference, and need to develop understanding of complex human interactions, rather than simplistic approaches to cultural competence.

A raised awareness of professional power, alongside a mismatch between behaviour and ethical principles, is likely to lead to a high level of dissonance among social workers (Jon Old, Chapter 4). If this is heightened by the human capacity to express thoughts, it may lead to poor judgements and decision-making. Theoretical ideas rooted in social psychology can help social workers to understand themselves in a societal context which is diverse and socially different. Greater consideration of thoughts, feeling and the spoken word are all critical to the development of social work practice.

Service user and carer perspectives are at the core of social work practice. Students benefit greatly from understanding the first-hand, narrative-based experiences in areas such as mental health and deaf-blind services. Lisa Armstrong and Angela Etherington (Chapter 9) applaud the insightful contributions made by those affected by severe and enduring mental illness to areas such as stigma and prejudice. They recommend greater involvement in educational processes, particularly with regard to ethical dilemmas which compromise respect, choice and self-determination.

Lucy Jacques and Rebecca Long (Chapter 10) offer a compelling insight into deaf-blind services for people with dual or combined sensory loss, suggesting that some people do not fit into the hearing world nor the deaf-signing world. Deaf-blind people can be excluded from social work as well as from society. However, the 2014 Care Act places a new responsibility for specialist assessments onto social workers.

The authors offer a range of insights – supported by activities, exercises and models – which can be replicated and developed by readers. The chapters are written from different perspectives and in a range of writing styles and approaches, but all the authors express commitment to long-term, real change – not just in social work practice, but more broadly within a multidimensional, caring society.

References

Abrams, D. and Hogg, M.A. (2010) Social identity and self-categorisation, in J.F. Dovidio, M. Hewstone, P. Glick and V.M. Esses (eds) *The SAGE Handbook of Prejudice, Stereotyping and Discrimination*. London: Sage.

Abrams, L.S. and Moio, J.A. (2009) Critical race theory and the cultural competence dilemma in social work education, *Journal of Social Work Education*, 45(2) (Spring/Summer): 245–62.

Adams, A., Hood, A. and Levell, P. (2014) *The Squeeze on Incomes in the IFS Green Budget 2014*. London: Institute for Fiscal Studies.

Adams, A. and Levell, A. (2014) *Measuring Poverty When Inflation Varies across Households*. London: Joseph Rowntree Foundation.

Ager, W., Dow, J., Ferguson, I., Gee, M., McPhail, M. and McSloy, N. (2005a) *Service User and Carer Involvement in Social Work Education: Good Practice Guidelines*. Glasgow: Scottish Institute for Excellence in Social Work Education.

Ager, W., Dow, J. and Gee, M. (2005b) Grassroots networks: a model for promoting the influence of service users and carers in social work education, *Social Work Education*, 24: 467–76.

Agnew, A. and Duffy, J. (2010) Innovative approaches to involving service users in palliative care social work education, *Social Work Education*, 29: 744–59.

Alaimo, K., Olson, C.M. and Frongillo, E.A., Jr. (2001) Food insufficiency and American school-aged children's cognitive, academic, and psychosocial development, *Pediatrics*, 108(1): 44–53.

Alexander, C., Redclift, V. and Hussain, A. (2013) *The New Muslims*. London: Runnymede Trust.

Alexander, H. (2003) Moral education and liberal democracy: spirituality, community and character in an open society, *Educational Theory*, 33(4): 367–87.

Allen, D. (2015) Protecting the cultural identity of Gypsy, Roma and Traveller children living in the public care system, *Today's Children Tomorrow's Parents*, 41(1): 122–39.

Allen, D. and Adams, P. (2013) *Social Work with Gypsy, Roma and Traveller Children*. London: British Association of Adoption and Fostering.

American Foundation for the Blind (2015) Available at: http://www.afb.org (accessed May 2017).

Anderson, B. (2013) *Us and Them*. Oxford: Oxford University Press.

Angell, C., Dennis, B. and Dumain, L. (1998) Spirituality, resilience and narrative: coping with parental death. *Families in Society: The Journal of Contemporary Social Sciences*, 79(6): 615–30.

APPG (All-Party Parliamentary Inquiry into Hunger in the United Kingdom) (2014) *Feeding Britain: A Strategy for Zero Hunger in England, Wales, Scotland and Northern Ireland*. The report of the All-Party Parliamentary Inquiry into Hunger in the United Kingdom. London: The Children's Society. Available at: https://foodpovertyinquiry.files.wordpress.com/2014/12/food-poverty-feeding-britain-final.pdf (accessed May 2017).

Armstrong, L. and Etherington, A. (2010) Squaring the Circle: considerations on Service User Involvement in Mental Health Education. 12th UK Joint Social Work Education Conference with the 4th UK Social Work Research Conference, June 2010, University of Hertfordshire.

Arnstein, S.R. (1969) A ladder of citizen participation, *Journal of the American Planning Association*, 35: 216–24.

Aronson, J., Cohen, G.L. and Nail, P.R. (1999) Self-affirmation theory: an update and appraisal, in E. Harmon-Jones and J. Mills (eds) *Cognitive Dissonance Theory: Revival with Revisions and Controversies*. Washington, DC: American Psychological Association.

Assagioli, R. (1991) *Transpersonal Development*. London: Crucible.

Atkinson, W., Roberts, S. and Savage, M. (eds) (2012) *Class Inequality in Austerity Britain: Power, Difference and Suffering.* Basingstoke: Palgrave Macmillan.

Barrott, J. (2008) Culture and diversity in counselling, in W. Dryden and A. Reeves (eds) *Key Issues for Counselling in Action*, 2nd edn. London: Sage.

Bassot, B. (2013) *The Reflective Journal.* Basingstoke: Palgrave Macmillan.

BASW (British Association of Social Workers) (2012) *The Code of Ethics for Social Work.* Available at: http://cdn.basw.co.uk/upload/basw_95243-9.pdf (accessed November 2015).

BASW (2015) *The Professional Capabilities Framework.* Available at: https://www.basw.co.uk/resource/?id=1137 (accessed December 2015).

Bauman, Z. (2006) *Liquid Times: Living in an Age of Uncertainty.* Cambridge: Polity Press.

Beckett, C. (2003) The language of siege: military metaphors in the spoken language of social work, *British Journal of Social Work*, 33: 625–39.

Bellisle, F. (2004) Effects of diet on behaviour and cognition in children, *British Journal of Nutrition*, 92(S2): S227–S32.

Beresford, P. (2000) Service users' knowledges and social work theory: conflict or collaboration? *British Journal of Social Work: The International Journal*, 30: 489–503.

Beresford, P. (2003) *It's Our Lives: A Short Theory of Knowledge, Distance and Experience.* London: Citizen Press in association with Shaping Our Lives.

Beresford, P. (2005) *Involving Service Users in Health and Social Care Research.* London: Routledge.

Beresford, P. (2014) Social work education leads the way on involving service users, *Guardian Online* (UK edition), 3 June. Available at: http://www.theguardian.com/social-care-network/2014/jun/03/social-work-education-leads-way-involving-service-users (accessed May 2017).

Beresford, P. (2016) *All Our Welfare: Towards Participatory Social Policy.* Bristol: Policy Press.

Beresford, P. and Andrews, E. (2012) *Caring for Our Future: What Service Users Say.* London: Joseph Rowntree Foundation.

Beresford, P. and Boxall, K. (2012) Service users, social work education and knowledge for social work practice, *Social Work Education*, 31(2): 155–67.

Beresford, P. and Campbell, J. (1994) Disabled people, service users, user involvement and representation, *Disability and Society*, 9: 315–25.

Beresford, P. and Croft, S. (2001) Service users' knowledges and the social construction of social work, *Journal of Social Work*, 1(3): 295–316.

Beresford, P., Page, L. and Stevens, A. (1994) *Changing the Culture: Involving Service Users in Social Work Education*, CCETSW Paper 32.2. London: CCETSW.

Bhatti-Sinclair, K. (2011) *Anti-Racist Practice in Social Work.* Basingstoke: Palgrave Macmillan.

Bhatti-Sinclair, K. (2015) Culturally appropriate interventions in social work, in J.D. Wright (ed.) *International Encyclopedia of the Social & Behavioural Sciences*, 2nd edn. Oxford: Elsevier.

Blyth, M. (2013) *Austerity: The History of a Dangerous Idea.* Oxford: Oxford University Press.

Bocock, R. (1977) *Freud and Modern Society.* London: Van Nostrand Reinhold.

Borton, T. (1970) *Reach, Touch and Teach.* London: Hutchinson.

Bowers, J. (2013) David Blunkett is Feeding Romaphobia, *Guardian*, 13 November.

Brandon, M., Bailey, S., Belderson, P. and Larsson, B. (2013) *Neglect and Serious Case Reviews.* London: NSPCC/University of East Anglia.

Branfield, F., Beresford, P. and Levin, E. (2007) *Common Aims: A Strategy to Support Service User Involvement in Social Work Education*, Social Work Education Position Paper 7. London: Shaping Our Lives and the Social Care Institute for Excellence (SCIE).

Brendtro, L.K. and Mitchell, M.L. (2013) Deep brain learning: healing the heart, *Reclaiming Children & Youth*, 22(1): 5–12.

Brenner, G., Bush, D. and Moses, J. (2009) *Creating Spiritual and Psychological Resilience: Integrating Care in Disaster Relief Work.* London: Routledge.

Brogan, B. (2010) Boris Johnson Interview, *Daily Telegraph*, 29 April.

Brophy, J., Jhutti-Johal, J. and Owen, C. (2003) *Significant Harm: Child Protection Litigation in a Multi-cultural Setting.* London: Department of Constitutional Affairs.

Brown, J.L. and Pollitt, E. (1996) Malnutrition, poverty, and intellectual development, *Scientific American,* 274: 38–43.

Brown, P., Dwyer, D. and Scullion, L. (2013) *The Limits of Inclusion? Exploring the Views of Roma and Non Roma in Six European Union Member States,* report for Roma SOURCE (Sharing of Understanding Rights and Citizenship in Europe) project. Salford: University of Salford.

Brown, P., Martin, P. and Scullion, L. (2014) Migrant Roma in the United Kingdom and the need to estimate population size, *People, Place and Policy,* 8(1): 19–33.

Browne, J., Hood, A. and Joyce, R. (2014) *Child and Working Age Poverty in Northern Ireland Over the Next Decade: An Update.* London: Institute for Fiscal Studies.

Burke, M., Hackney, H., Hudson, E., Miranti, J., Watts, G. and Epp, L. (1999) Spirituality, religion, and the CACREP curriculum standards, *Journal of Counseling and Development,* 77: 251–57.

Butler, I. and Drakeford, M. (2001) Which Blair project? Communitarianism, social authoritarianism and social work, *Journal of Social Work,* 1: 7–19.

Cameron, D. (2007) Address to Handsworth Mosque, Birmingham, 30 January 2007.

Cameron, D. (2011) *PM's Speech at Munich Security Conference,* 5 February 2011. Available at: https://www.gov.uk/government/speeches/pms-speech-at-munich-security-conference (accessed June 2017).

Campinha-Bacote, J. (1999) *The Process of Cultural Competence in the Delivery of Health Care Service: A Culturally Competent Mode of Care,* 3rd edn. Cincinnati, OH: Transcultural C.A.R.E. Associates.

Campinha-Bacote, J. (2002) The process of cultural competence in the delivery of healthcare services: a model of care, *Journal of Transcultural Nursing Care,* 13(3): 181–84.

Canda, E. and Furman, L. (1999) *Spiritual Diversity in Social Work Practice: The Heart of Helping.* New York: The Free Press.

Capra, F. (1982) *The Turning Point: Science, Society and the Rising Culture.* London: Harper Collins.

Carey, M. (2009) Critical commentary: happy shopper? The problem with service user and carer participation, *British Journal of Social Work,* 39(1): 179–88.

Carey, N. (2012) *The Epigenetics Revolution: How Modern Biology is Rewriting Our Understanding of Genetics, Disease, and Inheritance.* New York: Columbia University Press.

Carvalho, J., Eatwell, R. and Wunderlich, D. (2015) The politicisation of immigration in Britain, *The Politicisation of Migration,* 25: 159.

Cascio, T. (1998) Incorporating spirituality into social work practice: a review of what to do. *Journal of Contemporary Social Sciences,* 79(5): 523–31.

Casey, L. (2012) *Listening to Troubled Families: A Report by Louise Casey CB.* London: Department for Communities and Local Government. Available at: https://www.gov.uk/government/uploads/system/uploads/attachment_data/file/6151/2183663.pdf (accessed 23 September 2015).

Casey, L. (2013) Speech to Local Government Association, Manchester, 3 July.

Cesari, J. (2013) *Why the West Fears Islam: An Exploration of Muslims in Liberal Democracies.* London: Springer.

Chaddock, A., Thwaites, R., Bennett-Levy, L. and Freeston, M.H. (2014) Understanding individual differences in response to self-practice and self-reflection (SP/SR) during CBT training, *Cognitive Behaviour Therapist,* 7: 1–17.

Chase, E. and Walker, R. (2014) The discursive truth of poverty in Britain: how it frames the experience of shame, in E. Chase and G. Bantebya-kyomuhendo (eds) *Poverty and Shame Global Experiences.* Oxford: Oxford University Press.

Ciscel, D.H. and Heath, J.A. (2001) To market, to market: imperial capitalism's destruction of social capital and the family, *Review of Radical Political Economics,* 33(4): 401–14.

Citizens as Trainers Group, YIPPEE, Rimmer, A. and Harwood, K. (2004) Citizen participation in the education and training of social workers, *Social Work Education*, 22: 309–23.

Civil Exchange (2015) *Whose Society? The Final Big Society Audit*. London: Civil Exchange.

Clark, T. and Heath, A. (2014) *Hard Times: The Divisive Toll of the Economic Slump*. New Haven, CT: Yale University Press.

Clements, L. and Thompson, P. (2011) *Community Care and the Law*. London: Legal Action Group.

Cobb, M. (2001) *The Dying Soul*. Buckingham: Oxford University Press.

Cohen, S. (2002) *Folk Devils and Moral Panics*, 3rd edn. London: Routledge.

Conboy, M. (2002) *The Press and Popular Culture*. London: Routledge.

Conboy, M. (2006) *Tabloid Britain: Constructing a Community through Language*. London: Taylor & Francis.

Cooper, J. (2007) *Cognitive Dissonance: Fifty Years of a Classic Theory*. London: Sage.

Coote, A. and Himmelweit, J.M. (2013) The problem that has no name – work, care and time, *Soundings: A Journal of Politics and Culture*, 54(1): 90–103.

Corcoran, H., Lader, D. and Smith, K. (2015) *Hate Crime, England and Wales 2014/15*, Home Office Statistical Bulletin 05/15. London: Home Office.

Corey, G. (2005) *Theory and Practice of Counseling and Psychotherapy*. London: Thompson.

Corey, G., Corey, M. and Callanan, P. (2007) *Issues and Ethics in the Helping Professions*. Belmont, CA: Thompson Brooks/Cole.

Cornah, D. (2006) *The Impact of Spirituality on Mental Health*. London: Mental Health Foundation.

Coulter, S. (2014) (Re) Introducing themes of religion and spirituality to professional social work training in the land of 'saints and scholars', in *Irish Families and Globalisation: Conversations about Belonging and Identity across Space and Time*. Michigan: Michigan Publishing.

Cox, J., Campbell, A. and Fulford, B. (2007) *Medicine of the Person: Faith, Science and Values in Health Care Provision*. London: JKP.

Coyte, E., Gilbert, P. and Nicholls, V. (2007) *Spirituality, Values and Mental Health: Jewels for the Journey*. London: JKP.

CPAG (Child Poverty Action Group) (2014) *Child Poverty Facts and Figures*. London: Child Poverty Action Group. Available at: http://www.cpag.org.uk/child-poverty-facts-and-figures (accessed 20 August 2015).

Crenshaw, K. (1991) Mapping the margins: intersectionality, identity politics, and violence against women of color, *Stanford Law Review*, 43(6): 1241–99.

Crepaz-Keay, D., Binns, C. and Wilson, E. (1997) *Dancing with Angels*. London: Central Council for Education and Training in Social Work.

Crisp, B. (2008) Social work and spirituality in a secular society, *Journal of Social Work*, 8: 363–75.

Crisp, B. (2010) *Spirituality and Social Work*. Farnham: Ashgate.

Croft, S. and Beresford, P. (1990) Listening to the voice of the consumer: a new model for social services research, *Convergence: International Journal of Adult Education*, 23: 62–68.

Crofts, P. (2013) Critical race theory and exploring 'whiteness', in A. Bartolli (ed.) *Anti-racism in Social Work Practice*. St Albans: Critical Publishing Ltd.

Cross, T., Bazron, B., Dennis, K. and Isaacs, M. (1989) *Towards a Culturally Competent System of Care*, Volume I. Washington, DC: Georgetown University Child Development Center, CASSP Technical Assistance Center.

Crotty, J. (2009) Structural causes of the global financial crisis: a critical assessment of the 'new financial architecture', *Cambridge Journal of Economics*, 33(4): 563–80.

Cunningham, J. and Cunningham, S. (2014) *Sociology and Social Work*. Exeter: Learning Matters.

Currer, C. (1986) Concepts of well- and ill-being: the case of Pathan mothers in Britain, in C. Currer and M. Stacey (eds) *Concepts of Health and Illness*. Leamington Spa: Berg.

Cushway, D. (2009) Reflective practice and humanistic psychology: the whole is more than the parts, in J. Stedman and R. Dallos (eds) *Reflective Practice in Psychotherapy and Counselling.* Maidenhead: McGraw-Hill.

Dana, R.H., Behn, J.D. and Gonwa, T. (1992) A checklist for the examination of cultural competence in social services agencies, *Research in Social Work Practice,* 2: 220–33.

Dalrymple, J. and Burke, B. (2006) *Anti-Oppressive Practice: Social Care and the Law,* 2nd edn. Maidenhead: Open University Press.

Dein, S. (2004) Working with patients with religious beliefs, *Advances in Psychiatric Treatment,* 10: 287–94.

Department for Education (2014) *Departmental Advice on Promoting Basic Important British Values as Part of Pupils' Spiritual, Moral, Social and Cultural (SMSC) Development.* London: DfE. Available at: https://www.gov.uk/government/publications/promoting-fundamental-british-values-through-smsc (accessed May 2017).

Department for Education (2015) *Children looked after in England (including adoption and care leavers) year ending 31 March 2015.* Available at: https://www.gov.uk/government/uploads/system/uploads/attachment_data/file/464756/SFR34_2015_Text.pdf (accessed September 2015).

DH (Department of Health) (1999) *The Government's Objectives for Children's Social Services.* London: Department of Health.

DH (2002) *Requirements for Social Work Training.* London: Department of Health.

DH (2010) *Fair Society, Healthy Lives. The Marmot review. Strategic Review of Health Inequalities in England Post-2010.* London: Department of Health. Available at: http://www.instituteofhealthequity.org/resources-reports/fair-society-healthy-lives-the-marmot-review (accessed May 2017).

Department for Work and Pensions (2015) *Households Below Average Income: An Analysis of the Income Distribution 1994/95–2013/14 June 2015 (United Kingdom).* London: DWP.

Dingwall, R., Eekelaar, J. and Murray, T. (1983) *The Protection of Children: State Intervention and Family Life.* Oxford: Blackwell.

Dodd, S. (2013) Personalisation, individualism and the politics of disablement, *Disability & Society,* 28(2): 260–73.

Dominelli, L. (1988) *Anti-Racist Social Work.* Basingstoke: Macmillan.

Dominelli, L. (2002) *Anti-Oppressive Social Work Theory and Practice.* Basingstoke: Palgrave Macmillan.

Dominelli, L. (2008) *Anti-Racist Social Work,* 3rd edn. Basingstoke: Palgrave/Macmillan.

Dorey, P. (2010) *British Conservatism: The Politics and Philosophy of Inequality.* London: IB Tauris.

Du Bois, W.E.B. (1999) The souls of white folks, in W.E.B Du Bois (ed.) *Darkwater: Voices from Within the Veil.* Mineola, NY: Dover Publications.

Dyer, R. (1997) *White.* Abingdon: Routledge.

Eccleshall, R. (2002) *English Conservatism Since the Restoration: An Introduction and Anthology.* London: Unwin Hyman.

Elkins, D. (1998) *Beyond Religion: A Personal Programme for Building a Spiritual Life Outside the Walls of Traditional Religion.* Wheaton: Quest Books.

Elkins, D., Hedstrom, L., Hughes, L., Leaf, J. and Saunders, C. (1988) Towards a humanistic-phenomenological spirituality: definition, description and measurement, *Journal of Humanistic Psychology,* 28(4): 5–18.

Emmons, R. (1999) *The Psychology of Ultimate Concerns: Motivation and Spirituality in Personality.* New York: Guilford.

Erikson, E.H. (1982) *The Life Cycle Completed.* New York: WW Norton & Norton.

Essed, P. (2001) Towards a methodology to identify converging forms of everyday discrimination. *45th Session of the United Nations Commission on the Status of Women.* New York: United Nations.

Etherington, K. (2004) *Becoming a Reflexive Researcher: Using Our Selves in Research*. London: JKP.

European Commission (2011) *Working Together for Roma Inclusion – The EU Framework Explained*. Belgium: European Commission.

European Roma Rights Centre (2011) *A Life Sentence: Romani Children in Institutional Care*. Budapest: European Roma Rights Centre.

Evans, G. and Chzhen, K. (2013) Explaining voters' defection from labour over the 2005–2010 electoral cycle: leadership, economics and the rising importance of immigration, *Political Studies*, 61(1): 138–57.

Evans, G. and Tilley, J. (2016) *The New Class War: The Political and Social Marginalisation of the British Working Class*. Oxford: Oxford University Press.

Fairholm, G. (1997) *Capturing the Heart of Leadership: Spirituality and Community in the New American Workplace*. Connecticut: Praeger.

Faiver, C., Ingersoll, R., O'Brien, E. and McNally, C. (2001) *Explorations in Counselling and Spirituality: Philosophical, Practical and Personal Reflections*. Pacific Grove, CA: Brooks/Cole.

Featherstone, B., White, S., Morris, K. and White, S. (2014) *Re-Imagining Child Protection: Towards Humane Social Work with Families*. Bristol: Policy Press.

Feltham, C. (1999) *Understanding the Counselling Relationship*. London: Sage.

Feltham, C. (2002) A surveillance culture? *Counselling and Psychotherapy Journal*, 13(1): 26–27.

Ferguson, H. (2005) Working with violence, the emotions and the psycho-social dynamics of child protection: reflections on the Victoria Climbie case, *Social Work Education*, 24(7): 781–95.

Ferguson, H. (2009) Walks, home visits and atmospheres: risk and the everyday practices and mobilities of social work and child protection, *British Journal of Social Work*, 40(4): 1100–17.

Ferguson, H. (2011) *Child Protection Practice*. Basingstoke: Palgrave Macmillan.

Ferguson, I. (2007) Increasing user choice or privatizing risk? The antinomies of personalization, *British Journal of Social Work*, 37: 387–403.

Ferguson, I. (2012) Personalisation, social justice and social work: a reply to Simon Duffy, *Journal of Social Work Practice*, 26(1): 55–73.

Festinger, L. (1954) A theory of social comparison processes, *Human Relations*, 7: 117–40.

Festinger, L. (1957) *A Theory of Cognitive Dissonance*. Stanford, CA: Stanford University Press.

Fiese, B.H., Gundersen, C., Koester, B. and Washington, L. (2011) *Household Food Insecurity: Serious Concerns for Child Development*, Social Policy Report. Volume 25, Number 3. *Society for Research in Child Development*.

Fineman, S. (2000) *Emotion in Organisations*. London: Sage.

Foley, F. (2016) The UK is Pursuing French-Style Policies on Extremism – But It May Lead to More Frequent Terror Attacks. *The Independent*, 21 July 2016.

Fook, J. (2012) *Social Work: A Critical Approach to Practice*. London: Sage.

Fook, J. and Gardner, F. (2006) *Critical Reflection in Health and Social Care*. Buckingham: Open University Press.

Fook, J. and Gardner, F. (2007) *Practising Critical Reflection: A Resource Handbook*. Maidenhead: Open University Press.

Forbes, J. and Sashidharan, S.P. (1997) User involvement in services – incorporation or challenge, *British Journal of Social Work*, 27: 481–98.

Forrest, S., Risk, I., Masters, H. and Brown, N. (2000) Mental health service user involvement in nurse education, *Journal of Psychiatric and Mental Health Nursing*, 7(1): 51–57.

Fortier, A.M. (2013) Pride politics and multiculturalist citizenship, in M. Greco and P. Stenner (eds) *Emotions: A Social Science Reader*. London: Routledge.

Frankenberg, R. (1993) *The Social Construction of Whiteness: White Women, Race Matters*. London: Routledge.

Frankenberg, R. (1997) An introduction: local whiteness, localising whiteness, in R. Frankenberg (ed.) *Displacing Whiteness: Essays in Social and Cultural Criticisms*. London: Duke University Press.

Freud, S. (1959) *Civilisation and its Discontents*. London: Hogarth.

Friedli, L. and Stearn, R. (2015) Positive affect as coercive strategy: conditionality, activation and the role of psychology in UK government workfare programmes, *Medical Humanities*, 41(1): 40–47.

Fuhse, J.A. (2012) Embedding the stranger: ethnic categories and cultural differences in social networks, *Journal of Intercultural Studies*, 33(6): 639–55.

Furman, L., Benson, P., Grimwood, C. and Canda, E. (2004) Religion and spirituality in social work education and direct practice at the millennium: a survey of UK social workers, *British Journal of Social Work*, 34(6): 767–92.

Furness, S. (2003) Religion, belief and culturally competent practice, *Journal of Practice Teaching in Health and Social Care*, 15(1): 61–67.

Furness, S. (2005) Shifting sands: developing cultural competence, *Practice: Social Work in Action*, 17: 247–56.

Furness, S. and Gilligan, P. (2010) *Religion, Belief and Social Work: Making a Difference*. Bristol: The Policy Press.

Furness, S. and Gilligan, P. (2014) The state of play: religion and spirituality in social work education and practice in the UK, *Educación Social: Revista de Intervención Socioeducativa*, 56: 31–46.

Gale, F., Bolzan, N. and McRae-McMahon, B. (2007) *Spirited Practices: Spirituality and the Helping Professions*. Melbourne: Allen and Unwin.

Gall, T., Charbonneau, C., Clarke, N., Grant, K., Joseph, A. and Shouldice, L. (2005) Understanding the nature and role of spirituality in relation to coping and health: a conceptual framework, *Canadian Psychology*, 46(2): 88–104.

Garner, S. (2007) *Whiteness: An Introduction*. London: Routledge.

Garrett, P.M. (2012) Amplifying the 'white noise': a response to Dharman Jeyasingham, *British Journal of Social Work*, 42: 1406–15.

Garthwaite, K.A., Collins, P.J. and Bambra, C. (2015) Food for thought: an ethnographic study of negotiating ill health and food insecurity in a UK foodbank, *Social Science & Medicine*, 132: 38–44.

Geist-Martin, P., Ray, E. and Sharf, B. (2003) *Communicating Health: Personal, Cultural and Political Complexities*. Belmont, CA: Wadsworth.

George, L., Larson, D., Koenig, H. and McCullough, M. (2000) Spirituality and health: what we know, what we need to know, *Journal of Social and Clinical Psychology*, 19(1): 102–16.

Geron, S.M. (2002) Cultural competency: how is it measured? Does it make a difference? *Generations*, 62: 39–45.

Gibbs, G. (1988) *Learning by Doing: A Guide to Teaching and Learning Methods*. Oxford: Further Education Unit Oxford Polytechnic.

Gibson, M. (2014) Social worker shame in child and family social work: inadequacy, failure, and the struggle to practise humanely, *Journal of Social Work Practice*, 28(4): 417–31.

Giddens, A. (1991) *Modernity and Self-identity*. Stanford, CA: Stanford University Press.

Gigerenzer, G. and Engel, C. (eds) (2007) *Heuristics and the Law*. Cambridge: MIT Press.

Gilligan, P. (2003) It isn't discussed: religion, belief and practice teaching: missing components of cultural competence in social work education, *Journal of Practice Teaching in Health and Social Care*, 5(1): 75–95.

Gilligan, P. (2008) Child abuse and spirit possession: not just an issue for African migrants, *Childright*, 245: 28–31.

Gilligan, P. (2009) Considering religion and beliefs in child protection and safeguarding work: is any consensus emerging? *Child Abuse Review*, 18(2): 94–110.

Giorgi, A. (2008) Concerning a serious misunderstanding of the essence of the phenomenological method in psychology, *Journal of Phenomenological Psychology*, 39: 33–58.

Glasby, J. and Littlechild, R. (2009) *Direct Payments and Personal Budgets: Putting Personalisation into Practice*. Bristol: The Policy Press.

Goleman, D. (1996) *Emotional Intelligence*. London: Bloomsbury.

Gove, M. (2013) *Michael Gove Speech to the NSPCC: Getting It Right for Children in Need*. Available at: https://www.gov.uk/government/speeches/getting-it-right-for-children-in-need-speech-to-the-nspcc (accessed 29 October 2015).

Graham, M. (2007) *Black Issues in Social Work and Social Care*. Bristol: Policy Press.

Gray, M. (2008) Viewing spirituality in social work through the lens of contemporary theory, *British Journal of Social Work*, 38: 175–96.

Gray, M., Coates, J. and Yellow Bird, M. (2008) *Indigenous Social Work Around the World: Towards Culturally Relevant Education and Practice*. Aldershot: Ashgate.

Gray, M., Dean, M., Agllias, K., Howard, A. and Schubert, L. (2015) Perspectives on neoliberalism for human service professionals, *Social Service Review*, 89(2): 368–92.

Greater London Authority (2013) *A Zero Hunger City: Tackling Food Poverty in London*. London: GLA. Available at: https://www.london.gov.uk/sites/default/files/gla_migrate_files_destination/A%20Zero%20Hunger%20City.doc.pdf (accessed May 2017).

Gregoire, J. and Jungers, C. (2007) *The Counselor's Companion: What every Beginning Counsellor Needs to Know*. London: LEA.

Grey, A. (1994) The spiritual component of palliative care, *Palliative Medicine*, 8: 215–21.

Grieve, P. and Hogg, M.A. (1999) Subjective uncertainty and intergroup discrimination in the minimal group situation, *Personality and Social Psychology Bulletin*, 25: 926–40.

Gupta, A. and Blewett, J. (2008) Involving service users in social work training on the reality of family poverty: a case study of a collaborative project, *Social Work Education*, 27: 459–73.

Guru, S. (2012) Under Siege: families of counter-terrorism, *British Journal of Social Work*, 42: 1151–73.

Haddad, M. (2012) *The Perfect Storm: Economic Stagnation, the Rising Cost of Living, Public Spending Cuts, and the Impact on UK Poverty*. Oxford: Oxfam.

Hajek, C. and Giles, H. (2005) Intergroup communication schemas: cognitive representations of talk with gay men, *Language and Communication*, 25: 161–81.

Hall, T. and Edwards, K. (2002) The spiritual assessment inventory: a theistic model and measure for assessing spiritual development, *Journal for the Scientific Study of Religion*, 41: 341–57.

Hamilton, D. and Jackson, M. (1998) Spiritual development: paths and processes, *Journal of Instructional Psychology*, 25(4): 262–70.

Hanson, L. (1997) *Integrative Life Planning*. San Francisco: Jossey-Bass.

Harris, S. (2014) *Waking Up: A Guide to Spirituality Without Religion*. London: Simon & Schuster.

Harrison, P. and Burke, B. (2014) Same, same, but different, in M. Lavalette and L. Penketh (eds) *Race, Racism and Social Work: Contemporary Issues and Debates*. Bristol: Policy Press.

Harvey, D. (2005) *A Brief History of Neoliberalism*. Oxford: Oxford University Press.

Haslam, N., Loughnan, S., Kashima, Y. and Bain, P. (2008) Attributing and denying humanness to others, *European Review of Social Psychology*, 19(1): 55–85.

Hawkins, P. and Shohet, R. (2000) *Supervision in the Helping Professions*. Philadelphia: Oxford University Press.

Hay, D. (2006) *The Spirit of the Child*. London: JKP.

Hayden, C. and Jenkins, C. (2014) The 'Troubled Families' programme in England: 'wicked problems' and policy based evidence, *Policy Studies*, 35(6): 631–49.

Health and Care Professions Council (HCPC) (2012) *Standards of Proficiency: Social Workers in England*. London: HCPC. Available at: http://www.hpc-uk.org/assets/documents/10003b08 standardsofproficiency-socialworkersinengland.pdf (accessed May 2017).

Health and Care Professionals Council (HCPC) (2014a) *Standards of Education and Training.* London: HCPC.

Health and Care Professionals Council (HCPC) (2014b) *Standards of Education and Training Guidance.* London: HCPC.

Healy, K. (2001) Reinventing critical social work: challenges from practice, context and postmodernism, *Critical Social Work*, 2: 1–13.

Healy, K. (2012) *Social Work Methods and Skills: The Essential Foundations for Practice.* Palgrave: Basingstoke.

Healy, L.M. (2007) Universalism and cultural relativism in social work ethics, *International Social Work*, 50(1): 11–26.

Heath-Kelly, C. (2013) Counter-Terrorism and the Counterfactual: Producing the 'Radicalisation' Discourse and the UK PREVENT Strategy, *British Journal of Politics & International Relations*, 15(3): 394–415.

Heelas, P. and Woodhead, L. (2005) *The Spiritual Revolution: Why Religion is Giving Way to Spirituality.* Oxford: Blackwell.

Heidegger, M. (2005) *Being and Time.* London: Blackwell.

Helminiak, D. (1998) *Religion and the Human Sciences: An Approach via Spirituality.* Albany: New York Press.

Henley, A. and Schott, J. (1999) *Culture, Religion and Patient Care in a Multi-ethnic Society.* London: Age Concern England.

Hernandez, M., Nesman, T., Issacs, M., Callejas, M.A. and Mowery, D. (eds) (2006) *Examining the Research Base Supporting Culturally Competent Children's Mental Health Services*, FMH1 Pub 240–1. Tampa, FL: University of South Florida, Louis de la Parte Florida Mental Health Institute, Research & Training Center for Children's Mental Health.

Hernandez, M., Nesman, T., Mowery, D., Acevedo-Polakovich, I. and Callejas, L.M. (2009) Cultural competence: a literature review and conceptual model for mental health services, *Psychiatric Services*, 60(8): 1046–50.

Heron, J. (1998) In Heron, J. (2001) *Helping the Client: A Creative Practical Guide.* London: Sage.

Heron, J. (2001) *Helping the Client: A Creative Practical Guide.* London: Sage.

Hick, J. (2001) *Dialogues in the Philosophy of Religion.* Basingstoke: Palgrave McMillan.

Hill, P., Paragment, C., Hood, M., McCullough, M., Swyers, J., Larson, D. and Zinnbauer, B. (2000) Conceptualising religion and spirituality: points of commonality, points of departure, *Journal for the Theory of Social Behaviour*, 30: 51–77.

Hills, J. (2015) *Good Times, Bad Times: The Welfare Myth of Them and Us.* Bristol: Policy Press.

Hinterkopf, E. (1998) *Integrating Spirituality in Counselling: A Manual for using the Experiential Focussing Method.* Alexandria: American Counseling Association.

Hirsch, D., Sutton, L. and Beckhelling, J. (2012) *The Cost of a Child in the Twenty-First Century.* London: Child Poverty Action Group.

HM Government (2011) *Prevent Strategy*, Cm 8092. London: Stationery Office.

Hogan, D.E. and Mallott, M. (2005) Changing racial prejudice through diversity education, *Journal of College Student Development*, 46(2): 115–25.

Holloway, M. (2007) *Negotiating Death in Contemporary Health and Social Care.* Bristol: Polity Press.

Holloway, M. and Moss, B. (2010) *Spirituality and Social Work.* Basingstoke: Palgrave Macmillan.

Hoops, J.F., Thomas, R.J. and Drzewiecka, J.A. (2015) Polish 'Pawns' between nationalism and neoliberalism in British newspaper coverage of post-European Union enlargement Polish immigration, *Journalism*, 17(6): 727–43.

Howell, W. (1982) *The Empathic Communicator.* Minnesota: Wadsworth Publishing Company.

Hubble, M., Duncan, B. and Miller, S. (1999) *The Heart & Soul of Change: What Works in Therapy.* Washington: American Psychological Association.

Hugman, R. (1998) Service users as consumers, in R. Hugman (ed.) *Social Welfare and Social Value*: The Role of Caring Professions. London: Macmillan.

Humphreys, C. (2005) Service user involvement in social work education: a case example, *Social Work Education*, 24: 797–803.

Hunt, S. (2002) *Religion in Western Society*. Basingstoke: Palgrave Macmillan.

Hunter, S. and Ritchie, P. (eds) (2007) *Co-production and Personalisation in Social Care*, Research Highlights in Social Work 49. London: Jessica Kingsley.

Hussain, A. (2011) (Dis)locating Muslims in Britain today, in C. Alexander and M. James (eds) *New Directions: New Voices: Emerging Research on Race and Ethnicity*. London: Runnymede Trust.

Hyde, B. (2008) *Children and Spirituality: Searching for Meaning and Connectedness*. London: JKP.

IFS (Institute for Fiscal Studies) (2014) *The IFS Green Budget*. London: IFS. Available at: http://www.ifs.org.uk/budgets/gb2014/gb2014.pdf (accessed 1 October 2015).

IFSW (International Federation of Social Workers) (2014) *Global Definition of Social Work*. Available at: http://ifsw.org/policies/definition-of-social-work/ (accessed 19 July 2015).

IMF (International Monetary Fund) (2014) *World Economic Outlook (WEO)*. Available at: http://www.imf.org/external/Pubs/ft/weo/2014/01/ (accessed 16 September 2015).

Irvine, J., Molyneux, J. and Gillman, M. (2015) 'Providing a link with the real world': learning from the student experience of service user and carer involvement in social work education, *Social Work Education*, 34: 138–50.

Jay, A. (2014) *An Independent Inquiry into Child Sexual Exploitation in Rotherham, 1997–2013*. Rotherham: Rotherham Metropolitan Borough Council.

Jesse, E., Schoneboom, C. and Blanchard, A. (2007) The effects of faith or spirituality in pregnancy: a content analysis, *Journal of Holistic Nursing*, 25(3): 151–58.

Jeyasingham, D. (2012) White noise: a critical evaluation of social work education's engagement with whiteness studies, *British Journal of Social Work*, 42: 669–86.

Johnston, A. (1995) Resiliency mechanisms in culturally diverse families, *Counseling and Therapy for Couples and Families*, 3(4): 316–24.

Johnston, D.W. and Lordan, G. (2015) Racial prejudice and labour market penalties during economic downturns, *European Economic Review*, 84: 57–75.

Jones, C., Wainwright, J. and Yarnold, E. (2000) *The Study of Spirituality*. London: SPEK.

Jones, L. (2016) 'If a Muslim says "homo", nothing gets done': racist discourse and in-group identity construction in an LGBT youth group, *Language in Society*, 45(1): 113–33.

Jones, O. (2011) *Chavs: The Demonization of the Working Class*. London: Verso.

Jones, S. (1994) A constructive relationship for religion with the science and profession of psychology, *American Psychologist*, 49(3): 184–99.

Jordan, B. (2010) *Why the Third Way Failed: Economics, Morality and the Origins of the 'Big Society'*. Bristol: Policy Press.

Jordan, B. and Drakeford, M. (2012) *Social Work and Social Policy under Austerity*. Basingstoke: Palgrave Macmillan.

Josephen, A., Larson, D. and Juthani, N. (2000) What's happening in psychiatry regarding spirituality?, *Psychiatric Annuals: A Journal of Continuing Psychiatric Education*, 30(8): 533–41.

Joyce, R. (2014) *Child Poverty in Britain: Recent Trends and Future Prospects*, IFS Working Paper W15/07. London: IFS. Available at: http://www.ifs.org.uk/uploads/publications/wps/WP201507.pdf (accessed 16 September 2015).

Kassimeris, G. and Jackson, L. (2012) British Muslims and the discourses of dysfunction: community cohesion and counterterrorism in the West Midlands, *Critical Studies on Terrorism*, 5(2): 179–96.

Kaushik, K. (2015) Britain's Immigration Debate Has Taken a Turn for the Toxic, *New Statesman*, 20 April.

Keating, F. (2000) Anti-racist perspectives: what are the gains for social work?, *Social Work Education*, 19(1): 77–87.

Keddie, A. (2014) The politics of Britishness: multiculturalism, schooling and social cohesion, *British Educational Research Journal*, 40(3): 539–54.

Keesing, R. (1981) *Cultural Anthropology: A Contemporary Perspective*. New York: Rhinehart and Wineston.

Kennedy, S. (2013) White woman listening, in A. Bartoli (ed.) *Anti-Racism in Social Work Practice*. St Albans: Critical Publishing Ltd.

Khan, S. (2015) As an Ordinary British Muslim, Here's What I Plan to Do to Tackle Isis, *The Independent*, 17 November.

King, M. (2011) Mervyn King Quoted in P. Inman, Bank of England Governor Blames Spending Cuts on Bank Bailouts, *Guardian*, 1 March 2011.

Koenig, H., McCullough, M. and Larson, D. (2001) *The Handbook of Religion and Health*. New York: OUP.

Kornhauser, R. (2015) Economic individualism and punitive attitudes: a cross-national analysis, *Punishment & Society*, 17(1): 27–53.

Krajewski-Jaime, E.R., Brown, K.S., Zeifert, M. and Kaufman, E. (1996) Utilizing international clinical practice to build inter-cultural sensitivity in social work students, *Journal of Multicultural Social Work*, 4(2): 15–29.

Kuhelj, A. (2014) Conflict between declared Roma minority rights and European practice: why the legal framework doesn't work in reality, *Loyola of Los Angeles International & Comparative Law Review*, 36(1): 65–113.

Kumashiro, K. (2015) *Against Common Sense, Teaching and Learning Toward Social Justice*, 3rd edn. New York: Routledge.

Kuzawa, C. and Sweet, E. (2009) Epigenetics and the embodiment of race: developmental origins of US racial disparities in cardiovascular health, *American Journal of Human Biology*, 21(1): 2–15.

Ladson-Billings, G. (2015) Foreword, in K. Kumashiro (ed.) *Against Common Sense: Teaching and Learning Toward Social Justice*, 3rd edn. New York: Routledge.

Lago, C. and Smith, B. (2003) *Anti-Discriminatory Practice*. London: Sage.

Laird, S.E. (2008) *Anti-Oppressive Social Work: A Guide for Developing Cultural Competence*. London: Sage Publications.

Langley, M.E. and Brown, S.T. (2010) Perceptions of the use of reflective learning journals in online graduate nursing education, *Nursing Education Perspective*, 31(1): 12–17.

LaPierre, L. (1994) A model for describing spirituality, *Journal of Religion and Health*, 33: 153–61.

Lavalette, M. and Penketh, L. (eds) (2014) *Race, Racism and Social Work: Contemporary Issues and Debates*. Bristol: Policy Press.

Law, I. (2010) *Racism and Ethnicity: Global Debates, Dilemmas, Directions*. Harlow: Pearson Education.

Lawler, S. (2005) Disgusted subjects: the making of middle-class identities, *The Sociological Review*, 53(3): 429–46.

Lazarus, R. and Folkman, S. (1984) In Pargament (1997) *The Psychology of Religion and Coping*. New York: Guilford.

Lazzarato, M. (2009) Neoliberalism in action inequality, insecurity and the reconstitution of the social, *Theory, Culture & Society*, 26(6): 109–33.

Leadbeater, C. (2004) *Personalisation Through Participation: A New Script for Public Services*. London: DEMOS.

Lee, M. and Zaharlick, A. (2013) *Culturally Competent Research*. New York: Oxford University Press.

Levin, E. (2004) *Involving Service Users and Carers in Social Work Education*. London: SCIE.

Levitas, R. (2005) *The Inclusive Society? Social Exclusion and New Labour*. Basingstoke: Palgrave Macmillan.

Levitas, R., Pantazis, C., Fahmy, E., Gordon, D., Lloyd, E. and Patsios, D. (2007) *The Multi-Dimensional Analysis of Social Exclusion*. London: Department for Communities and Local Government (DCLG).

Lines, D. (2006) *Spirituality in Counselling and Psychotherapy*. London: Sage.

Lirola, M.M. (ed.) (2014) *Discourses on Immigration in Times of Economic Crisis: A Critical Perspective*. Cambridge: Scholars Publishing.

Littler, J. (2013) Meritocracy as plutocracy: the marketising of 'equality' within neoliberalism, *New Formations: A Journal of Culture/Theory/Politics*, 80–1: 52–72. doi:10.3898/NewF.80/81.03.2013.

Logie, C.H., Bogo, M. and Katz, E. (2015) 'I didn't feel equipped': social work students' reflections on a simulated client 'coming out', *Journal of Social Work Education*, 51(2): 315–28.

Lorenz, W. (1996a) The education of the nation: racism and the nation state, in A. Aluffi-Pentini and W. Lorenz (eds) *Anti-Racist Work with Young People*. Dorset: Russell House Publishing.

Lorenz, W. (1996b) Pedagogical principles for anti-racist strategies, in A. Aluffi-Pentini and W. Lorenz (eds) *Anti-Racist Work with Young People*. Dorset: Russell House Publishing.

Lupton, R. and Thomson, S. (2015) *The Coalition's Record on Schools: Policy, Spending and Outcomes 2010–2015*. London: Centre for Analysis of Social Exclusion, LSE. Available at: http://sticerd.lse.ac.uk/dps/case/spcc/WP13.pdf (accessed 9 September 2015).

Lyall, D. (1995) *Counselling in the Pastoral and Spiritual Context*. Buckingham: OUP.

Lynch, G. (2002) *Pastoral Care and Counselling*. London: Sage.

Mac an Ghaill, M. (1999) *Contemporary Racisms and Ethnicities: Social and Cultural Transformations*. Buckingham: Open University Press.

Macey, M. and Moxon, E. (1996) An examination of anti-racist and anti-oppressive theory and practice in social work education, *British Journal of Social Work*, 26(3): 297–314.

MacInnes, T., Aldridge, H., Bushe, S., Kenway, P. and Tinson, A. (2013) *Monitoring Poverty and Social Exclusion*. London: Joseph Rowntree Foundation.

Mackay, K. (2002) From Consultation to Participation: A Study of User/Survivors as Co-producers of Mental Health Services. MSc Dissertation, University of Stirling.

MacKinlay, E. (2006) *Spiritual Growth and Care in the Fourth Age of Life*. London: JKP.

Maddox, D. (2016) Vote to Curb Sharia Courts, *Daily Express*, 11 March: 5.

Magaletta, P. and Duckro, P. (1996) Prayer in the medical encounter, *Journal of Religion and Health*, 35: 203–09.

Mahoney, M. and Graci, G. (1999) The meaning and correlates of spirituality: suggestions from an exploratory survey of experts, *Death Studies*, 23(6): 521–28.

Mailoo, V. (2015) Common sense or cognitive bias and groupthink: does it belong in our clinical reasoning?, *British Journal of General Practice*, 65(630): 27.

Mainstone, F. (2014) *Mastering Whole Family Assessment in Social Work: Balancing the Needs of Children, Adults and their Families*. London: Jessica Kingsley Publishers.

Man Ng, S. and Chan, C. (2005) Intervention, in R. Adams, L. Dominelli and M. Payne (eds) *Social Work Futures: Crossing Boundaries, Transforming Practice*. Basingstoke: Palgrave Macmillan.

Mansager, E. (2000) Individual psychology and the study of spirituality, *Journal of Individual Psychology*, 56: 371–88.

Manthorpe, J. (2000) Developing carers' contributions to social work training, *Social Work Education*, 19: 19–27.

Martin, L., Brady, G., Kwhali, J., Brown, S.J., Crowe, S. and Matouskova, G. (2014) *Social Workers' Knowledge and Confidence when Working with Cases of Child Sexual Abuse: What are the Issues and Challenges?* London: NSPCC/Coventry University.

Martorano, B., Natali, L., de Neubourg, C. and Bradshaw, J. (2014) Child well-being in advanced economies in the late 2000s, *Social Indicators Research*, 118(1): 247–83.

Masocha, S. (2016) Challenging the 'Othering', *Professional Social Work*, February: 22–23.

Mason, J.L., Benjamin, M.P. and Lewis, S. (1996) The cultural competence model: implications for child and family mental health services, in C.A. Heflinger and C.T. Nixon (eds) *Families and the Mental Health System for Children and Adolescents*. Thousand Oaks, CA: Sage Publications.

Masson, J. (1989) *Against Therapy*. London: Harper Collins.

Matthews, E. (1998) Integrating the spiritual dimension into traditional counsellor education programs, *Counseling and Values*, 43: 3–18.

Matthews, L. (1996) Culturally competent models in human services organisations, *Journal of Multi-Cultural Social Work*, 4(4): 131–35.

Maxime, J.E. (1986) Some psychological models of black self-concept, in S. Ahmed, J. Cheetham and J. Small (eds) *Social Work with Black Children and their Families*. London: B T Batsford Publishers.

McCormack, M. (2012) *The Declining Significance of Homophobia*. Oxford: Oxford University Press.

McIntosh, P. (1988) *White Privilege and Male Privilege: A Personal Account of Coming to See Correspondences through Work in Women's Studies*, working paper no. 189. Wellesley, MA: Center for Research on Women, Wellesley College.

McIntyre, L., Williams, J.V.A., Lavorato, D.H. and Patten, S. (2013) Depression and suicide ideation in late adolescence and early adulthood are an outcome of child hunger, *Journal of Affective Disorders*, 150(1): 123–29.

McKay, S. (2014) Benefits, poverty and social justice, *Journal of Poverty and Social Justice*, 22(1): 3–10.

McLaren, L.M. (2013) Immigration and perceptions of the political system in Britain, *Political Quarterly*, 84(1): 90–100.

McLaughlin, H. (2009) What's in a name: 'client', 'patient', 'customer', 'consumer', 'expert by experience', 'service user'—what's next?, *British Journal of Social Work*, 39(6): 1101–17.

McLeod, J. (2001) Counselling as a social process, in P. Milner and S. Palmer (eds) *Counselling: The BACP Counselling Reader*. London: Sage.

McNicholl, A. (2016) Social work must challenge Cameron's reforms with a critical eye and an open mind, *Community Care*, 19 January.

McPhatter, A.R. (1997) Cultural competence in child welfare. What is it? How do we achieve it? What happens without it?, *Child Welfare*, 76: 255–78.

Meaney, M. (2001) Maternal care, gene expression, and the transmission of individual differences in stress reactivity across generations, *Annual Review of Neuroscience*, 24: 1161–92.

Mearns, D. and Thorne, B. (2002) *Person-Centred Therapy Today: New Frontiers in Theory and Practice*. London: Sage.

Medvec, V. H., Madey, S. F. & Gilovich, T. (1995). When less is more: Counterfactual thinking and satisfaction among Olympic medalists [sic]. *Journal of Personality and Social Psychology*, 69, 603–610.

Meer, N. (2014) *Key Concepts in Race and Ethnicity*. London: Sage.

Meer, N. and Modood, T. (2009) The multicultural state we're in: Muslims, 'Multiculture' and the 'Civic Re-balancing' of British Multiculturalism, *Political Studies*, 57(3): 473–97.

Meisenhelder, J. (2002) Terrorism, posttraumatic stress, and religious coping, *Issues in Mental Health Nursing*, 23: 771–82.

Merali, A. and Shadjareh, M. (2002) *Islamophobia – The New Crusade*. London: Islamic Human Rights Commission.

Miller, C. (2006) *Souldrama: A Journey into the Heart of God*. Raleigh, NC: Lulu.Com.

Miller, C. (2008) *Souldrama: Awakening to Your Life's Purpose – Putting Spirituality into Action*. Available at: http://www.souldrama.com (accessed June 2017).

Miller, G. (1999) The development of the spiritual focus in counseling and counselor education, *Journal of Counseling & Development*, 77(4): 498–501.

Miller, W. (1999) *Integrating Spirituality into Treatment: Resources for Practitioners*. Washington, DC: American Psychological Association.

Miller, W. and Thoresen, C. (2003) Spirituality, religion and health: an emerging research field, *American Psychologist*, 58(1): 24–35.

Modood, T. (1992) *Not Easy Being British: Colour, Culture and Citizenship*. London: Runnymede Trust and Trentham Books.

Molyneux, J. and Irvine, J. (2004) Service user and career involvement in social work training: a long and winding road?, *Social Work Education*, 23: 293–308.

Moore, T. (2003) *The Soul's Religion: Cultivating a Profoundly Spiritual Way of Life*. London: Bantam Books.

Moreton-Robinson, A. (ed.) (2004) *Whitening Race: Essays in Social and Cultural Criticism*. Canberra: Aboriginal Studies Press.

Morrall, P. (2008) *The Trouble with Therapy: Sociology and Psychotherapy*. Maidenhead: McGraw-Hill.

Morrison, T. (1970/1981) *The Bluest Eye*. London: Triad Panther.

Moss, B. (2002) Spirituality: a personal perspective, in N. Thompson (ed.) *Grief and Loss: A Guide for Human Services Practitioners*. Basingstoke: Palgrave.

Moss, B. (2005) *Religion and Spirituality*. Lyme Regis: Russell House.

Murray, C. and Field, F. (1990) *The Emerging British Underclass*. London: IEA Health and Welfare Unit.

Mursell, G. (2001) *The Story of Christian Spirituality: Two Thousand Years from East to West*. Minneapolis: Fontana.

Myatt, M. (2014) *Talking to Leaders about Spiritual Leadership: Seeing it Through to the Shadows*. London: 157 Group.

Myers, J. and Williard, K. (2003) Integrating spirituality into counsellor preparation: a developmental, wellness approach, *Journal of Counseling and Values*, 47: 2003.

Nandi, A. and Platt, L. (2013) *Britishness and Identity Assimilation among the UK's Minority and Majority Ethnic Groups*, Understanding Society Working Paper Series No. 2013-08. Colchester: Institute for Social and Economic Research, University of Essex.

Narey, M. (2014) *Making the Education of Social Workers Consistently Effective: Report of Sir Martin Narey's Independent Review of the Education of Children's Social Workers*. London: Department for Education. Available at: https://www.gov.uk/government/uploads/system/uploads/attachment_data/file/287756/Making_the_education_of_social_workers_consistently_effective.pdf (accessed 12 September 2015).

NASWUT (2014) *The Impact of Financial Pressures on Children and Young People*. Birmingham: NASWUT. Available at: http://www.nasuwt.org.uk/consum/groups/public/@press/documents/nas_download/nasuwt_012429.pdf (accessed 12 September 2015).

National Library of Wales (2015) website. Available at: https://www.llgc.org.uk/discover/digital-gallery/printedmaterial/thebluebooks/ (accessed November 2015).

Nelson-Jones, R. (1992) *The Intimate Connection,*. London: SPCK.

Newton, R. (2015) *The Little Book of Thinking BIG*. Chichester: John Wiley & Sons Ltd.

National Health Service Training Directorate (1992) *Training and User Involvement in Mental Health Services*. Bristol: National Health Service Training Directorate.

Nickels, H.C., Thomas, L., Hickman, M.J. and Silvestri, S. (2012) De/Constructing 'Suspect' Communities: a critical discourse analysis of British newspaper coverage of Irish and Muslim communities, 1974–2007, *Journalism Studies*, 13(3): 340–55.

Noll, H.H. and Lemel, Y. (eds) (2003) *Changing Structures of Inequality: A Comparative Perspective*. London: Mcgraw Hill.

Norton, P. and Aughey, A. (1981) *Conservatives and Conservatism*. London: Temple Smith.

Nouwen, H. (1972) *The Wounded Healer*. New York: Doubleday and Co.

Nylund, D. (2006) Critical multiculturalism, whiteness, and social work: towards a more radical view of cultural competence, *Journal of Progressive Human Services*, 17(2): 27–42.

Observer (2002) Editorial, 10 November.

O'Connell and Leonard (2014) Decision making in children and families social work: the practitioner's voice, *British Journal of Social Work*, 44: 1805–22.

O'Hara, M. (2014) *Austerity Bites: A Journey to the Sharp End of Cuts in the UK*. Bristol: Policy Press.

Oliver, M., Sapey, B. and Thomas, P. (2012) *Social Work with Disabled People*. Basingstoke: Palgrave Macmillan.

O'Nions, H. (2011) Roma expulsions and discrimination: the elephant in Brussels, *European Journal of Migration & Law*, 13(4): 361–88.

ONS (Office of National Statistics) (2014) *Annual Survey of Hours and Earnings, 2013 Revised Results*. Available at: http://www.ons.gov.uk/ons/rel/ashe/annual-survey-of-hours-and-earnings/2013-revised-results/index.html (accessed 05 October 2015).

Opotow, S. (1995) Drawing the line: social categorization, moral exclusion, and the scope of justice, in B.B. Bunker and J.Z. Rubin (eds) *Conflict, Cooperation, and Justice*. San Francisco: Jossey-Bass.

Osborne. G. (2013) Online blog by D. Blackburn. Available at: https://blogs.spectator.co.uk/2013/04/george-osbornes-benefits-speech-full-text/ (accessed June 2017).

OSCE/ODIHR (Office for Democratic Institutions and Human Rights) (2011) *Guidelines for Educators on Countering Intolerance and Discrimination Against Muslims*. Warsaw, Poland: OSCE.

Otten, S. and Dirk Wentura, D. (1999) About the impact of automaticity in the minimal group paradigm: evidence from affective priming tasks, *European Journal of Social Psychology*, 29(8): 1049–71.

Owusu-Bempah, K. and Howitt, D. (2000) *Psychology beyond Western Perspectives*. Leicester: BPS.

Palmer, S. and Laungani, P. (1999) *Counselling in a Multicultural Society*. London: Sage.

Paradies, Y. (2016) Whither anti-racism?, *Ethnic and Racial Studies*, 39(1): 1–15.

Pargament, K. (1997) *The Psychology of Religion and Coping*. New York: Guilford.

Parrott, L. (2010) *Values and Ethics in Social Work Practice*. Essex: Learning Matters.

Parton, N. and O'Byrne, P. (2000) What do we mean by constructive social work?, in N. Parton and P. O'Byrne (eds) *Constructive Social Work: Towards a New Practice*. London: McMillan.

Patrick, R. (2014) Working on welfare: findings from a qualitative longitudinal study into the lived experiences of welfare reform in the UK, *Journal of Social Policy*, 43(4): 705–25.

Pattison, S. (2002) Foreword, in G. Lynch (ed.) *Pastoral Care and Counselling*. London: Sage.

Pawson, R., Boaz, A., Grayson, L., Long, A., and Barnes, C. (2003) *Types and Quality of Knowledge in Social Care*, Knowledge Review 3. London: Social Care Institute for Excellence.

Payne, M. (2007) Performing as a 'wise person' in social work practice, *Practice*, 19(2): 85–96.

Payne, M. (2012) *Citizenship Social Work with Older People*. Chicago, IL: Lyceum Books.

Payne, M. (2014) *Modern Social Work Theory*, 4th edn. Basingstoke: Palgrave Macmillan.

Peace, T. (ed.) (2015) *Muslims and Political Participation in Britain*. London: Routledge.

Pearson, C. (2006) *Direct Payments and Personalisation of Care*. Edinburgh: Dunedin Academic Press.

Perry, B. (2001) *In the Name of Hate: Understanding Hate Crimes*. New York: Routledge.

Perry, B. and Szalavitz, M. (2011) *Born for Love*. New York: William Morrow.

Peterson, C. and Seligman, M. (2003) Character strengths before and after September 11, *Psychological Science*, 14(4): 381–84.

Peterson, C. and Seligman, M. (2004) *Character Strengths and Virtues: A Handbook and Classification*. Buckingham: Oxford University Press.

Petrides, K., Frederickson, N. and Furnham, A. (2004) The role of trait emotional intelligence in academic performance and deviant behaviour at school, *Personality and Individual Differences*, 36: 277–93.

Phillips, T. (2015) Ten Things About Race that are True but We Can't Say, *The Sunday Times*, 15 March.

Phillips, T. (2016) An Inconvenient Truth, *The Sunday Times Magazine*, 10 April.

Pilkington, A. (2003) *Radical Disadvantage and Ethnic Diversity in Britain.* London: Sage.

Pinker, S. (2005) So how does the mind work?, *Mind & Language*, 20(1): 1–24.

Pitt, V. (2011) Promoting diversity in social work practice to combat oppression, *Community Care*, 25 February 2011.

Postle, K. (2002) Working 'Between the Idea and the Reality': ambiguities and tensions in care managers' work, *British Journal of Social Work*, 32(3): 335–51.

Priestland, D. (2013) *Merchant, Soldier, Sage: A New History of Power.* London: Penguin.

Pritchard, J. (2000) *Good Practice in Supervision.* London: JKP.

Purnell, L. (2002) The Purnell model of cultural competence, *Journal of Transcultural Nursing*, 13(3): 193–96.

Purnell, L. and Paulanka, B. (2003) *Transcultural Health and Social Care: A Culturally Competent Approach.* Philadelphia: Davis Company.

Purtilo, R. and Haddad, A. (2002) *Health Professional and Patient Interaction.* Pennsylvania: Saunders.

Quarmby, K. (2011) *Scapegoat.* London: Granta Books.

Randolph, S.M. and Banks, H.D. (1993) Making a way out of no way. The promise of Africentric approaches to HIV prevention, *Journal of Black Psychology*, 19: 204–14.

Rattansi, A. (2005) Changing the subject? Racism, culture and education, in J. Donald and A. Rattansi (eds) *'Race', Culture and Difference*, 3rd edn. London: Sage.

Reamer, F. (2015) *Wrestling with faith in social work education.* Available at: http://www.socialworktoday.com/news/eoe_052013.shtml (accessed June 2017).

Reynolds, J. and Read, J. (1999) Opening minds: user involvement in the production of learning materials on mental health and distress, *Social Work Education*, 18: 417–31.

Richards, P. and Bergin, A. (1997) *A Spiritual Strategy for Counseling and Psychotherapy.* Washington, DC: American Psychological Association.

Riddell, S., Priestley, M., Pearson, C., Mercer, G., Barnes, C., Jolly, D. and Williams, V. (2006) *Disabled People and Direct Payments: A UK Comparative Study.* Edinburgh: College of Humanities & Social Science, University of Edinburgh.

Robinson, K. and Webber, M. (2013) Models and effectiveness of service user and career involvement in social work education: a literature review, *British Journal of Social Work*, 43: 925–44.

Robinson, S. (2007) *Spirituality, Ethics and Care.* London: JKP.

Rogers, C. (1950) A current formulation of client-centered therapy, *Social Science Review*, 24(4): 442–50.

Rogers, C. (1980) *A Way of Being.* Boston: Houghton-Mifflin.

Rogowski, S. (2011) Social work with children and families: challenges and possibilities in the neo-liberal world, *British Journal of Social Work*, 42(5): 921–40.

Rogowski, S. (2013) *Critical Social Work with Children and Families: Theory, Context and Practice.* Bristol: Policy Press.

Roth, M. and Toma, S. (2014) The plight of Romanian social protection: addressing the vulnerabilities and well-being in Romanian Roma families, *International Journal of Human Rights*, 18(6): 714–34.

Rowson, J. (2013) *Taking spirituality seriously.* Available at: https://www.thersa.org/discover/publications-and-articles/rsa-blogs/2013/10/taking-spirituality-seriously (accessed May 2017).

Rowson, J. (2014) *Spiritualise: Revitalising Spirituality to Address 21st Century Challenges.* London: RSA. Available at: file:///C:/Users/Owner/Downloads/Report-spiritualise-report-feb-15.pdf (accessed May 2017).

Ruch, G. (2007) Reflective practice in contemporary child-care social work: the role of containment, *British Journal of Social Work*, 37(4): 659–80.

Rummery, K. (2016) Equalities: the impact of welfare reform by gender disability and age, in M. Bochel and M. Powell (eds) *The Coalition Government and Social Policy: Restructuring the Welfare State*. Bristol: Policy Press.

Runnymede Trust (1997) *Islamophobia: A Challenge for us All: Report of the Runnymede Trust Commission on British Muslims and Islamophobia*. London: Runnymede Trust.

Rutstein, N. (2001) *The Racial Conditioning of Our Children*. Albion: National Resource Centre for Healing Racism, Starr Commonwealth.

Ryan, F. (2015) It is Shameful that Labour Buys into the Rhetoric that People Who Need Welfare are Scum, *New Statesman*, 19 March.

Ryder, A., Cemlyn, S., Greenfields, M., Richardson, J. and Van Cleemput, P. (2012) *A Critique of UK Coalition Government Policy on Gypsy, Roma and Traveller Communities*. Available at: http://www.edf.org.uk/report-on-coalition-gypsies-roma-and-travellers-policy/ (accessed May 2017).

Sadd, J. (2011) *We are More than our Story: Service User and Career Participation in Social Work*. SCIE Report 42. London: SCIE.

Said, E. (1978) *Orientalism*. London: Routledge and Kegan Paul.

Salihu, H.M. and Wilson, R.E. (2007) Epidemiology of prenatal smoking and perinatal outcomes, *Early Human Development*, 83(11): 713–20.

Savage, M., Devine, F., Cunningham, N., Taylor, M., Li, Y., Hjellbrekke, J. et al. (2013) A new model of social class? Findings from the BBC's Great British Class Survey experiment, *Sociology*, 47(2): 219–50.

Sawatzky, R. and Pesut, B. (2005) Attributes of spiritual care in nursing practice, *Journal of Holistic Nursing*, 23(1): 19–33.

Scambler, G. (2009) Health-related stigma, *Sociology of Health and Illness*, 31: 441–55.

Scambler, G. and Scambler, A. (2011) Underlying the riots: the invisible politics of class, *Sociological Research Online*, 16(4): 25.

Schiele, J.H. (1996) Afrocentricity: an emerging paradigm in social work practice, *Social Work*, 41: 284–94.

Schön, D. (1987) *Educating the Reflective Practitioner*. London: Falmer.

Schön, D.A. (1991) *The Reflective Turn: Case Studies In and On Educational Practice*. New York: Teachers Press, Columbia University.

Schreurs, A. (2002) *Psychotherapy and Spirituality: Integrating the Spiritual Dimension into Therapy Practice*. London: JKP.

Sealey, C. (2016) Wither multiculturalism? An analysis of the impact on welfare practice and theory of policy responses to an increasingly multicultural society in the UK, *Revista de Asistenta Sociala*, 14(1): 11–26.

Seawright, D. (2010) *The British Conservative Party and One Nation Politics*. London: Continuum.

Seligman, M. (1990) *Learned Optimism: How to Change Your Mind and Your Life*. New York: Vintage Books.

Sengupta, K. (2016) Munich Shooting: Gunman Ali Sonboly was 'Obsessed' with Mass Killings, Say Police. *The Independent*, 24 July 2016.

Sense (2015) Available at: http://www.sense.org.uk (accessed May 2017).

Sherman, D.K. and Cohen, G.L. (2006) The psychology of self-defense: self-affirmation theory, *Advances in Experimental Social Psychology*, 38: 183–243.

Shipman, T. (2013) No Hiding Place for Those Who Opt for a Life on Benefits, Says Duncan Smith. *Daily Mail*, 27 December 2013.

Shohet. R. (2007) *Passionate Supervision*. London: JKP.

Sinclair, S., Raffin, R., Pereira, M. and Guebert, N. (2006) Collective soul: the spirituality of an interdisciplinary palliative care team, *Palliative and Supportive Care*, 4: 13–24.

Singh, G. (2014) Rethinking anti-racist social work in a neoliberal age, in M. Lavalette and L. Penketh (eds) *Race, Racist and Social Work: Contemporary Issues and Debates*. Bristol: Policy Press.

Singh, S. (2014) What are the experiences and outcomes of anti-racist social work education? Unpublished doctoral thesis, University of Sussex.

Skeggs, B. (2004) *Class, Self, Culture*. London: Routledge.

Skelton, G. (2012) *An Interview with Gerry Skelton on Social Work and Spirituality*, video 9 minutes, 45 seconds). Social Care Institute of Excellence. Available at: http://www.scie-socialcareonline.org.uk/an-interview-with-gerry-skelton-on-social-work-and-spirituality/r/a11G0000002WHCgIAO (accessed May 2017).

Slife, B., Hope, C. and Nebeker, R. (1999) Examining the relationship between religious spirituality and psychological science, *Journal of Humanistic Psychology*, 39(2): 51–65.

Sloan, R. and Bagiella, E. (2000) Claims about religious involvement and health outcomes, *Annals of Behavioral Medicine*, 24: 14–21.

Smart, B. (1999) *Facing Modernity: Ambivalence, Reflexivity and Morality*. London: Sage.

Smethurst, C. (2012) Contextualising the experience of older people, in B. Hall and T. Scragg (eds) *Social Work with Older People: Approaches to Person-Centred Practice*. Maidenhead: McGraw-Hill Education.

Smith, H. (1995) *The Illustrated World's Religions: A Guide to our Wisdom Traditions*. New York: Harper Collins.

Smith, M. (2005) *Surviving Fears in Health & Social Care*. London: Jessica Kingsley.

Snyder, M. and Swann, W.B. (1978) Behavioral confirmation in social interaction: from social perception to social reality, *Journal of Experimental Psychology*, 14: 148–62.

Spalek, B. and Imtoual, A. (2008) *Religion, Spirituality and the Social Sciences: Challenging Marginalisation*. Bristol: Policy Press.

Spencer, S. (2006) *'Race' and Ethnicity: Culture, Identity and Representation*. London: Routledge.

Sperry, L. (2000) Spirituality and psychiatry: incorporating the spiritual dimension into clinical practice, *Psychiatric Annals: A Journal of Continuing Psychiatric Education*, 30(8): 518–23.

Spiro, M.E. (2001) Cultural determinism, cultural relativism, and the comparative study of psychopathology, *Ethos*, 29(2): 218–34.

Standing, G. (2009) *Work After Globalization: Building Occupational Citizenship*. Cheltenham: Edward Elgar.

Standing, G. (2011) *The Precariat: The New Dangerous Class*. London: Bloomsbury Academic.

Standing, G. (2014) The Precariat and Class Struggle [published as: O precariado e a luta de classes, *Revista Crítica de Ciências Sociais*, 103: 9–24].

Stationery Office (2015) *Counter-Terrorism and Security Act 2015: Chapter 6*. London: TSO. Available at: http://www.tsoshop.co.uk.

Steele, C.M. (1988) The psychology of self-affirmation: sustaining the integrity of the self, in L. Berkowitz (ed.) *Advances in Experimental Social Psychology* (vol. 21). New York: Academic Press.

Stevenson, L. (2016) Children's social work reform: what the social work sector thinks: the sector's views on accreditation, training, outsourcing, and a new regulator, *Community Care*, 23 March. Available at: http://www.communitycare.co.uk/2016/03/23/childrens-social-work-reform-social-work-sector-thinks/ (accessed May 2017).

Stewart, M. (2012) *The Gypsy 'Menace': Populism and the New Anti-Gypsy Politics*. New York: Columbia University Press.

Stirling, B., Furman, L.D., Benson, P.W., Canda, E.R. and Grimwood, C.A. (2009) Comparative survey of Aotearoa New Zealand and UK social workers on the role of religion and spirituality in practice, *British Journal of Social Work*, 40(2): 602–21. doi: 10.1093/bjsw/bcp008.

Sue, D. (2006) *Multicultural Social Work Practice*. New Jersey: John Wiley.

Sutton-Spence, R. and Woll, B. (1998) *The Linguistics of British Sign Language*. Cambridge: Cambridge University Press.

Sweeney, A. and Morgan, L. (2009) The levels and stages of service user/survivor involvement in research, in J. Wallcraft, B. Schrank and M. Amering (eds) *Handbook of Service User Involvement in Mental Health Research*. Chichester: John Wiley.

Swinton, J. (2001) *Spirituality and Mental Health: Rediscovering a 'Forgotten' Dimension*. London: JKP.

SWRB (Social Work Reform Board) (2010a) *Building a Safe and Confident Future: One Year On*. London: SWRB.

SWRB (2010b) *Building a Safe and Confident Future: One Year On: Improving the Quality and Consistency of the Social Work Degree in England*. London: SWRB. Available at: https://www.gov.uk/government/uploads/system/uploads/attachment_data/file/180803/DFE-00602-2010-5.pdf (accessed May 2017).

Tacey, D. (2004) *The Spiritual Revolution: The Emergence of Contemporary Spirituality*. London: Routledge.

Tajfel, H. and Turner, J.C. (1979) An Integrative Theory of Intergroup Conflict, in W.G. Austin and S. Worchel (eds) *The Social Psychology of Intergroup Relations*. Monterey, CA: Brooks/Cole.

Taylor, C. and White, S. (2000) *Practising Reflexively in Health and Welfare*. Buckingham: Open University Press.

Teater, B. (2014) *An Introduction to Applying Social Work Theories and Methods*, 2nd edn. Maidenhead: Open University Press.

Tesser, A. and Campbell, J. (1982) Self-evaluation maintenance and the perception of friends and strangers, *Journal of Personality*, 50: 261–79.

Tew, J., Gell, G. and Foster, S. (2004) *Learning from Experience: Involving Service Users and Carers in Mental Health Education and Training. A Good Practice Guide*. London: Mhhe (Mental health in higher education)/NHS (National Institute for Mental Health in England)/Trent NHS Workforce Development Confederation.

Tew, J., Holley, T. and Caplen, P. (2012) Dialogue and challenge: involving service users and carers in small group learning with social work and nursing students, *Social Work Education*, 31: 316–30.

Thoburn, J., Chand, A. and Procter, J. (2005) *Child Welfare Services for Minority Ethnic Families: The Research Reviewed*. London: Jessica Kingsley.

Thompson, N. (2010) *Theorising Social Work Practice*. Basingstoke: Palgrave Macmillan.

Thompson, N. (2012) *Anti-Discriminatory Practice: Equality, Diversity and Social Justice*, 5th edn. Basingstoke: Palgrave Macmillan.

Thompson, N. (2015) Social democracy and the apotheosis of the consumer, in N. Thompson (ed.) *Social Opulence and Private Restraint: The Consumer in British Socialist Thought Since 1800*. Oxford: Oxford University Press.

Thompson, N. and Thompson, S. (2008) *The Critically Reflective Practitioner*. Basingstoke: Palgrave Macmillan.

Thoresen, C., Harris, A. and Oman, D. (2001) Spirituality, religion and health, in T. Plant and A. Sherman (eds) *Faith and Healing: Psychological Perspectives*. New York: Guilford Press.

Thorne, B. (1998) *Person-Centred Counselling and Christian Spirituality*. London: Whurr.

Thorne, B. (2000) *Person-Centred Counselling and Christian Spirituality: The Secular and the Holy*. London: Whurr.

Thorne, B. (2002) *The Mystical Power of Person-centred Therapy*. London: Whurr.

Todd, S. (2014) The Working Classes Don't Want to be 'Hard-working Families', *Guardian*, 10 April 2014.

Trevithick, P. (2011) Understanding defences and defensiveness in social work, *Journal of Social Work Practice*, 25(4): 389–412.

Trevithick, P. (2012) *Social Work Skills and Knowledge: A Practice Handbook*. Maidenhead: Open University Press.

Turbott, J. (2004) Religion, spirituality and psychiatry: steps towards rapprochement, *Australasian Psychiatry*, 12(2): 145–47.

Turner, J.C. (1999) Current issues in research on social identity and self-categorization theories, in N. Ellemers, R. Spears and B. Doosje (eds) *Social Identity: Context, Commitment, Content*. Oxford: Blackwell.

Turner, W. (2000) Cultural considerations in family-based primary prevention programs in drug abuse, *Journal of Primary Prevention*, 21(2): 285–303.

Tyson, J. and Hall, N. (2015) The perpetrators of disability hate crime, in P. Giannasi and P. Shah (eds) *Tackling Disability Discrimination and Disability Hate Crime: A Multidisciplinary Guide*. London: Jessica Kingsley Publishing.

Uberoi, V. and Modood, T. (2013) Has multiculturalism in Britain retreated? *Soundings: A Journal of Politics and Culture*, 53(1): 129–42.

Urh, Š. (2011) Ethnic sensitivity: a challenge for social work, *International Social Work*, 54(4): 471–84.

Verhaeghe, P. (2014) *What About Me? The Struggle for Identity in a Market Based Society*. London: Scribe.

Vince. R. (1998) Behind and beyond Kolb's learning cycle, *Journal of Management Education*, 22(3): 304–19.

Vygotsky, L. (1962) *Thought and Language*. Cambridge, MA: MIT Press.

Waggoner, M.R. and Uller, T. (2015) Epigenetic determinism in science and society, *New Genetics & Society*, 34(2): 177–95.

Wagler-Martin, W. (2005) Listening to our stillness: giving voice to our spirituality, *Journal of Critical Social Work*, 6(2): 135–42.

Waite, P., Hawks, S. and Gast, J. (1999) The correlation between spiritual well-being and health behaviors, *American Journal of Health Promotion*, 13(3): 159–62.

Walby, S. (2007) *A Review of Theory and Methodology for the Analysis of the Implications of Intersectionality for Gender Equality Policies in the EU*, Report D13 and D14. Vienna: QUING.

Walker, A. and Corbett, S. (2013) *The 'Big Society', Neoliberalism and the Rediscovery of the 'Social' in Britain*. Sheffield: Sheffield Political Economy Research Institute.

Wallcraft, J., Fleischmann, P. and Schofield, P. (2012) *The Involvement of Users and Carers in Social Work Education: A Practice Bench Marking Study*. London: Social Care Institute of Excellence.

Walter, N. (1998) *The New Feminism*. London: Little, Brown.

Walter, N. (2010) I Believed Sexism in Our Culture Would Wither Away. I was Entirely Wrong, *Guardian*, 25 January 2010.

Walter, N. (2011) *Living Dolls: The Return of Sexism*. London: Hachette.

Warner, J. (2013) Social work, class politics and risk in the moral panic over Baby P, *Health, Risk & Society*, 15(3): 217–33.

Warner, J. (2015) *The Emotional Politics of Social Work and Child Protection*. Bristol: Policy Press.

Weaver, H. (1999) Indigenous people and the social work profession: defining culturally competent services, *Social Work*, 44(3): 217–25.

Webber, M. and Robinson, K. (2012) The meaningful involvement of service users and carers in advanced-level post-qualifying social work education: a qualitative study, *British Journal of Social Work*, 42(7): 1256–74.

Webster, R. (2005) *Why Freud was Wrong: Sin, Science and Psychoanalysis*. Oxford: Orwell Press.

Weightman, A. L., Morgan, H. E., Shepherd, M. A., Kitcher, H., Roberts, C. and Dunstan, F. D. (2012) Social inequality and infant health in the UK: systematic review and meta-analyses, *BMJ Open*, 2(3): e000964.

Weinreb, L., Wehler, C., Perloff, J., Scott, R., Hosmer, D., Sagor, L. and Gundersen, C. (2002) Hunger: its impact on children's health and mental health, *Pediatrics*, 110(4): e41.

Welbourne, P. (2011) Twenty-first century social work: the influence of political context on public service provision in social work education and service delivery, *European Journal of Social Work*, 14(3): 403–20.

West, W. (1997) Integrating counselling, psychotherapy and healing: an inquiry into counsellors and psychotherapists whose work includes healing, *British Journal of Guidance and Counselling*, 25(3): 291–311.

West, W. (2000) *Psychotherapy and Spirituality: Crossing the Line between Therapy and Religion*. London: Sage.

West, W. (2004) *Spiritual Issues in Therapy*. Basingstoke: Palgrave MacMillan.

White, G. (2006) *Talking about Spirituality in Health Care Practice*. London: JKP.

White, S., Fook, J. and Gardner, F. (2006) *Critical Reflection in Health and Social Care*. Maidenhead: Open University Press.

Whitehead, D. (2003) Beyond the metaphysical: health-promoting existential mechanisms and their impact on the health status of clients, *Journal of Clinical Nursing*, 12: 678–88.

Wilber, K. (1979) A developmental view of consciousness, *Journal of Transpersonal Psychology*, 7(2): 1–21.

Williams, C. (1999) Connecting anti-racist and anti-oppressive theory and practice: retrenchment or reappraisal? *British Journal of Social Work*, 29: 211–30.

Williams, F. (1996) Racism and social policy: a critique of welfare theory, in D. Taylor (ed.) *Critical Social Policy: A Reader*. London: Sage.

Williams, S. and Rutter, L. (2007) *Enabling and Assessing Work Based Learning for Social Work: Supporting the Development of Professional Practice*. Birmingham: Learn to Care.

Willows, D. and Swinton, J. (2000) *Spiritual Dimensions of Pastoral Care*. London: JKP.

Wilson, G. and Kelly, B. (2010) Evaluating the effectiveness of social work education: preparing students for practice learning, *British Journal of Social Work*, 40(8): 2431–49.

Wilson, K., Ruch, G., Lymbery, M. and Cooper, A. (2008) *Social Work: An Introduction to Contemporary Practice*. Harlow, Essex: Pearson.

Wolf, M. (2014) *The Shifts and the Shocks: What We've Learned – and Have Still to Learn – from the Financial Crisis*. London: Allen Lane.

Wolfe, I. (2014) Disproportionate disadvantage of the young: Britain, the Unicef report on child well-being, and political choices, *Archives of Disease in Childhood*, 99(1): 6–9.

Wolfe, I., MacFarlane, A., Donkin, A., Marmot, M. and Viner, R. (2014) *Why Children Die: Death in Infants, Children and Young People in the UK*, Part A. London: Royal College of Paediatrics and Child Health.

Woodward, K. (2003) *Social Sciences: The Big Issues*. London: Routledge.

Woolf, L.M. and Hulsizer, M.R. (2005) Psychosocial roots of genocide: risk, prevention, and intervention, *Journal of Genocide Research*, 7(1): 101–28.

World Bank (2014) *Global Economic Prospects*. Washington, DC: World Bank. Available at: http://pubdocs.worldbank.org/en/767961448980802634/Global-Economic-Prospects-June-2014-Shifting-priorities.pdf (accessed May 2017).

Yalom, I. (2008) *Staring at the Sun: Overcoming the Terror of Death*. San Francisco: Jossey-Bass.

Yip, K.-S. (2006) Self-reflection in reflective practice: a note of caution, *British Journal of Social Work*, 36: 777–88.

Young, J. (2011) Moral panics and the transgressive other, *Crime, Media, Culture*, 7(3): 245–58.

Zappone, K. (1991) *The Hope for Wholeness: A Spirituality for Feminists*. Connecticut: Twenty-Third Publications.

Zinnbauer, B., Pargament, K., Cole, B., Rye, M., Butter, E., Belavich, T., Hipp, K., Scott, A. and Kadar, J. (1997) Religion and spirituality: unfuzzying the fuzzy, *Journal for the Scientific Study of Religion*, 36(4): 549–64.

Zohar, D. and Marshall, I. (2001) *SQ: The Ultimate Intelligence*. London: Bloomsbury.

Zohar, D., Mitchell, L. and Calder, L. (2000) *Spiritual Intelligence*. London: Bloomsbury.

Index

Ethics, Values and Social Work Practice

Linda Bell and Hafford-Letchfield

ISBN: 978-0-335-24529-I (Paperback)
eBook: 978-0-335-24530-7

2015

Ethics, Values and Social Work Practice is a brand new text offering
students and social work practitioners a contemporary and relevant
introduction to the central role of ethics and values in their work. This book
offers a fresh perspective on ethics and values in the context of everyday
social work practice, and provides an accessible route into the key theories,
as well as useful strategies, tips and tools for practice.

Key features include:

- Discussion points for individual reflection or ethical debates
- Case studies based on likely scenarios from practice
- Chapter summaries and key points for social work practice

www.openup.co.uk

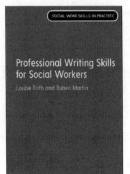

Professional Writing Skills for Social Workers

Louise Frith and Ruben Martin

ISBN: 978-0-335-26392-9 (Paperback)
eBook: 978-0-335-26393-6
2015

Communicating in writing is a highly valued skill, and now more than ever social workers are required to improve their standards of writing so that they can communicate effectively with multiple audiences. This book gives social workers practical guidance and advice on how to write analytically, stressing that writing skills are important to the professional lives of social workers and to facilitating decision making.

Key topics include:

- Planning and organizing writing
- Using professional language and vocabulary
- Technical aspects of writing

www.openup.co.uk